UNDERSTANDING BECKETT

A Study of Monologue and Gesture in the Works of Samuel Beckett

Peter Gidal

M

MACMILLAN
PRESS

First published 1986
Reprinted 1988

Published by
THE MACMILLAN PRESS LTD
Houndmills, Basingstoke, Hampshire RG21 2XS
and London
Companies and representatives
throughout the world

Printed in Hong Kong

British Library Cataloguing in Publication Data
Gidal, Peter
Understanding Beckett: a study of monologue
and gesture in the works of Samuel Beckett.–
Language, discourse, society)
1. Beckett, Samuel – Criticism and interpretation
I. Title   II. Series
822′.912   PR6003.E282Z/
ISBN 0–333–31278–3 (hardcover)
ISBN 0–333–45530–4 (paperback)

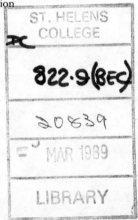

Artistic activity is the supreme act of despising everything
that is inside and outside of us, everything that is obvious.
Olga Rozanova, *Suprematism and the Critics*, 1918

Practices give words their meanings.
Ludwig Wittgenstein, *Remarks on Colour*, 1951 (III, 317)

It is absurd to oppose polemic to theory for one very simple
reason: no new idea appears in a void.
Christine Delphy, 'A Materialist Feminism is Possible',
Feminist Review, no. 4, 1980

Sally Harding's practical and theoretical work as a radical materialist feminist has taught me so much over the years; valuing no less two decades of friendship

Contents

List of Illustrations

Acknowledgements

Anne Friedberg carefully and critically read the first half of the manuscript in its second-to-last stage, making important points, all of which necessarily led to manuscript revision and precision. Gratitude for this and for introducing me to and sharing the work of H.D. and Bryher.

Gratitude to Billie Whitelaw and Samuel Beckett for so generously allowing me to use, and reprint here, the working script of *Not I*. And thanks to Sophie Muller for in the first place telling me of the colour-annotated script and for recounting her rehearsals with Billie Whitelaw.

I thank Lucy Bailey, Terry Eagleton, Jay Leyda and Rene Gimpel for allowing quotes from letters, Deke Dusinberre for allowing the lengthy quotation from his *Screen* piece, and Steve Dwoskin for bringing the Schiller Theatre *Godot* programme for me from Berlin in 1975.

Each photographer was extremely helpful with the obtaining of stills.

Last but not least, Stephen Heath deserves thanks, he without whom, etc. – and for depositing doughnuts on my doorstep, fresh from the bakery.

The author and publishers wish to thank the following who have kindly given permission for the use of copyright material:

Basil Blackwell Ltd, on behalf of the Literary Executors, for the extracts from *Remarks on Colour* by Ludwig Wittgenstein.

John Calder (Publishers) Ltd and Grove Press Inc., for the extracts from *Proust, How It Is, Company, Watt, Ill Seen Ill Said* and *Enough* by Samuel Beckett.

Faber and Faber Ltd and Grove Press Inc., for the extracts from *Not I, Endgame, Waiting for Godot* and *A Piece of Monologue* by Samuel Beckett.

Routledge & Kegal Paul PLC and the Johns Hopkins University Press, for the extract from *The Act of Reading* by Wolfgang Iser.

The author and publishers have tried to contact all the relevant copyright-holders, but if any have been inadvertently overlooked, they will be pleased to make the necessary arrangements at the first opportunity.

Introduction

As with many books it might be useful not to start at the beginning. Perhaps Chapter XVIII or XX, and certainly the Notes (pp. 251–78). Then from p. 1.

P.G.

I

Quote: *A Piece of Monologue*

Speech as Channel of Communication, or Not

The Natural

The Reader's 'I' in Language

Birth was the death of him. Again. Words are few. Dying too.
Birth was the death of him. Ghastly grinning ever since. Up at
the lid to come. In cradle and crib. At suck first fiasco. With the
first totters. From mammy to nanny and back. All the way.
Bandied back and forth. So ghastly grinning on. From funeral
to funeral. To now. This night. Two and a half billion seconds.
Hard to believe so few.

> (opening words of Beckett's *A Piece of Monologue*)

Is speech a channel of communication or not? Is the notion of a
'channel' a kind of naturalism, channel asserting a kind of
communication, wherein communication posits a move from *a* to
b? Channel as a notion of communication would also posit the
possibility of not only moving from *a* to *b* but also back again, and
again. The notion of transformation or of dialectic is absent from
such a notion of communication and its channels. That which is to
be communicated, under such a rubric, always must by definition
pre-exist the act of communication, the material move of such a
possibility. Facilitating such a notion, which is an impossible
notion, is the concept of the given *natural*.

This concept allows for a codification to take place, thereby
making of the supposedly natural the in fact natural*ised*. An
interior, formal, hold, a stasis outside of contradiction-in-
duration, is set up. Action and description are naturalised for the

1

viewer within the linear forward movement of time, a movement annihilated in order for the 'natural' to exist outside of any concrete process. Thus existence becomes ineluctably pre-existence.

In the viewer is inculcated a sense of suspension of disbelief, not necessarily in relation to a mimesis of *the* real or supposed real, but rather in terms of a perceptually and logically verifiable reality-*effect*. This reality-effect becomes a basis for the code of the natural, a 'natural' thus instigated without of necessity bearing any resemblance to real or imagined reality *outside* the theatre.

In the opening words of *A Piece of Monologue* and in much of Beckett's writing the move is from the seemingly identifiable, that which the reader can identify (if not identify with), to a distanciation produced by the structures of sound and image, the latter processed as in difficult relation, if any. Any relation, better said, that is established through such a process, both *in*-text, and text-to-reader/viewer, is done through a series of acts/ movements/labours rememorated time after time, at the time. This separates *presentation* of certain images, meanings, sounds, devices, from a concept of *usage* wherein unreflected use is made of something that pre-exists the labour-work, the production, the theatrics or languag*ing*.

What must then be divided from the concept of *presentation* is any essentialism, anything pre-existing and 'natural' and given. And what the concept must retain is the oxymoronic contradiction which, for example, explicated Lenin's unity (which is not such) of opposites.[1] Also separated from the concept of presentation is any notion of constant and un- and a-historical *presence*, as if some object, or meaning, or theatric comment, or language fragment were simply to exist, i.e. all meaning ad- and in-hering prior to any construction. Such an idealist object with inherent seeming meaning and function is what a bourgeois literature has as its base, usually in the form of metaphor or unquestioned representation.

'A representation being a true being with certain qualities such as qua qua qua.' Well, if not that how that 'not that' in this Beckett piece *A Piece of Monologue*? ('an old piece reworked recently').

'Birth was the death of him; again . . . words a few dying to birth was the death of him.'[2] Already 'I' am not able to put myself into the sentence. To identify with (thus into) meaning becomes problematic. And no great difference exists between identification with, and into, character, and identification with, and into, ideas/intellectual constructs. Identification with and into ideas/ intellectual constructs would simply allow for a series of apparent identities of the reader/viewer with the languages or theatrics, only to be 'later' deconstructed, reassembled, or unassembled, thereby making of the production in question an alibi for a series of anterior motives. In that sense the communication and the concept of the channel would be reinsisting itself against the materiality of other possible operations.

The emotive has its own teleologies, as does the realm of 'ideas'. The rational as represented in language becomes thereby an academic decoy (in place of production) for the reader/viewer being part of a process both in and against any moment to moment representation and meaning. The contradictions of subjectivity and objectivity which operate all our histories become repressed through notions of 'character' as being always '*a* character' in the realm of the given (or, to simply extend that, always a series of characters which in no way make difficult the whole concept of such illusionist representatives of something *anterior* and preconstructed). Dialectic becomes repressed via (also) the repression of the viewer in the process, his or her sex, attempts of placement, memory, and the power of meaning and meaninglessness.[3] For a materialist process to function it necessitates certain mechanisms and not others.

'Birth was the death of him. Again . . . words a few dying to birth was the death of him.' Already (again) 'I' am not able to put myself into the sentence, to identify with (thus into) meaning or the character(s), or the idea(s), or the potential regress or progress of what is going on or going to go on. After the first few words 'birth was the death of him again' I am back here thinking how could birth be the death of him again. Or: is the 'again' a demand for a repeat and if that, then whose demand if not the speaker's. Then there is someone else a demander. If a demander (but I am not sure if) then first: what do I identify, secondly, how do I identify it. Before I can do anything with that thought other than have it, the following words (on the listened-to tape of *A Piece of Monologue*): 'words a few dying to birth was the death of him'. This places me for a second time within the first five seconds of this piece (duration one spoken hour, on tape) in a questionable position: (a), does 'words a few' refer to the general possibility and paucity of few words' existence, or (b) the possibility and paucity of few words' use, or (c) does 'words a few' become *another* demand or (d) is it a description by the speaker who is 'dying to'?[4]

The latter would be a double meaning as in 'I am dying to say such and such' or dying too. At this one moment of listening we are *in* the unknowing, *in conflict with* the need to know.

Then repeat: 'birth was the death of him'. In retrospect it can (if illogically though empirically) be deduced that there was a voice making a demand; there is a demander who is being here acknowledged, as the sentence is being repeated *as previously demanded*. The demanding voice is the subjective voice of the one monologuist – no evidence pointing to anything else. There is no reason outside one needing metaphor (and its dominant literary acculturations) to assume a persona or personae is/are allowing the main speaker to somehow stand for (incarcerate) other characters, their figments, the (ostensible) author's one amongst 'them'. The opposite of this is the case.[5]

II

Quote: *A Piece of Monologue*

Quote: *Der Blaue Reiter Almanach*

New Contents/New Forms

SPEAKER. Birth was the death of him. Again. Words are few. Dying too. Birth was the death of him. Ghastly grinning ever since. Up at the lid to come. In cradle and crib. At suck first fiasco. With the first totters. From mammy to nanny and back. All the way. Bandied back and forth. So ghastly grinning on. From funeral to funeral. To now. This night. Two and a half billion seconds. Again. Two and a half billion seconds. Hard to believe so few. From funeral to funeral. Funerals of ... he all but said of loved ones. Thirty thousand nights. Hard to believe so few. Born dead of night. Sun long sunk behind the larches. New needles turning green. In the room dark gaining. Till faint light from standard lamp. Wick turned low. And now. This night. Up at nightfall. Every nightfall. Faint light in room. Whence unknown. None from window. No. Next to none. No such thing as none. Gropes to window and stares out. Stands there staring out. Stock still staring out. Nothing stirring in that black vast. Gropes back in the end to where the lamp is standing. Was standing. When last went out. Loose matches in right-hand pocket. Strikes one on his buttock the way his father taught him. Takes off milkwhite globe and sets it down. Match goes out. Strikes a second as before. Takes off chimney. Smoke-clouded. Holds it in left hand. Match goes out. Strikes a third as before and sets it to wick. Puts back chimney. Match goes out. Puts back globe. Turns wick low. Backs away to edge of light and turns to face east. Blank wall. So nightly. Up. Socks. Nightgown. Window. Lamp. Backs away to edge of light and

5

stands facing blank wall. Covered with pictures once.
Pictures of ... he all but said of loved ones. Unframed.
Unglazed. Pinned to wall with drawing-pins. All shapes and
sizes. Down one after another. Gone. Torn to shreds and
scattered. Strewn all over the floor. Not at one sweep. No
sudden fit of ... no word. Ripped from the wall and torn to
shreds one by one. Over the years. Years of night. Nothing on
the wall now but the pins. Not all. Some out with the wrench.
Some still pinning a shred. So stands there facing a blank wall.
Dying on. No more no less. No. Less. Less to die. Ever less.
Like light at nightfall. Stands there facing east. Blank
pinpocked surface once white in shadow. Could once name
them all. There was father. That grey void. There mother.
That other. There together. Smiling. Wedding day. There all
three. That grey blot. There alone. He alone. Not now.
Forgotten. All gone so long. Gone. Ripped off and torn to
shreds. Scattered all over the floor. Swept out of the way
under the bed and left. Thousand shreds under the bed with
the dust and spiders. All the ... he all but said the loved ones.
Stands there facing the wall staring beyond. Nothing there
either. Nothing stirring there either. Nothing stirring
anywhere. Nothing to be seen anywhere. Nothing to be heard
anywhere. Room once full of sounds. Faint sounds. Whence
unknown. Fewer and fainter as time wore on. Nights wore on.
None now. No. No such thing as none. Rain some nights still
slant against the panes. Or dropping gentle on the place
beneath. Even now. Lamp smoking through wick turned low.
Strange. Faint smoke issuing through vent in globe. Low
ceiling stained by night after night of this. Dark shapeless
blot on surface elsewhere white. Once white. Stands facing
wall after the various motions described. That is up at
nightfall and into gown and socks. No. In them already. In
them all night. All day. All day and night. Up at nightfall in
gown and socks and after a moment to get his bearings gropes
to window. Faint light in room. Unutterably faint. Whence
unknown. Stands stock still staring out. Into black vast.
Nothing there. Nothing stirring. That he can see. Hear.
Dwells thus as if unable to move again. Or no will left to move
again. Not enough will left to move again. Turns in the end
and gropes to where he knows the lamp is standing. Thinks
he knows. Was last standing. When last went out.

(first half of Beckett's *A Piece of Monologue*)

What is a monologue? 'Two and a half billion seconds.' Again. 'Two and a half billion seconds.' 'Hard to believe so few.' 'One thinks that one is tracing the outline of the thing's nature over and over again, and one is merely tracing round the frame through which we look at it' (Ludwig Wittgenstein, *Philosophical Investigations* (Oxford: Blackwell, 1953) p. 48). Beckett: '. . . wall. Covered with pictures once . . . he all but said loved ones. Unframed. Unglazed. Pinned to wall with drawing-pins. All shapes and sizes. Down one after another.'

What is expressionism and how is Samuel Beckett not the last expressionist? In *Der Blaue Reiter Almanach* the polemic is against 'the abstract', for 'content'. This problematises the issue of expressionism because in the form (and the formal) of representation in (*as*) the abstract can be figured either a new content in terms of a new relation to signification, meaning (-lessness), and to the production process of articulation, *or* the abnegation and disavowal of such. The materialist operation of the abstract, *the anti-expressionist*, does not maintain Kandinsky's new contents and contentments. In explanation, first the *Blaue Reiter* 'new contents' quote:

> In practice the 'Blaue Reiter' was correct: that which arose formally has died. It lived barely two years – supposedly lived. . . . the question of Art is mainly a question of content. And in this way life, reality, goes its own way. These thundering signs of a heroic period are ignored in an almost inexplicable manner: the public (to which many art theorists belong) continues more than ever to consider, to analyse, to systematize exclusively the formal element, in opposition to the spiritual strivings of the times. So perhaps the time for 'hearing' and 'seeing' is not yet ripe. (V. Kandinsky, *Der Blaue Reiter Almanach* (Munich: R. Piper, 1914, 2nd edn) p. ix.)

III

Quote: 'Critics and the Public' (Nadezhda Udalzova)

Does this not mean quite simply that such people have absolutely no idea of what constitutes artistic form? . . . But they are always mistaken, and each time they are obliged to look backwards. Art, however, does not wait, but ever advances, now denying, now asserting. If Cezanne had been properly understood in his time, then the great realist Picasso would have avoided the mystical haze, the grace of astral bodies and similar theosophical magic that now surrounds him. Both the public and the critics would have realized now that black and red squares are the result of the introduction of the painterly plane into the cubist composition. Form is what gives life to art, form and form alone. (Nadezhda Udalzova, 'How Critics and the Public Relate to Contemporary Russian Art' (1915), anthologised in *Women Artists of the Russian Avantgarde* (Galerie Gmurzynska, Cologne, 1979))

(See Illustrations 1 and 2.)

Illus. 1   Olga Rozanova, *Exploding Suitcase*, collage, 1916 (20.8 × 30.7 cm)

Illus. 2 Vasilii Kandinsky, Panel II for Edwin R. Campbell, *Painting no. 199*, 1914 (162.6 × 122.7 cm)

IV

It is important to consider briefly the way Beckett's novels (which, it might be argued, form the substance of his literary achievement – as opposed to the more familiar plays) have not only intensified the role of the first-person narrator as the sole speaking subject, but have simultaneously extended the strategies of contradiction and hyperbole at every level of construction, effectively undermining what would otherwise appear as simple – and relentlessly pessimistic – solipsism. On the broadest level a major shift can easily be traced through the early novels, *More Pricks than Kicks*, *Murphy*, *Watt* – in which the speaking subject develops from an omniscient narrator to a fully participating witness, up to the magnificent mature trilogy – *Molloy*, *Malone Dies*, *The Unnamable* – in which each speaking subject limits his discourse to an internalized monologue. But those monologues incorporate contradictions which interrogate the very act of relating, of speaking as a unified subject. Thus *Molloy* is organized as two long monologues, ostensibly by discrete characters (Molloy and Moran), although as the latter monologue progresses the convergence of the two is suggested on several planes (did Molloy and Moran meet? Are they perhaps identical? Does the latter monologue historically precede the former?) and each monologue offers an increasingly fragmented and disintegrated notion of speaking subject which is unquestionably tantamount to the fragmentation of the authorial voice of Beckett.

11

Molloy begins: 'I am in my mother's room. It's I who live there
now. I don't know how I got there. Perhaps in an ambulance,
certainly a vehicle of some kind. I was helped. I'd never have
got there alone.' The repetition and substitution (note how the
implicit 'here' of the first sentence is replaced by the
contradictory 'there') create a sense of ambivalence and
distance on the part of the speaking subject which is reiterated
twenty pages later: 'Not to want to say, not to know what you
want to say, and never stop saying, or hardly ever, that is the
thing to keep in mind, even in the heat of composition.' And
again, another twenty pages on: 'Yes, the words I heard, and
heard distinctly, having quite a sensitive ear, were heard a first
time, then a second, and often even a third, as pure sounds, free
of all meaning, and this is probably one of the reasons why
conversation was unspeakably painful to me. And the words I
uttered myself, and which must nearly always have gone with
an effort of the intelligence, were often to me as the buzzing of an
insect.' The subversion of the unified authorial voice is simple
and explicit in the latter monologue (Moran's) in which the
closing sentences ('It was not midnight. It was not raining')
challenge the authority of the opening sentences ('It is
midnight. The rain is beating on the windows'). Both voices are
authorial, neither authoritative.

Beckett further exposed the fabric of his fiction – indeed, of all
writing – by stressing repetition and contradiction more
insistently. Number III of the *Texts for Nothing* commences:
'Leave, I was going to say leave all that. What matter who's
speaking, someone said what matter who's speaking. There's
going to be a departure. I'll be there, I won't miss it, it won't be
me, I'll be here, I'll say I'm far from here, it won't be me, I
won't say anything, there's going to be a story, someone's going
to try and tell a story'. Or, more starkly, *The Unnamable*: 'Where
now? Who now? When now? Unquestioning. I, say I.
Unbelieving. Questions, hypotheses, call them that. Keep
going, going on, call that going, call that on.' The carefully
balanced syntax of repetition and contradiction effectively
increases the stress on the speaking subject until that
subjectivity ironically disintegrates. There is no single, unified,
speaking subject – not even an ultimate authorial voice – there
is only the fragmentary composite of subjective voices.   (Deke

Dusinberre, 'Consistent Oxymoron, Peter Gidal's Theoretical Strategy', *Screen*, Summer 1977, pp. 80–1)

So the attempt against expressionism, and how Beckett is not the last expressionist, hinges on the function and effect of the whole matter not being a matter of individual subjectivity/authority, nor of any intercommunal 'collectivity'. A theorisation of ideology makes obvious how $1 + 1 + 1 + 1$ is not necessarily more collective than 1, or '1'.

An analogue would be the demands of the collective British Women's Movement which are precisely each adherent's demands; this operates *against* individualism *and* against the notion of *re*-presentation of some fictionally non-contradictory totality.

If it is not a matter of individual subjectivity and the complete author that that always of necessity represents, then we have a de-authored monologue. De-authored writing, de-authored effects. But de-authorisation (in both senses) has to be produced, *worked*. Certain forms of monologue produce that in immediate radical opposition to monologue as dominant patriarchal form of truth.

De-authorisation has to be produced against the possession-effect of conventional, authorial, authorised material. The written product, the monologue, for example, *as commodity* for the reader/viewer, means the given (in this case language) is the effect of a prior ownership. A contract for furtherance of ownership in whatever transmuted form is the result of such a possession-effect.

V

Quote: Beckett's *Proust*

Possessive Space

Nothing to Express

Material(ist) Process and Identification

we are faced by the problem of an object whose mobility is not merely the function of the subject's, but . . . two separate and immanent dynamisms related by no system of synchronization. So that whatever the object, our thirst for possession is, by definition, insatiable. . . . No object prolonged (in Time) tolerates possession, only to be achieved by the complete identification of subject and object. (Samuel Beckett, *Proust* (London: Chatto and Windus, 1931) pp. 17, 57)

Does an author produce, inserting him-/her-/itself[6] in the production process, a non-possessive space? And if so, *where* then is any author? 'Masson himself, having remarked that Western perspective is no more than a series of traps for the capture of objects declares that their possession does not interest him. He congratulates Bonnard for having, in his last works, "gone beyond possessive space in every shape and form, far from surveys and bounds, to the point where all possession is dissolved" ' (Beckett, *Three Dialogues with George Duthuit*, in *Transition*, Paris, 1946).

Once a space is a web of differences, of constant constitution– reconstitution of movement supplying point for point, scrape for scrape, scratch for scratch, erasure for erasure, addition subtraction etc., the traces somehow retrospectively not adumbrated, the object not as circumscribed separateness, discrete, but as an object producing the specific effects on the

14

viewer of non-possessive space: were that the case where then the author? (with monologue similarly).

The question in the quote about Masson, Bonnard, is that of Western perspective as a trap for capture of objects, and of representation as a functional model, effecting something, affecting something. Disregarding for a moment (a) the truth of the assertion about Bonnard's work (having gone beyond possessive space), there is (b) the question as to what it means to not any longer have an *interest* in possession. Does this come from being overpossessed, overluxuriating, decadent, or from being in need, with no hope of such fulfilment? (c) What does 'going beyond' mean (disregarding whether it is true)?

'There is nothing to express', *and* it is impossible, not least because one medium does not adequately represent another. Only through elaborate systems of machining illusion 'into place' through mechanisms effaced can even a beginning of expression be effected. Expression is the specific effect of an immense work of repression, a repression-mechanism, its ends being those of holding the identification, the suspension of disbelief. Weary of that is stating 'nothing to paint, nothing to paint with'. That *nothing*, thus, is literally inexpressable, as is the *non-meaning* (as opposed to the expression) of language.

Material(ist) process is both in the world, is the world (i.e. art production is material) *and* is simultaneously analysis-*of*. Neither 'alone' suffices. The basis is operation of contradiction (as in materialist monologue and gesture). Thus, nothing to *represent* with (nothing to paint with, nothing to write with) literally, because it is always something other which a representation represents, or presents; an image of an image; *of*. It is not where you think it is, nor are you where it is (you are not speaking from where I hear you). Here is the break: between the construction for you of meaning for you *and* the enunciation, the production. All the above is only to somehow literalise this statement of nothing to paint with, nothing to write with, because I don't think what's referred to is brushes and pencils.

'B: (*A fortnight later*) Yes.' This in answer to: 'Inexpressive?' It thus takes time, or, rather, the narrative being enunciated here is that it takes time to construct inexpressivity, or even the possibility of inexpressivity as a concept. The sentence speaks of the time for construction of (a) belief. Expression is an impossible act. What has been 'lost', what is no longer in this 'impossible act of expression' is the author as author of the act of expression, and its referents (that which the words refer to in the world, as opposed to the concepts they signify). What has also been lost are the world's symbolisations, metaphors, projections, stand-ins. 'Escape from the sense of failure by means of less exclusive relations between representor and representee' (*Dialogue with George Duthuit*, ibid.), evicting author yet again.

> One has one's own laundry and one washes it.
> One doesn't have one's own words, and one doesn't wash them.
> In the beginning was not the word,
> The word is at the end.   (Brecht, entry for September 1920,
>   *Tagebücher* (Frankfurt: Suhrkamp, 1978) p. 55)

Do the bones of your fingers when you clasp your hands together and *feel* have to be stand-in for '*you*', fragments *for*, or *of*, your character, your ego, that then to be identified with you into that image (clear or vague) of yourself, *or* via representation by another? 'We must do away with explanation and description must take its place' (Wittgenstein, *Philosophical Investigations*, p. 47).

The description of the hands above, your hands, to be taken not as metaphor, also relates concretely for example to self description and its mechanisms in Beckett's monologues: monologue-as-presentation not representation. This concrete concept does not 'somehow' hold for *any* monologue, or any simple piece of description, but holds specifically for certain structures which make difficult and then impossible the sustaining of character as capable vehicle (even via absence or fragment or imaginary moment).

VI

Quote: *Not I* (Billie Whitelaw's Complete Annotated Typescript)

Quote: *How It Is*

Quote: *Company*

Quote: *Watt*

Quote: *Everybody's Autobiography* (Gertrude Stein)

Quote: *Tender Buttons* (Gertrude Stein)

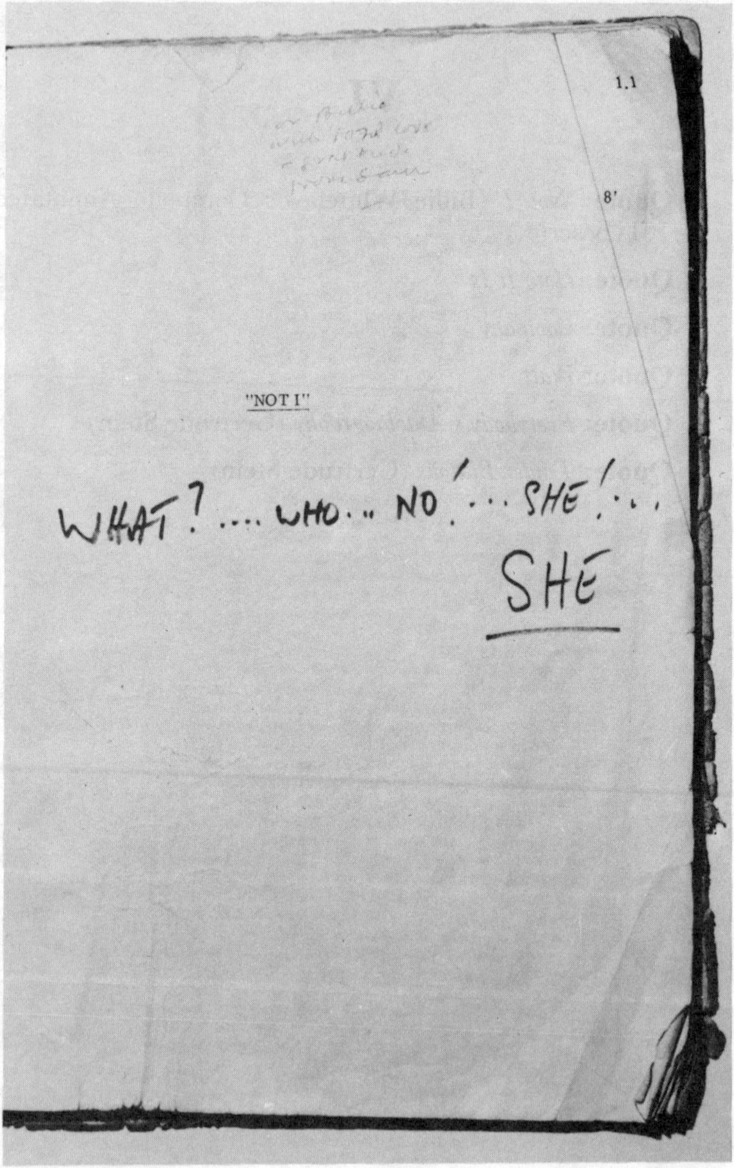
1.1
8'
"NOT I"
WHAT? .... WHO.. NO!... SHE!...
SHE

1.1

ACT ONE

Stage in darkness but for

MOUTH, upstage audience right, about 8'
above stage level, faintly lit from close
up and below, rest of face in shadow.
Invisible microphone.

AUDITOR, downstage audience left, tall
standing figure, sex undeterminable,
enveloped from head to foot in loose
black djellaba, with hood, fully faintly
lit, standing on invisible podium about
4' high, shown by attitude alone to be
facing diagonally across stage intent on
MOUTH, dead still throughout but for
four brief movements where indicated.
See Note 1.

As house lights down MOUTH's voice
unintelligible behind curtain. House
lights out. Voice continues unintelligible
behind curtain, 10 seconds. With rise of
curtain ad-libbing from text as required
leading when curtain fully up and attention
sufficient into:

MOUTH: ... out ... into this world ... this world ... tiny
little thing ... before its time ... in a godfor ...
what? ... girl? ... yes ... tiny little girl ... into
this ... out into this ... before her time ... godforsaken hole called ... called ... no matter ...
parents unknown ... unheard of ... he having
vanished ... thin air ... no sooner buttoned up his
breeches ... she similarly ... eight months later
... almost to the tick ... so no love ... spared that
... no love such as normally vented on the ...
speechless infant ... in the home ... no ... nor
indeed for that matter any of any kind ... no love
of any kind ... at any subsequent stage ... so
typical affair ... nothing of any note till coming up
to sixty when ... what? ... seventy? ... good
God! ... coming up to seventy when ... wandering
in a field ... looking aimlessly for cowslips ... to
make a ball ... a few steps then stop ... stare
into space ... stop and stare again ... so on ...
drifting around ... when suddenly ... gradually ...
all went out ... all that early April morning light
... and she found herself in the ... what? ...

1.2

MOUTH: who? ... what? ... no ... no! ... SHE! ...
(contd)   (pause and movement 1) ... found herself in the
          dark ... and if not exactly ... insentient ... in-
          sentient ... for she could still hear the buzzing
          ... so-called! ... in the ears ... and a ray of
          light came and went ... came and went ... such
          as the moon might cast ... drifting ... in and out
          of cloud ... but so dulled ... feeling ... feeling
          so dulled ... she did not know ... what position
          she was in! ... imagine! ... what position she was
          in! ... whether standing ... or sitting ... but the
          brain – what? ... kneeling? ... yes ... whether
          standing ... or sitting ... or kneeling ... but the
          brain – ... what? ... lying? ... yes ... whether
          standing ... or sitting ... or kneeling ... or lying
          ... but the brain still ... still ... in a way ... for
          her first thought was ... oh long after! ... sudden
          flash ... brought up as she had been to believe ...
          with the other waifs ... in a merciful ... (brief
          laugh) ... God ... (good laugh) ... first thought
          was ... oh long after ... she was being punished
          ... for her sins ... a number of which then ...
          further proof if proof were needed ... flashed through
          her mind ... one after another ... then dismissed as
          foolish ... oh long after! ... this thought dismissed
          ... as she suddenly realized ... gradually realized
          ... she was not suffering... imagine! ... not suffering!
          ... indeed could not remember ... off-hand ... when
          she had suffered less ... unless of course she was
          ... meant to be suffering ... ha! ... thought to be
          suffering ... just as the odd time ... in her life ...
          when clearly intended to be having pleasure ... she
          was in fact ... having none ... not the slightest ...
          in which case of course ... that notion of punishment
          ... for some sin or other ... or for the lot ... or no
          particular reason ... for its own sake ... thing
          she understood perfectly ... that notion of punish-
          ment ... which had first occurred to her ... brought
          up as she had been to believe ... with the other waifs
          ... in a merciful ... (brief laugh) ... God ...
          (good laugh) ... first occurred to her ... then dis-
          missed ... as foolish ... was perhaps not so foolish
          ... after all ... so on ... all that ... vain reason-
          ings ... till another thought ... oh long after! ...
          sudden flash ... very foolish really but – ... what?
          ... the buzzing? ... yes ... all the time the buzzing
          ... so-called! ... in the ears ... though of course

1.3

MOUTH:
(contd)

actually ... not in the ears at all ... in the skull
... dull roar in the skull ... and all the time this
ray or beam ... like moonbeam ... but probably
not ... certainly not ... always the same spot ...
now bright ... now shrouded ... but always the
same spot ... as no moon could ... no ... no
moon ... just all part of the same wish to ...
torment ... though actually in point of fact ... not
in the least ... not a twinge ... so far ... ha! ...
so far ... this other thought then ... oh, long after
... sudden flash ... very foolish really but so like
her ... in a way ... that she might do well to
groan ... on and off ... writhe she could not ...
as if in actual ... agony ... but could not ... could
not bring herself ... some flaw in her make-up ...
incapable of deceit ... or the machine ... more
likely the machine ... so disconnected ... never
got the message ... or powerless to respond ...
like numbed ... couldn't make the sound ... not
any sound ... no sound of any kind ... no screaming
for help for example ... should she feel so inclined
... scream ... (screams) ... then listen ...
(silence) ... scream again ... (screams again)
... listen again ... (silence) ... no ... spared
that ... all silent as the grave ... no part - ...
what? ... the buzzing? ... yes ... all silent but
for the buzzing ... so-called ... no part of her
moving ... that she could feel ... just the eyelids
... presumably ... on and off ... shut out the
light ... reflex they call it ... no feeling of any
kind ... but the lids ... even best of times ... who
feels them? ... opening ... shutting ... all that
moisture ... but the brain still ... still sufficient-
ly ... oh very much so! ... at this stage ... in
control ... under control ... to question even this
... for on that April morning ... so it reasoned
... that April morning ... she fixing with her eye
... a distant bell ... as she hastened towards it ...
fixing it with her eye ... lest it elude her ... had
not all gone out ? ... all that light ... of itself ...
without any ... any ... on her part ... so on ...
so on it reasoned ... vain questionings ... and all
dead still ... sweet silent as the grave ... when
suddenly ... gradually ... she realiz - ... what?
... the buzzing? ... yes ... all dead still but for
the buzzing ... when suddenly she realized ...
words were - ... what? ... who? ... what? ...
no ... no! ... SHE! ... (pause and movement 2)

1.4

MOUTH:
(contd)

... realized ... words were coming ... words were
coming! ... a voice she did not recognize ... at
first ... so long since it had sounded ... then finally
had to admit ... could be none other ... than her
own ... certain vowel sounds ... she had never
heard ... elsewhere ... so that people would stare
... the rare occasions ... once or twice a year ...
always winter some strange reason ... stare at her
uncomprehending ... and now this stream ...
steady stream ... she who had never ... on the
contrary ... practically speechless ... all her
days ... how she survived! ... even shopping ...
busy shopping centre ... supermart ... just handed
in the list ... with the bag ... old black shopping
bag ... then stood there waiting ... any length of
time ... middle of the throng ... motionless ...
staring into space ... mouth half open as usual ...
till it was back in her hand ... the bag back in her
hand ... then pay and go ... not as much as goodbye
... how she survived! ... and now this stream ...
not catching the half of it ... not the quarter ... no
idea ... what she was saying ... imagine! ... no
idea what she was saying! ... till she began trying
to ... delude herself ... it was not hers at all ...
not her voice at all ... and ▮▮▮▮▮▮ no doubt ...
vital she should ... was on the point ... after long
efforts ... when suddenly she felt ... gradually the
felt ... her lips moving ... imagine! ... her lips
moving! ... as of course till then she had not ...
and not alone the lips ... the cheeks ... the jaws
... the whole face ... all those ... what? ...
the tongue? ... yes ... the tongue in the mouth
... all those contortions without which ... no speech
possible ... and yet in the ordinary way ... not
felt at all ... so intent one is ... on what one is
saying ... the whole being ... hanging on its words)
... so that not only she had ... had she ... not only
had she ... to give up ... admit hers alone ... her
voice alone ... but this other awful thought ... sudden
flash ... oh long after ... even more awful if
possible ... that feeling was coming back ... feeling
coming back! ... starting at the top ... then
working down ... the whole machine ... but no ...
spared that ... the mouth alone ... so far ... ha!
... so far ... then thinking ... oh long after! ...
sudden flash ... it can't go on ... all this ... all
that ... steady stream ... straining to hear ... make
something of it ... and her own thoughts ... make
something of them ... all that. What? ... the buzzing?

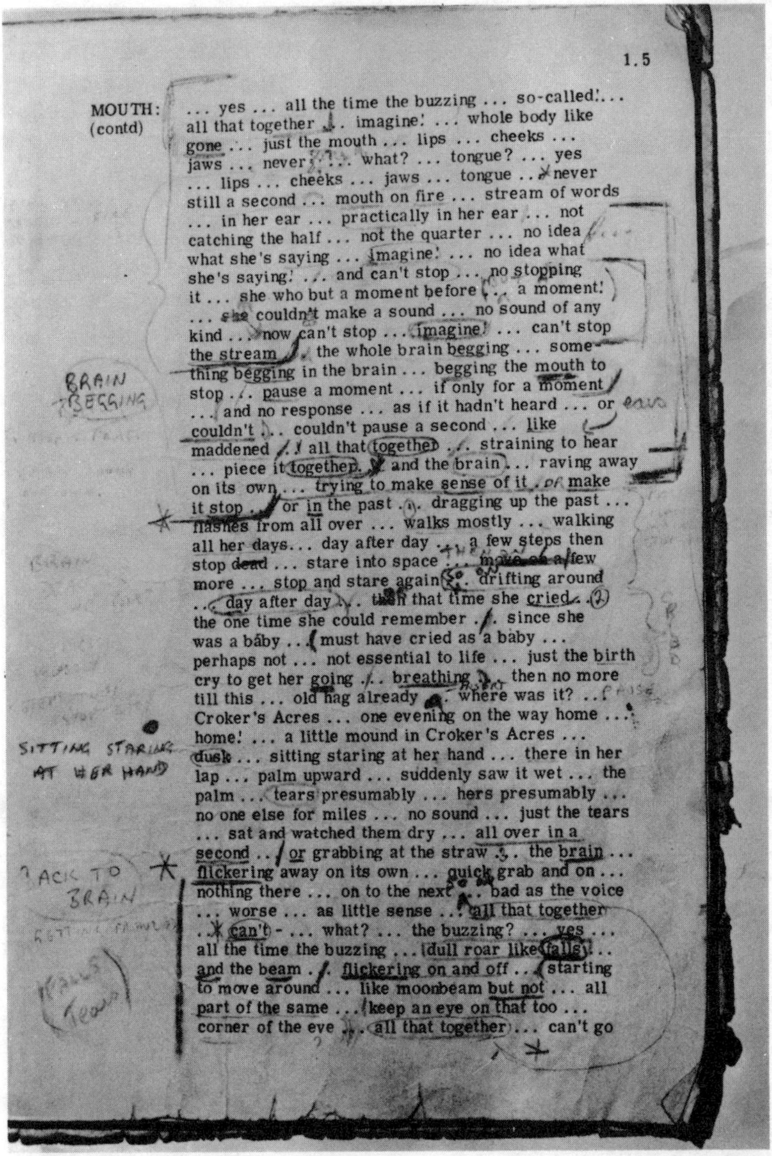

1.5

MOUTH: ... yes ... all the time the buzzing ... so-called ...
(contd) all that together .. imagine ... whole body like
gone ... just the mouth ... lips ... cheeks ...
jaws ... never .... what? ... tongue? ... yes
... lips ... cheeks ... jaws ... tongue .. never
still a second ... mouth on fire ... stream of words
... in her ear ... practically in her ear ... not
catching the half ... not the quarter ... no idea
what she's saying ... imagine ... no idea what
she's saying ... and can't stop ... no stopping
it ... she who but a moment before ... a moment
... she couldn't make a sound ... no sound of any
kind ... now can't stop ... imagine ... can't stop
the stream ... the whole brain begging ... something begging in the brain ... begging the mouth to
stop .. pause a moment ... if only for a moment
... and no response ... as if it hadn't heard ... or
couldn't ... couldn't pause a second ... like
maddened ... all that together ... straining to hear
... piece it together ... and the brain ... raving away
on its own ... trying to make sense of it ... or make
it stop ... or in the past ... dragging up the past ...
flashes from all over ... walks mostly ... walking
all her days... day after day ... a few steps then
stop dead ... stare into space ... move on a few
more ... stop and stare again ... drifting around
... day after day ... then that time she cried ...
the one time she could remember ... since she
was a baby .. must have cried as a baby ...
perhaps not ... not essential to life ... just the birth
cry to get her going ... breathing ... then no more
till this ... old hag already ... where was it? ..
Croker's Acres ... one evening on the way home ...
home ... a little mound in Croker's Acres ...
dusk ... sitting staring at her hand ... there in her
lap ... palm upward ... suddenly saw it wet ... the
palm ... tears presumably ... hers presumably ...
no one else for miles ... no sound ... just the tears
... sat and watched them dry ... all over in a
second .. or grabbing at the straw ... the brain ...
flickering away on its own ... quick grab and on ...
nothing there ... on to the next ... bad as the voice
... worse ... as little sense ... all that together
... can't - ... what? ... the buzzing? ... yes ...
all the time the buzzing ... dull roar like falls ...
and the beam ... flickering on and off ... starting
to move around ... like moonbeam but not ... all
part of the same ... keep an eye on that too ...
corner of the eye ... all that together ... can't go

[Handwritten marginal annotations: "BRAIN BEGGING", "SITTING STARING AT HER HAND", "BACK TO BRAIN"]

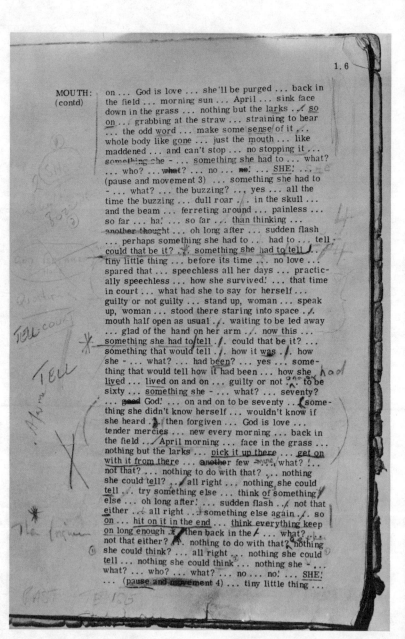

1.6

MOUTH:
(contd)

on ... God is love ... she'll be purged ... back in the field ... morning sun ... April ... sink face down in the grass ... nothing but the larks .. so on ... grabbing at the straw ... straining to hear ... the odd word ... make some sense of it ... whole body like gone ... just the mouth ... like maddened ... and can't stop ... no stopping it ... something she - ... something she had to ... what? ... who? ... what? ... no ... no! ... SHE! ... (pause and movement 3) ... something she had to - ... what? ... the buzzing? .. yes ... all the time the buzzing ... dull roar .. in the skull ... and the beam ... ferreting around ... painless ... so far ... ha! ... so far ... than thinking ... another thought ... oh long after ... sudden flash ... perhaps something she had to ... had to ... tell ... could that be it? .. something she had to tell ... tiny little thing ... before its time ... no love ... spared that ... speechless all her days ... practically speechless ... how she survived! ... that time in court ... what had she to say for herself ... guilty or not guilty ... stand up, woman ... speak up, woman ... stood there staring into space .. mouth half open as usual .. waiting to be led away ... glad of the hand on her arm .. now this ... something she had to tell .. could that be it? ... something that would tell .. how it was .. how she - ... what? ... had been? ... yes ... something that would tell how it had been ... how she had lived ... lived on and on ... guilty or not .. to be sixty ... something she - ... what? ... seventy? ... good God! ... on and on to be seventy .. something she didn't know herself ... wouldn't know if she heard .. then forgiven ... God is love ... tender mercies ... new every morning ... back in the field .. April morning ... face in the grass ... nothing but the larks ... pick it up there ... get on with it from there ... another few .. what? ... not that? ... nothing to do with that? .. nothing she could tell? .. all right ... nothing she could tell .. try something else ... think of something else ... oh long after! ... sudden flash .. not that either .. all right .. something else again .. so on ... hit on it in the end ... think everything keep on long enough .. then back in the .. what? ... not that either? .. nothing to do with that? nothing she could think? ... all right ... nothing she could tell ... nothing she could think ... nothing she - ... what? ... who? ... what? ... no ... no! ... SHE! ... (pause and movement 4) ... tiny little thing ...

1.7

MOUTH:
(contd)

out before its time ... godforsaken hole ... no love
... spared that ... speechless all her days ...
practically speechless ... even to herself ... never
out loud ... but not completely ... sometimes
sudden urge ... once or twice a year ... always
winter some strange reason ... the long evenings
... hours of darkness ... sudden urge to ... tell
... then rush out it stop the first she saw ...
nearest lavatory ... start pouring it out ... steady
stream ... mad stuff ... half the vowels wrong ...
no one could follow ... till she saw the stare she
was getting ... then die of shame ... crawl back in
... once or twice a year ... always winter some
strange reason ... long hours of darkness ... now
this ... this ... quicker and quicker ... the words
... the brain ... flickering away like mad ... quick
grab and on ... nothing there ... on somewhere else
... try somewhere else ... all the time something
begging ... something in her begging ... begging it
all to stop ... unanswered ... prayer unanswered
... or unheard ... too faint ... so on ... keep on
trying ... not knowing what ... what she was trying
... what to try ... whole body like gone ... just the
mouth ... like maddened ... soon ... keep ...
what? ... the buzzing? ... yes ... all the time the
buzzing ... dull roar like falls ... in the skull ...
and the beam ... poking around ... painless ... so
far ... ha! ... so far ... all that ... keep on ...
not knowing what ... what she was - ... what? ...
who? ... what ... no ... no! ... SHE! .. (pause)
... what she was trying ... what to try ... no
Matter ... keep on ... (curtain starts down) ...
hit on it in the end ... then back ... God is love ...
tender mercies ... new every morning ... back in
the field ... April morning
... face in the grass ... nothing but the larks ...
pick it up - *Get on with it from there -*

(Curtain fully down. House dark.
Voice continues behind curtain,
unintelligible, 10 seconds, ceases as
house lights up)

a few more years / out -
INTO THIS WORLD - / THIS WORLD

How It Is
   of this old tale quaqua on all sides then in me bits and scraps try
   and hear a few scraps two or three each time per day and night
   string them together make phrases more phrases the last how it
   was after Pim how it is something wrong there end of part three
   and last

   this voice these voices no knowing not meaning a choir no no
   only one but quaqua meaning on all sides megaphones possibly
   technique something wrong there

   wrong for never twice the same unless time vast tracts aged out
   of recognition no for often fresher stronger after than before
   unless sickness sorrow they sometimes pass one feels better less
   wretched after than before

   unless recordings on ebonite or suchlike a whole life generations
   on ebonite one can imagine it nothing to prevent one mix it all
   up change the natural order play about with that

   unless unchanging after all the voice we're talking of the voice
   and all my fault lack of attention want of memory the various
   times mixed up in my head all the various times before during
   after vast tracts of time

   and always the same old thing the same old things possible and
   impossible or me my fault who can find nothing else when the
   panting stops hear nothing else the same old things four or five a
   few adornments life above little scenes

   things said to me said of me to whom else of whom else clench
   the eyes try and see another to whom of whom to whom of me of
   whom to me or even a third clench the eyes try and see a third
   mix up all that   (Samuel Beckett, *How It Is* (London: Calder
   and Boyars, 1964) p. 107)

Company
   A voice comes to one in the dark. Imagine.

   To one on his back in the dark. This he can tell by the pressure on his hind parts and by how the dark changes when he shuts his eyes and again when he opens them again. Only a small part of what is said can be verified. As for example when he hears, You are on your back in the dark. Then he must acknowledge the truth of what is said. But by far the greater part of what is said cannot be verified. As for example when he hears, You first saw the light on such and such a day. Sometimes the two are combined as for example, You first saw the light on such and such a day and now you are on your back in the dark. A device perhaps from the incontrovertibility of the one to win credence for the other. That then is the proposition. To one on his back in the dark a voice tells of a past. With occasional allusion to a present and more rarely to a future as for example, You will end as you now are. And in another dark or in the same another devising it all for company. Quick leave him.

Use of the second person marks the voice. That of the third that cantankerous other. Could he speak to and of whom the voice speaks there would be a first. But he cannot. He shall not. You cannot. You shall not.

Apart from the voice and the faint sound of his breath there is no sound. None at least that he can hear. This he can tell by the faint sound of his breath. . . . For with what right affirm of a faint sound that it is a less faint made fainter by farness and not a true faint near at hand? Or of a faint fading to fainter that it recedes and not in situ decreases? If with none then no light from the voice on the place . . . (Samuel Beckett, *Company* (London: John Calder, 1980) pp. 1, 45)

Watt

And it was just this hairbreadth departure from the nature of a true pot that so excruciated Watt. For if the approximation had been less close, then Watt would have been less anguished. For then he would not have said, This is a pot, and yet not a pot, no, but then he would have said, This is something of which I do not know the name. And Watt preferred on the whole having to do with things of which he did not know the name, though this too was painful to Watt, to having to do with things of which the known name, the proven name, was not the name, any more, for him. For he could always hope, of a thing of which he had never known the name, that he would learn the name, some day, and so be tranquillized. But he could not look forward to this in the case of a thing of which the true name had ceased, suddenly, or gradually, to be the true name for Watt. For the pot remained a pot, Watt felt sure of that, for everyone but Watt. For Watt alone it was not a pot, any more. (Samuel Beckett, *Watt* (Paris: Olympia Press, 1953) p. 78)

And is it not strange that one says of a thing that it is full, when it is not full at all, but not of a thing that it is empty, if it is not empty? And perhaps the reason for this is this, that when one fills, one seldom fills quite full, for that would not be convenient, whereas when one empties one empties completely, holding the vessel upside down, and rinsing it out with boiling water if necessary, with a kind of fury. (ibid., p. 92)

What distressed Watt in this incident of the Galls father and son, and in subsequent similar incidents, was not so much that he did not know what had happened, for he did not care what had happened, as that nothing had happened, that a thing that was nothing had happened, with the utmost formal distinctness, and that it continued to happen, in his mind, he supposed, though he did not know exactly what that meant, and though it seemed to be outside him, before him, about him, and so on, inexorably to unroll its phases, beginning with the first (the knock that was not a knock) ending with the last (the door closing that was not a door closing), and omitting none, uninvoked, at the most unexpected moments, and the most inopportune. Yes, Watt could not accept, as no doubt Erskine could not accept, and as no doubt Arsene and Walter and Vincent and the others had been unable to accept, that nothing had happened, with all the clarity and solidity of something, and that it revisited him in such a way that he was forced to submit to it all over again, to hear the same sounds, see the same light, touch the same surfaces, and so on, as when they had first involved him in their unintelligible intricacies. If he had been able to accept it, then perhaps it would not have revisited him, and this would have been a great saving of vexation, to put it mildly. But he could not accept it, could not bear it. One wonders sometimes where Watt thought he was. In a culture-park? (ibid., p. 73)

The moon was now up. It was not far up, but it was up. It was of an unpleasant yellow colour. Long past the full, it was waning, waning. Watt's way of advancing due east, for example, was to turn his bust as far as possible towards the north and at the same time to fling out his right leg as far as possible towards the south, and then to turn his bust as far as possible towards the south and at the same time to fling out his left leg as far as possible towards the north, and then again to turn his bust as far as possible towards the north, and to fling out his right leg as far as possible towards the south, and then again to turn his bust as far as possible towards the south and to fling out his left leg as far as possible towards the north, and so on, over and over again, many many times, until he reached his destination and could sit down. So, standing first on one leg, and then on the other, he moved forward, a headlong tardigrade, in a straight line. The knees, on these occasions, did not bend. They could have, but they did not. No knees could bend better than Watt's, when they chose, there was nothing the matter with Watt's knees, as may appear. But when out walking they did not bend, for some obscure reason.   (ibid., p. 30)

For if there were two things that Watt disliked, one was the moon, and the other was the sun.   (ibid., p. 31)

Everybody's Autobiography

There is a bother about that you get more familiar with a thing when you say it than when you write it, when you say it you repeat it when you write it you never do because when you write it is in you and when you say it they hear you. After two weeks I wondered if I heard what I said or if I only heard them hearing what I said. When I write I write and when I talk I talk and the two are not one, no not for any one and when they come near being one, then the inside is not inside and the outside is not outside and I like the inside to be inside and the outside to be outside, it makes it more necessary to be one. . . . I think I write so clearly that I worry about it. . . . The landlord at the boarding house was funny, he sat at the end of the table and he did not like low lights, he said if they had another light like that he would be in total darkness. He did not say funny things. . . . Well feudal days were the days of fathers and now once more

these days are the days of fathers. . . . And fathers come up and
fathers go down. That is natural enough when nobody has had
fathers they begin to long for them and then when everybody
has had fathers they begin to long to do without them . . .
perhaps the twenty-first century like the eighteenth century will
be a nice time when everybody forgets to be a father or to have
been one. The Jews and they come into this because they are
very much given to having a father and to being one and they
are very much given not to want a father and not to have one,
and they are an epitome of all this that is happening the
concentration of fathering to the perhaps there not being one
. . . when we come to England that is what she finds most
exciting that and everything else done by women. . . . She
might have been important that summer when everything was
different, what else does she say yes it is nature but that does
not make it natural. She says also that whenever she is comfortably seated she is not comfortable unless everybody else is
comfortably sitting, but after all she never is sitting comfortably
so perhaps quite naturally everybody else is not comfortably
sitting.   (Gertrude Stein, *Everybody's Autobiography*, 1931 (New
York: Vintage Books, Random House, 1973) pp. 139–42)

Tender Buttons

Act so that there is no use in a centre. . . . A fact is that when the
place was replaced all was left that was stored and all was
retained that would not satisfy more than another. The
question is this, is it possible to suggest more to replace that
thing. This question and this perfect denial does make the time
change all the time.

. . . it does there is no doubt that to be right is more than perfect
there is no doubt and glass is confusing it confuses the substance
which was of a color. . . . A silence is not indicated by any
motion, less is indicated by a motion, more is not indicated it is
enthralled. So sullen and so low, so much resignation, so much
refusal and so much place for a lower and an upper, so much
and yet more silence why is not sleeping a feat why is it not and
when is there some discharge when. There never is.

If comparing a piece that is a size that is recognized as not a size but a piece, comparing a piece with what is not recognized but what is used as it is held by holding, comparing these two comes to be repeated. Suppose they are put together, suppose that there is an interruption, supposing that beginning again they are not changed as to position, suppose all this and suppose that any five two of whom are not separating suppose that the five are not consumed. Is there an exchange, is there a resemblance to the sky which is admitted to be there and the stars which can be seen. Is there. That was a question. There was no certainty. Fitting a failing meant that any two were indifferent and yet they were all connecting that, they were all connecting that consideration. This did not determine rejoining a letter. This did not make letters smaller. It did. . . . Why is a pale white not paler than blue, why is a connection made by a stove, why is the example which is mentioned not shown to be the same. (Gertrude Stein, 'Rooms', *Tender Buttons* (New York: Marie Claire Editions, 1914) p. 63)

VII

Quote: Phrases from *A Piece of Monologue*

Listening

Observing, and the 'Through-whom'

'Truth'

Effects of/in language

Listening to phrases from a soundtape from *A Piece of Monologue*: 'Nothing there' . . . 'nothing stirring that he can see here' . . . 'then slow fade up of a form' . . . '*fade up*' being the allusion to the use of an apparatus for making visible, i.e. stagelights, or stagelights imagined. Thus, 'no, no such thing as no light' is a concept here of non-invisibility (tape ft 380). 'Word no different from Image in necessarily explaining things' (Wittgenstein). Whilst listening to the tape, the following: 'then slow fade up' . . . 'no, no such thing as no light'. One is in the position as listener of having to *disrupt the process of hearing* and go with the linear continuance within the narrative, in order to switch to a code which allows for the apparatus ('fade') to become part of the story (but only with difficulty). Saying 'fade up' is not the same as saying 'switches light on in order to make visible'. One is referring within the mental imaginary space of the 'narrative' (the diegesis) to a set of accepted codes, the other is referring from outside of the (constructed) mental imaginary space of the narrative. More precisely, by *seeming* to be outside the diegesis (nothing is extradiegetic) there is the changing parameter of what is the diegetic. 'Fade up' is a seemingly extra or non-diegetic element, as is 'no, no such thing as no light' – a negation of the previous sentence (a previous representation) by 'no, no such thing'. The statement is in contradiction to the fiction; therefore, 'no, no such thing as no light' (and the first 'no' can equal the meaning of 'yes',

32

as in 'yes, no such thing as no light'). 'No, no such thing as no light' at first contradicts the given diegetic sentences and then extends the parameters of what is for this monologue allowable as diegetic. This construction *re*places the listener, and that shift has disallowed the listener's 'going with' the descriptive referential fiction which would have been at the expense of the materiality of the process of producing here for you meaning via such language structuration.

The problematic of the, or an, omniscient observer as centre of knowledge is not yet answered by this critique. This connects directly to the question of the speaker, speaking the monologue, as the centre of knowledge. The speaker (monologuer) may not be the traditional omniscient observer–speaker of the short-story genre, but rather may still be omniscient inasmuch as being the only, or main, character through whom the monologue is spoken. 'It dreamed him . . .' (Leib Perez, *Chassidic Stories*, trans. Ludwig Strauss (Berlin: Schocken, 1936) p. 8).[7] The through-whom is a double-edged concept, still positing a knower, *can*-er, speaker–producer-god, who speaks, or through whom is spoken, akin to the Althusserian concept of people through whom history is made, rather than some humanistic notion of 'individual people make history'. The speaking-through forces an ideology and a politics which sees individual subjectivities and the voices of speech of individual subjectivities as constructed within a historical and dialectical process, rather than as individuals in a vacuum. History is thus a process without a subject; humans do not make language, it is through humans that speech is languaged (the opposite of which would be to see each individual human as somehow the source of language and identity, pre-existing the objective contradictions of material life and its histories, sexual, economic, ideological, etc.).

The question for both notions of the 'through-whom' must be whether this 'character' can be identified with/into, and for how *long*. The latter becomes a crucial question of duration as material process. The possibility for the listener, within a monological identification mechanism (through and via the speaker) of a constant rememoration attempt, depends on the locus in time necessary for functioning as a locus in space. The unfunctioning, the un-understanding is thus basic to the subject's break from monological identity.[8] What is left is the material at hand in all process, of both the subject-matter's form and the subject-matter's subject, thus of the history of 'subjects', and the material rememoration attempts (of such histories) under no matter what guise.

To reiterate: the scientific fact (truth another matter) given by the speaker when stating 'no, no such thing as no light' undermines by negation a poesis of shadow and darkness, the holding of any of this as some perfect poetic metaphor. When a previous truth of the speaker's statement is negated, 'no such thing as no light', the piece paradoxically retains its *non-naturalism* for the listener, because once the speaker's truth has been questioned (together with the 'truth' of the fading figure), that example's hold on our feelings and thoughts is made impossible precisely as the truth of the speaker is no longer credible. The paradox being that the hold of those figurations of expressionist aloneness was based on the speaker's metaphors, characterisations, dramas. Followed by a scientific theory: a concept of 'total darkness' is not viable. This annihilates the specific possibility of existence, *and consequent disappearance* (absence), disallows those imaginary existences, no longer allows for the positing of the almost-gone, undermines the possibility of total absence. *Gone* as impossible now, but not because of the speaker's 'no, no such thing as no light' but because of the non-believability any longer of anything the speaker says except for its momentary subjectivity-effect, its subject-*ness*, paralleled by simultaneous unbelief, unknowing.

This position undermines subjective *and* scientific 'truth'. Scientific facts exist even if others, opposing ones, exist differently, in different periods. Einstein and Galileo were scientists not poets in spite of this. Both were at times scientifically incorrect as to facts known prior to, and after, their 'time'. The time of an acceptability of a scientific truth is not an endless time outside of history and ideology. Related to this, Brecht's being wrong about Galileo did not, at that point, and for *that* reason, constitute Brecht as a poet (!) though Brecht was a poet. Various (all ideological) theoretical facts can be posited outside of perception or discovery. Metaphysical idealism is always at hand, as is god, when the material cause is unobtainable for historical, ideological, technological, theoretico-philosophical, reasons.

colour, it turns white to green, red to black, yellow to greenish yellow, blue to greenish blue. The white pane should, therefore, make everything whitish, i.e. it should make everything *pale*; and, then, why shouldn't it turn black to grey? – Even a yellow glass makes things darker, should a white glass make things darker too?

196.   Grey is not poorly illuminated white, dark green is not poorly illuminated light green. It is true that we say 'At night all cats are grey', but that really means: we can't distinguish what colour they are and they *could* be grey.

200.   White seen through a coloured glass appears with the colour of the glass. That is a rule of the appearance of transparency. So white appears white through white glass, i.e. as through uncoloured glass.

96.   We say 'Let's imagine human beings who don't know *this* language-game'. But this does not give us any clear idea of the life of these people, of where it deviates from ours. We don't yet know what we have to imagine; for the life of these people *is* supposed to correspond to ours for the rest, and it first has to be determined what we would call a life that corresponds to ours under the new circumstances. . . .   (Ludwig Wittgenstein, *Remarks on Colour* (1951) (Oxford: Blackwell, 1977; Frankfurt: Suhrkamp, 1977) pp. 46–116)

foregoing about language or about the absence of light? Is it specifics of colour or about language's inability to posit its mechanisms and any object described as truth? Said ntly, language can posit itself as truth only whilst aneously unable to evidence itself as that in any way other hrough a series of mechanisms which by the writing ate a reader to an illusionist practice. How, then, is the r's truth questioned? How long does it take for an 'I' to *not* ts power as giver of meaning or reproducer of such, to the that the reader is *not* producing his or her reading, equal, e, different. Rather, now, than a battle of two (or more) s, 'a reading' is a production constantly in process, with no

'Scientific truth' has causes and effects in language. As there is (in 1985) no such thing as no light there is always some light, and the approach of total darkness which one infers from shadowlike figures, present or absent, is annihilated. 'No, no such thing as no light' thus makes impossible the reinscription of the listener into an on-going narrative identification which would be necessary for a continuum of the scene (*ex-vacuo* and *in-vacuo*).

As the effects are in language, are they also about language? The 'shadows' produced are/were literary productions. The lack of light similarly. The listener is inculcated by language in a contradictory mental labour process through certain usages of negation, repetition and the reification of the referent in and through structures of the spoken, the speed of speech, etc.

Language's incapacity to cover the world outside language militates against the 'pro-theatric' being describable, the 'pro-theatric' that which is empirically real, on stage or off. Yet this impossibility of description does not stop things being 'describ*ed*', a narrative of events being set forth.

we construct a geometry. And 'ideal' doe
something specially good, but only somethi
extremes.

36. And of course such a construct can in t
something about the actual use.

43. In philosophy it is not enough to learn in
is to be said about a subject, but also *how*
about it. We are always having to begin
method of tackling it.

132. In a particular meaning of 'white' whi
colour of all. In a painting in which a pie
gets its lightness from the blue sky, the s
the white paper. And yet in another
darker and white the lighter colour (G
palette, white is the lightest colour.

136. By analogy with the other colours, a
white background seen through a tra
would have to appear unchanged as a
white background. For the black mu
the white, because it is also the colo
body, remains unchanged.

146. A body that is actually transparen
white to us; but it cannot seem wh

153. We don't say of something which
it looks white.

160. If I say a piece of paper is pure wh
next to it and it then app
surroundings and for ordinary
white and not light grey.

174. In the places where there is on
white paper it doesn't seem at a

191. If a pane of green glass gives t

VIII

Quote: *Remarks on Colour* (Wittgenstein)[9]

About Language or about Light?

On *White*

An Example: Canvas and Memory

Ideology as Material

Subjective Histories as Objective Histories

Women Speaking and Reflexivity, and Resistance

Sexual Difference, So-called, and Identity

Negation

I:

24. It is not immediately clear of which transparent glass we should say it has the same colour as an opaque colour sample. If I say 'I am looking for glass of *this* colour' (pointing to a piece of coloured paper) that would mean roughly that something white seen through the glass should look like my sample.

30. Every coloured medium darkens that which is seen through it, it swallows light: now is my white glass also supposed to darken? And the more so the thicker it is? So it would really be a dark glass!

III:

35. Lichtenberg says that very few people have ever seen pure white. Do most people use the word wrong, then? And how did *he* learn the correct use? – On the contrary: he constructed an ideal use from the actual one. The way

possibilities of notions like 'many interpretations'. It is now no more a matter of that.

> Runge says (in the letter that Goethe reproduced in his *Theory of Colours*) there are transparent and opaque colours. White is an opaque colour. (ibid., I, 17)

> Hand ... in light of spill ... white (Beckett, *A Piece of Monologue*, p. 75)

White, as separate from 'the human' in certain theatrical usages, as not human, inhuman, antihuman, the way a white figure, or a white space, or a white hand, or a white face, *looks*, as much as in the *ideology* within which exist adhering meanings and positions for the reader/viewer. Ideology is material. White: Fear. When Bert Brecht asked Karl Valentin what to do with a scene of soldiers in war, how to show fear, Valentin's response was 'Paint their faces white, blank white.' This was the genesis for Brecht of the notion of 'quoting' a feeling, a thought, a position, simultaneous with the notion of 'acting' it out. The *distanciation* produced by such an acting technique found its origin in such mechanisms as the flat-white-painted faces. Brechtian theatre and its politics, from the specific to the general, is inseparable from Valentin's expressionist/anti-expressionist *collectivising* notion of the usage of the colour white. Once that concept of 'white' becomes utilised, specifics (*from* the general) must be worked out, so that the characterisations are not just illustrations of a set of ideas anterior to the play, the process of theatre, and theatrics. A specific is a white face as unmoving, frozen (iconic?), desexualised, fetish – hysterical stasis – the dehumanised form (the human figure) in constant conflict with language, movement, theatrical context. One can see how such a notion of the usage of the colour *white* sets up a theoretical, abstract, concreteness. Wittgenstein's impossible empiricisms were trying to define precisely and being unable, setting up the kind of dialectic that, in a different arena, Valentin and Brecht worked out. The Beckettian whited Mouth in *Not I* and whited face in *Rockaby* are inseparable from such a problematic.

The examples of 'the white' in various representational practices (writing, painting, theatre, film) are given not as analogies for something else but as usages inscribed in the process of making, constructing, producing, *as artifice*, as opposed to experiencing 'what is' as natural, as somehow always already everpresent with its meanings, political intents, effectivities.

To give another example: if a certain single image, for example the tower at Prague airport is seen from a plane, and at that moment for the viewer (passenger) a memory-construct is formed replacing him/her to a time and place when the same image was previously seen, and the surround, the environs, the fog, the other buildings, the closer presences (planes, people, objects, present time and space) are repressed, then that is a transporting of one to an imaginary position, i.e. the past, but a past which does not admit to subjective and objective historical process. As if one could now still be in the prior time, oneself no different and it no different. If that same image of the Prague tower is seen, silkscreened onto a section of mainly white canvas, the whole 'picture' (for example) six feet square, most of the surface white canvas, and the 'same' process of rememoration takes place for the same viewer when seeing the image of the tower, then that is occurring within and against reproduction and representation. The illusion, via repression, of a previous time and space, a previous thought and feeling, for one, is at once present, via a perception of this representation, yet it disallows a fullness to the representation, and disallows the meanings the same power of repression, the same force to transport one, as what occurs occurs in the face of representation, the canvas, the spaces and materiality *there*, facing one. The *image* of the tower, i.e. the instigator of the specifically described process as image-*of*, is co-present and in conflict with the illusionary reintegration into a non-historical, unchanged past.

The memory-trace via the canvas, or via the white face, or via a moment of speech in *A Piece of Monologue* is against that, against and in relation to that work of attempted representation and *its* materiality. Whereas in daily-life experience (neither, in fact, is outside of representation but one is outside of the primarily aesthetic realm) an image, the Prague tower, triggers a memory and a replacing of the self into a past, utilising (via repression) the image as metaphor, a repressed metaphor for 'memory-back-to-something/somewhere *else*'. The daily-life image thus functions as metaphor, synechdochally (part for whole, the image of the tower for (a segment of) previous life). It also functions as nostalgia when not in relation to a specific construction-attempt of pictorial representation, i.e. when simply reseen and setting off memory in daily life. It functions as nostalgia with no measure against a present history of the self, with no measure of the dialectical historical distance and difference from the rememorated time, as the transformations, in between, are elided for this transport-back. The function of the illusionist moves back via a stimulus in the world thus becomes an attempt at (and a feeling of) timelessness, a past futurised (as 'now', or 'now again') or a future anteriorised (from *then*, the time of the initial recognition of the tower, to the meaning it gathers now, as if that first experience could have been moved forward to now). The ideological quest involved precisely pertains to an illusionary sameness being produced, the acknowledgement of transformation and struggle, i.e. history, subjectivity and historical materiality (materialism) negated. A sameness thus which functions only at the expense of the material process engaged, and at the expense of one's life as anything other than a series of (ideological) desires, some stage of 'pure' thought whose fulfilment is directly related to repressive mechanisms that negate (social) practice in a material world. This 'lesson' though can not be learnt by reliving the perception somehow of this or that moment from life but only by a force of abstract thought and the reperceiving of the opposition between perception (the construction of ideological positions and feelings) and knowledge (the process and processes articulated on stage, in film, on canvas, in writing, against which by its structures of material repetition, process, construction, etc., the spectator can be positioned in contradiction and opposition), and from that produce a position against conventions of the natural, real, true. The white as other, as a wedge against identification into the naturalised (and self-identification), the obliteration of which it is predicated upon. 'Hand, in light of spill, white' is thus not an expressionist metaphor, but a reification of the represented object (hand) and further exaggeration of its uselessness, its break from human body and human nature, break from the current theatrical-verbal-imaginative codes and forces such is predicated upon.[10]

The notion of a verbal-monological/theatrical anti-humanist practice is only thinkable within a notion of ideology as material process. Ideology is material and material is ideological (not simply, for example, economic). What are the political meanings of this for language? How is this concretely connected to the viewer's being situated in patriarchal speech and patriarchal positions formed thereby? Implicit and explicit paternal signification, in structures and forms of phallocratic 'truth', are the material of ideology. 'Individual' positions are never individual positions.

Different histories produced onto different categories of body (men, women, black men, black women, working class, managerial class, etc.) have their insistences when it comes to meanings (pre-)existing for them. Within such objective categories, specific subjectivities are motored. A politico-aesthetic materialism (theatre, painting, music, writing)[11] could attempt whilst not relegating to irrelevance their categories of collectivity to produce subjective histories' effects as specific problematics through figure(s) and absence(s), through each's subjectivity, making of the resulting a person/category who/which is then inscribed in contradiction through ('*vis à vis*') the given piece of work.

The theatrics and the language of *Not I*, its repetitions and various forms of attempted descriptive speech and that attempt's impossibility, inscribe the viewer–listener in a reflexive process. This structuration of the viewer as ineluctable effect of the theatrical text, without denying her–his causality and her–his history, produces unending opposition through fracturing expectation and unity, for male and female. The viewer never reaches a state of 'end'. Yet there is a constant power/opposition dialectic. Sexual 'difference', having a vagina or having a penis, having a vagina and breasts or having a penis, *is* the figuration upon which one group asserts its power and authority, another its opposition. Such reflexiveness inscribed in ('in', i.e. through, with and against) the viewer also differentiates between a reflexiveness within narration, and reflexion in and against the viewer–listener's (conscious and unconscious) *specific* historical/economic/sexual context. A main concern in the Beckettian text is the relation of female viewer to female speaker/actress, and the latter's language and gesture. The specific effects of that reflexive process of (in and through) *Not I* instantiates the loss of male power-positions, and instantiates the power of a woman's speech and gesture as materially dialectic.

Resistance, for example, is formulated against the conscious and unconscious theatrical–political context. There are possibilities, for example, of the unconscious being untrammelled, thereby allowing images, words, works, their force whilst simultaneously *conscious* resistances are maintained. Or certain meanings heard and viewed (the oppression by ideological meaning) could be allowed on the conscious level, in, for example, a group defined as women-only, whilst in a mixed group both the unconscious and the conscious resistances would be politically necessary. Certain suppressions and repressions, and oppressions, obviously function differently in different contexts; that has its effects on the unconscious (which, too, is historical) as well as on the conscious. A position differing from this one would have to be the reactionary one that maintains some kind of 'free' unconscious, where some 'free' desire, some notion of contextless 'liberation' and libertarianism still persists. The *un*conscious differentiation for each viewer is not predetermined by some general context but by the history of the spectator(s) in relation to the work's attempted effects, its processes; will that not effect conscious positionings and critiques in relation to the unconscious identifications? The relation of the male and female viewer to the Beckettian speaking female is thus imbricated in a complexity of the politics of language and the politics against language, and its constructions, both of which disallow a consumption of the theatric process outside of a material(ist) history – unless an immense work of repression is effected, and the bourgeois conventions allowed to overdetermine the specificity of the work at hand.

The concept of *sexual* difference is one figuration upon which one group asserts its power, another its opposition. To label such a position biologistic would be to assume the philosophically strictly idealist possibility that patriarchy is oppressive to *anyone* via certain constraints regardless of sex, thereby denying and disavowing the ideological material basis upon which such function is predicated. Revolutionary would be to not be defined by the sexual. To be defined as same, not different. It is by the body's sex that 'woman' is defined, that 'man' is defined, that

women and men are defined. It is politically specific to reduce to
its sex a series of techniques (reification) in a seamless continuum
of power, which were it a stasis would provide its own destruction.
It is the movement and *its* ineluctableness, its dynamics, like
capitalism's, which makes for such a necessary long-term battle in
opposition. How does this conceptualisation exist in written work,
in language, in Beckett? It has to do with the reification of a
repeated fragment of language, the reification of the referent:
'Hand, in light of spill, white', such a phrase finding its
contradictory power against sexual archetypes, sexual–political
archetypes, in the very artifice of the process which positions itself
against the 'image' or 'imaginary' or 'scene' or 'fiction' produced.
Such a reification in language through language disallows the
'natural dynamic', the 'dynamic of the natural' with its
hegemonic structures of truth, as truth, to obtain. True as Good.
'Stare into space ... then on ... a few more ... stop and stare again ...
so on ... drifting around ... when suddenly ... gradually ... all went
out ... all that early' (ten words per second). 'Stare into space ...
then on ... a few more ... stop and stare again ... so on ... drifting
around ... when suddenly ... gradually ... all went out ... all that
early.' Even the 'hysterical' (speed – 'wildness' – repression –
gestural symptom – hallucinated hearing – paralysis – etc.) in
such repetitive representation as to sound, as to image, as to
(impossible) attempt to focus on one moment, one *non*-movement
disallows the production of a coherent image of hysteria. Instead,
opposed to this (for 'images of hysteria' as for anything else), a
process of material difference from *any* real outside of the real of
the process of representation-attempts – disillusioning those
attempts.

To come to the dead-end of identificatory pleasure is what is
radical in these structuring processes. The constant impossibility
is the dead end. All heard, all seen, all struggle no longer collapsed
onto the conventions of ideology of power, and its material
enactments and reproductions through the individual listener-
spectator as representative for, and part of, the social totality's
hegemonic state. Thus the last gasp of a 'dying' patriarchy, like
the last gasp of a 'dying' capitalism, has theoretical truth whilst it
is empirically untrue. Virtual hegemony is assured simultaneous
with the dead-end. And that as a process in which a viewer–
listener functions, in that dialectic mental movement, is the

'Scientific truth' has causes and effects in language. As there is (in 1985) no such thing as no light there is always some light, and the approach of total darkness which one infers from shadowlike figures, present or absent, is annihilated. 'No, no such thing as no light' thus makes impossible the reinscription of the listener into an on-going narrative identification which would be necessary for a continuum of the scene (*ex-vacuo* and *in-vacuo*).

As the effects are in language, are they also about language? The 'shadows' produced are/were literary productions. The lack of light similarly. The listener is inculcated by language in a contradictory mental labour process through certain usages of negation, repetition and the reification of the referent in and through structures of the spoken, the speed of speech, etc.

Language's incapacity to cover the world outside language militates against the 'pro-theatric' being describable, the 'pro-theatric' that which is empirically real, on stage or off. Yet this impossibility of description does not stop things being 'describ*ed*', a narrative of events being set forth.

VIII

Quote: *Remarks on Colour* (Wittgenstein)[9]

About Language or about Light?

On *White*

An Example: Canvas and Memory

Ideology as Material

Subjective Histories as Objective Histories

Women Speaking and Reflexivity, and Resistance

Sexual Difference, So-called, and Identity

Negation

I:

24. It is not immediately clear of which transparent glass we should say it has the same colour as an opaque colour sample. If I say 'I am looking for glass of *this* colour' (pointing to a piece of coloured paper) that would mean roughly that something white seen through the glass should look like my sample.

30. Every coloured medium darkens that which is seen through it, it swallows light: now is my white glass also supposed to darken? And the more so the thicker it is? So it would really be a dark glass!

III:

35. Lichtenberg says that very few people have ever seen pure white. Do most people use the word wrong, then? And how did *he* learn the correct use? – On the contrary: he constructed an ideal use from the actual one. The way

36

we construct a geometry. And 'ideal' does not mean something specially good, but only something carried to extremes.

36. And of course such a construct can in turn teach us something about the actual use.

43. In philosophy it is not enough to learn in every case *what* is to be said about a subject, but also *how* one must speak about it. We are always having to begin by learning the method of tackling it.

132. In a particular meaning of 'white' white is the lightest colour of all. In a painting in which a piece of white paper gets its lightness from the blue sky, the sky is lighter than the white paper. And yet in another sense blue is the darker and white the lighter colour (Goethe). . . . On the palette, white is the lightest colour.

136. By analogy with the other colours, a black drawing on a white background seen through a transparent *white* glass would have to appear unchanged as a black drawing on a white background. For the black must remain black and the white, because it is also the colour of the transparent body, remains unchanged.

146. A body that is actually transparent can, of course, seem white to us; but it cannot seem white and transparent.

153. We don't say of something which looks transparent that it looks white.

160. If I say a piece of paper is pure white and then place snow next to it and it then appears grey, in normal surroundings and for ordinary purposes I would call it white and not light grey.

174. In the places where there is only a little less light on the white paper it doesn't seem at all grey, but always white.

191. If a pane of green glass gives the things behind it a green

colour, it turns white to green, red to black, yellow to greenish yellow, blue to greenish blue. The white pane should, therefore, make everything whitish, i.e. it should make everything *pale*; and, then, why shouldn't it turn black to grey? – Even a yellow glass makes things darker, should a white glass make things darker too?

196. Grey is not poorly illuminated white, dark green is not poorly illuminated light green. It is true that we say 'At night all cats are grey', but that really means: we can't distinguish what colour they are and they *could* be grey.

200. White seen through a coloured glass appears with the colour of the glass. That is a rule of the appearance of transparency. So white appears white through white glass, i.e. as through uncoloured glass.

296. We say 'Let's imagine human beings who don't know *this* language-game'. But this does not give us any clear idea of the life of these people, of where it deviates from ours. We don't yet know what we have to imagine; for the life of these people *is* supposed to correspond to ours for the rest, and it first has to be determined what we would call a life that corresponds to ours under the new circumstances. . . . (Ludwig Wittgenstein, *Remarks on Colour* (1951) (Oxford: Blackwell, 1977; Frankfurt: Suhrkamp, 1977) pp. 46–116)

Is the foregoing about language or about the absence of light? Is it about specifics of colour or about language's inability to posit its own mechanisms and any object described as truth? Said differently, language can posit itself as truth only whilst simultaneously unable to evidence itself as that in any way other than through a series of mechanisms which by the writing inculcate a reader to an illusionist practice. How, then, is the speaker's truth questioned? How long does it take for an 'I' to *not* retain its power as giver of meaning or reproducer of such, to the extent that the reader is *not* producing his or her reading, equal, opposite, different. Rather, now, than a battle of two (or more) readings, 'a reading' is a production constantly in process, with no possibilities of notions like 'many interpretations'. It is now no more a matter of that.

> Runge says (in the letter that Goethe reproduced in his *Theory of Colours*) there are transparent and opaque colours. White is an opaque colour.   (ibid., I, 17)

> Hand . . . in light of spill . . . white (Beckett, *A Piece of Monologue*, p. 75)

White, as separate from 'the human' in certain theatrical usages, as not human, inhuman, antihuman, the way a white figure, or a white space, or a white hand, or a white face, *looks*, as much as in the *ideology* within which exist adhering meanings and positions for the reader/viewer. Ideology is material. White: Fear. When Bert Brecht asked Karl Valentin what to do with a scene of soldiers in war, how to show fear, Valentin's response was 'Paint their faces white, blank white.' This was the genesis for Brecht of the notion of 'quoting' a feeling, a thought, a position, simultaneous with the notion of 'acting' it out. The *distanciation* produced by such an acting technique found its origin in such mechanisms as the flat-white-painted faces. Brechtian theatre and its politics, from the specific to the general, is inseparable from Valentin's expressionist/anti-expressionist *collectivising* notion of the usage of the colour white. Once that concept of 'white' becomes utilised, specifics (*from* the general) must be worked out, so that the characterisations are not just illustrations of a set of ideas anterior to the play, the process of theatre, and theatrics. A specific is a white face as unmoving, frozen (iconic?), desexualised, fetish – hysterical stasis – the dehumanised form (the human figure) in constant conflict with language, movement, theatrical context. One can see how such a notion of the usage of the colour *white* sets up a theoretical, abstract, concreteness. Wittgenstein's impossible empiricisms were trying to define precisely and being unable, setting up the kind of dialectic that, in a different arena, Valentin and Brecht worked out. The Beckettian whited Mouth in *Not I* and whited face in *Rockaby* are inseparable from such a problematic.

The examples of 'the white' in various representational practices (writing, painting, theatre, film) are given not as analogies for something else but as usages inscribed in the process of making, constructing, producing, *as artifice*, as opposed to experiencing 'what is' as natural, as somehow always already everpresent with its meanings, political intents, effectivities.

To give another example: if a certain single image, for example the tower at Prague airport is seen from a plane, and at that moment for the viewer (passenger) a memory-construct is formed replacing him/her to a time and place when the same image was previously seen, and the surround, the environs, the fog, the other buildings, the closer presences (planes, people, objects, present time and space) are repressed, then that is a transporting of one to an imaginary position, i.e. the past, but a past which does not admit to subjective and objective historical process. As if one could now still be in the prior time, oneself no different and it no different. If that same image of the Prague tower is seen, silkscreened onto a section of mainly white canvas, the whole 'picture' (for example) six feet square, most of the surface white canvas, and the 'same' process of rememoration takes place for the same viewer when seeing the image of the tower, then that is occurring within and against reproduction and representation. The illusion, via repression, of a previous time and space, a previous thought and feeling, for one, is at once present, via a perception of this representation, yet it disallows a fullness to the representation, and disallows the meanings the same power of repression, the same force to transport one, as what occurs occurs in the face of representation, the canvas, the spaces and materiality *there*, facing one. The *image* of the tower, i.e. the instigator of the specifically described process as image-*of*, is co-present and in conflict with the illusionary reintegration into a non-historical, unchanged past.

The memory-trace via the canvas, or via the white face, or via a moment of speech in *A Piece of Monologue* is against that, against and in relation to that work of attempted representation and *its* materiality. Whereas in daily-life experience (neither, in fact, is outside of representation but one is outside of the primarily aesthetic realm) an image, the Prague tower, triggers a memory and a replacing of the self into a past, utilising (via repression) the image as metaphor, a repressed metaphor for 'memory-back-to-something/somewhere *else*'. The daily-life image thus functions as metaphor, synechdochally (part for whole, the image of the tower for (a segment of) previous life). It also functions as nostalgia when not in relation to a specific construction-attempt of pictorial representation, i.e. when simply reseen and setting off memory in daily life. It functions as nostalgia with no measure against a present history of the self, with no measure of the dialectical historical distance and difference from the rememorated time, as the transformations, in between, are elided for this transport-back. The function of the illusionist moves back via a stimulus in the world thus becomes an attempt at (and a feeling of) timelessness, a past futurised (as 'now', or 'now again') or a future anteriorised (from *then*, the time of the initial recognition of the tower, to the meaning it gathers now, as if that first experience could have been moved forward to now). The ideological quest involved precisely pertains to an illusionary sameness being produced, the acknowledgement of transformation and struggle, i.e. history, subjectivity and historical materiality (materialism) negated. A sameness thus which functions only at the expense of the material process engaged, and at the expense of one's life as anything other than a series of (ideological) desires, some stage of 'pure' thought whose fulfilment is directly related to repressive mechanisms that negate (social) practice in a material world. This 'lesson' though can not be learnt by reliving the perception somehow of this or that moment from life but only by a force of abstract thought and the reperceiving of the opposition between perception (the construction of ideological positions and feelings) and knowledge (the process and processes articulated on stage, in film, on canvas, in writing, against which by its structures of material repetition, process, construction, etc., the spectator can be positioned in contradiction and opposition), and from that produce a position against conventions of the natural, real, true. The white as other, as a wedge against identification into the naturalised (and self-identification), the obliteration of which it is predicated upon. 'Hand, in light of spill, white' is thus not an expressionist metaphor, but a reification of the represented object (hand) and further exaggeration of its uselessness, its break from human body and human nature, break from the current theatrical-verbal-imaginative codes and forces such is predicated upon.[10]

The notion of a verbal-monological/theatrical anti-humanist practice is only thinkable within a notion of ideology as material process. Ideology is material and material is ideological (not simply, for example, economic). What are the political meanings of this for language? How is this concretely connected to the viewer's being situated in patriarchal speech and patriarchal positions formed thereby? Implicit and explicit paternal signification, in structures and forms of phallocratic 'truth', are the material of ideology. 'Individual' positions are never individual positions.

Different histories produced onto different categories of body (men, women, black men, black women, working class, managerial class, etc.) have their insistences when it comes to meanings (pre-)existing for them. Within such objective categories, specific subjectivities are motored. A politico-aesthetic materialism (theatre, painting, music, writing)[11] could attempt whilst not relegating to irrelevance their categories of collectivity to produce subjective histories' effects as specific problematics through figure(s) and absence(s), through each's subjectivity, making of the resulting a person/category who/which is then inscribed in contradiction through ('*vis à vis*') the given piece of work.

The theatrics and the language of *Not I*, its repetitions and various forms of attempted descriptive speech and that attempt's impossibility, inscribe the viewer–listener in a reflexive process. This structuration of the viewer as ineluctable effect of the theatrical text, without denying her–his causality and her–his history, produces unending opposition through fracturing expectation and unity, for male and female. The viewer never reaches a state of 'end'. Yet there is a constant power/opposition dialectic. Sexual 'difference', having a vagina or having a penis, having a vagina and breasts or having a penis, *is* the figuration upon which one group asserts its power and authority, another its opposition. Such reflexiveness inscribed in ('in', i.e. through, with and against) the viewer also differentiates between a reflexiveness within narration, and reflexion in and against the viewer–listener's (conscious and unconscious) *specific* historical/economic/sexual context. A main concern in the Beckettian text is the relation of female viewer to female speaker/actress, and the latter's language and gesture. The specific effects of that reflexive process of (in and through) *Not I* instantiates the loss of male power-positions, and instantiates the power of a woman's speech and gesture as materially dialectic.

Resistance, for example, is formulated against the conscious and unconscious theatrical–political context. There are possibilities, for example, of the unconscious being untrammelled, thereby allowing images, words, works, their force whilst simultaneously *conscious* resistances are maintained. Or certain meanings heard and viewed (the oppression by ideological meaning) could be allowed on the conscious level, in, for example, a group defined as women-only, whilst in a mixed group both the unconscious and the conscious resistances would be politically necessary. Certain suppressions and repressions, and oppressions, obviously function differently in different contexts; that has its effects on the unconscious (which, too, is historical) as well as on the conscious. A position differing from this one would have to be the reactionary one that maintains some kind of 'free' unconscious, where some 'free' desire, some notion of contextless 'liberation' and libertarianism still persists. The *un*conscious differentiation for each viewer is not predetermined by some general context but by the history of the spectator(s) in relation to the work's attempted effects, its processes; will that not effect conscious positionings and critiques in relation to the unconscious identifications? The relation of the male and female viewer to the Beckettian speaking female is thus imbricated in a complexity of the politics of language and the politics against language, and its constructions, both of which disallow a consumption of the theatric process outside of a material(ist) history – unless an immense work of repression is effected, and the bourgeois conventions allowed to overdetermine the specificity of the work at hand.

The concept of *sexual* difference is one figuration upon which one group asserts its power, another its opposition. To label such a position biologistic would be to assume the philosophically strictly idealist possibility that patriarchy is oppressive to *anyone* via certain constraints regardless of sex, thereby denying and disavowing the ideological material basis upon which such function is predicated. Revolutionary would be to not be defined by the sexual. To be defined as same, not different. It is by the body's sex that 'woman' is defined, that 'man' is defined, that

women and men are defined. It is politically specific to reduce to
its sex a series of techniques (reification) in a seamless continuum
of power, which were it a stasis would provide its own destruction.
It is the movement and *its* ineluctableness, its dynamics, like
capitalism's, which makes for such a necessary long-term battle in
opposition. How does this conceptualisation exist in written work,
in language, in Beckett? It has to do with the reification of a
repeated fragment of language, the reification of the referent:
'Hand, in light of spill, white', such a phrase finding its
contradictory power against sexual archetypes, sexual–political
archetypes, in the very artifice of the process which positions itself
against the 'image' or 'imaginary' or 'scene' or 'fiction' produced.
Such a reification in language through language disallows the
'natural dynamic', the 'dynamic of the natural' with its
hegemonic structures of truth, as truth, to obtain. True as Good.
'Stare into space ... then on ... a few more ... stop and stare again ...
so on ... drifting around ... when suddenly ... gradually ... all went
out ... all that early' (ten words per second). 'Stare into space ...
then on ... a few more ... stop and stare again ... so on ... drifting
around ... when suddenly ... gradually ... all went out ... all that
early.' Even the 'hysterical' (speed – 'wildness' – repression –
gestural symptom – hallucinated hearing – paralysis – etc.) in
such repetitive representation as to sound, as to image, as to
(impossible) attempt to focus on one moment, one *non*-movement
disallows the production of a coherent image of hysteria. Instead,
opposed to this (for 'images of hysteria' as for anything else), a
process of material difference from *any* real outside of the real of
the process of representation-attempts – disillusioning those
attempts.

To come to the dead-end of identificatory pleasure is what is
radical in these structuring processes. The constant impossibility
is the dead end. All heard, all seen, all struggle no longer collapsed
onto the conventions of ideology of power, and its material
enactments and reproductions through the individual listener-
spectator as representative for, and part of, the social totality's
hegemonic state. Thus the last gasp of a 'dying' patriarchy, like
the last gasp of a 'dying' capitalism, has theoretical truth whilst it
is empirically untrue. Virtual hegemony is assured simultaneous
with the dead-end. And that as a process in which a viewer–
listener functions, in that dialectic mental movement, is the

working out/playing *out* of constant repetition. Instead of identity, another process institutes itself: projecting you whilst failing, time and time again, as necessary conventions of narrative are relinquished. That negation, that failure, is the literary move of language, producing each time again a question of identity, sentence by sentence.

Negation operates always as *more*, re-vision is re-materialising the constructs of discoherence. Its processing of you means an intervention occurs in the writing and reading. This processing of your subjectivity is the opposite of a finding of oneself or of losing one self. Individualism as myth. The myth of individualism is the notion of a subjectivity as *not* specific, historical, sexual, economic and dialectical. It is myth as truth, living us in every real way, no less mythical for being real. The power of materialist process is against the identities of such myth.

IX

Quote: *How It Is*

Narratives

Erasure (Palimpsestuality)

Quick then end at last of part two how it was with Pim leaving
at last only part three and last how it was after Pim before Bom
how it is saying as I hear it that one day all that every word
always as I hear it in me that was without quaqua the voice of us
all when the panting stops and murmur in the mud to the mud
that one day come back to myself to Pim why not known not
said from the nothing come back from the nothing the surprise
to find myself alone at last no more Pim me alone in the dark the
mud end at last of part two how it was with Pim leaving at last
only part three and last how it was after Pim before Bom how it
is that's how it was with Pim

III.

here then at last I quote on part three how it was after Pim how
it is part three at last and last towards which lighter than air an
instant flop fallen so many vows sighs prayers without words
ever since the first word I hear it the word how

No more time I say it as I hear it murmur it in the mud I'm
sinking sinking fast too strong no more head imagination spent
no more breath

The vast past near and far the old today of the extreme old even
the humming-bird known as the passing moment all that . . .

good good end at last of part three and last that's how it was end
of quotation after Pim how it is.   (Beckett, *How It Is*, pp. 99,

46

103, 147, last paragraph of pt II, first paragraph of pt III, last sentence of pt III).

There is the necessity in certain monologues, and the materiality of certain monological structures of repetition and sameness, never to allow a syntactical structure a full phrase which would complete a fiction (of truth or of fiction). It is the *segment* which must not function as complete, in order for it not to suddenly turn into its overdetermined opposite, 'the flow of the story'. A full phrase of subject and object must not stand. Such materialist monologue thus has a dual hold. As a postmodernist* text it has a specific force against itself, continually. It is constantly what it is not, and operates that reflection constantly via the reader–listener. Thus whilst 'it' is monologue, it formulates constant impossibilities of narrative functioning. The short staccato sentences of Stein, H.D., Beckett, in some instances, form a hermetic precision, the inaccessibility of which is nothing but lack of telos.

In order to operate such a system, the erasure (which palimpsest is) and the redundancy of repetition are necessitated. The lack of full phrase would not maintain its power without the return of the same and the non-assimilability into forward movement of time according to ('orderly') principles of veracity. The specificity of the history of you and the history of the attempted represented in the 'novel' or 'play' or 'monologue' would merely, otherwise, find points of relation, for a continuum, in the interests of moving time (both represented and real) along. Instead one must have an interrupting, precisely, of both represented and real time, for a disturbed cathexis of reading. Such remnant of realism is what can then, now, be defined as a realism neither annihilatory of materialist practice nor decidedly in the interests of colonising fragments to conglomerate narrative.

*I use the term *not* to mean '(return of) narrative expression(ism)', but to mean a step after (conventionalised) modernism, engaging 'it'. *Post* should not mean *to forget*.

X

Quote: *Kora and Ka* (H.D.)
Quote: *Ill Seen Ill Said*
Short Sentence Structures

Ka wears me to a shred. It is I who am bone thin. Soul is, I have proved it, octopus. Nevertheless, octopus cannot devour utterly. I am frame still, allbeing, bone and sinew. I stretch arms. I, I am John Helforth. . . . I have a right, like any man, like any woman, like any other ill-begotten creature, to a body. . . . There are two things mitigate* against me, one is my mind, one is the lack of it. Kora brought me here. She thinks that I am overworked. I am overworked. . . . Kora is everything. Without Kora, Ka would HAVE GOT ME. Sometimes I call Kora, Ka, or reverse the process and call Ka, Kora. I am on familiar terms with Kora, with Ka, likewise. . . . Colour has rotated in his mind but he now discards it. His eyes are at rest in silver and in green and in a rotation of silver–green, green–silver. He sees a space of long room with a low ceiling. He sees the curtain Kora has drawn, now open. He sees Kora (in a chiffon sort of robe) draw aside the curtains. He sees shadow wavering across diminished sunlight and sunlight filtering through diminished green. He sees shadow wavering slightly like fern-fronds under water. He sees that the red and blue cluster of field flowers, stamped on the chiffon that Kora has drawn on, lie here, there, across bare arm, bare shoulder, the gallant little bulge her back makes, like field flowers, flung onto a statue sprayed with water. The chiffon robe is light, rain-colour or the texture of a sprayed-out garden fountain. The

---

*In the original edition of 100 privately printed copies this was sometimes pencilled in as 'militate'.

flowers seem to lie along the shoulder of Kora as if she had been rolling in a meadow. I see Kora as she steps into a pool of sunlight that is stippled over with leaf-shadow. Her feet are bare. They are whiter than her legs and the strap of her shoe has left a white strap on her foot. Her bare foot is shot in a whiter sheaf of white flesh. I see that the strap on the other foot is also white. (H.D., *Kora and Ka* (Berkeley, Calif.: Bios, 1978) ch. 3, pt 1)

From where she lies she sees Venus rise. On. From where she lies when the skies are clear she sees Venus rise followed by the sun. Then she rails at the source of all life. On. At evening when the skies are clear she savors its star's revenge. At the other window. Rigid upright on her old chair she watches for the radiant one. Her old deal spindle-backed kitchen chair. It emerges from out the last rays and sinking ever brighter is engulfed in its turn. On. She sits on erect and rigid in the deepening gloom. Such helplessness to move she cannot help. Heading on foot for a particular point often she freezes on the way. Unable till long after to move on not knowing whether or for what purpose. Down on her knees especially she finds it hard not to remain so forever. Hand resting on hand on some convenient support. Such as the foot of her bed. And on them her head. There then she sits as though turned to stone face to the night. Save for the white of her hair and faintly bluish white of face and hands all is black. For an eye having no need of light to see. All this in the present as had she the misfortune to be still of this world. (Samuel Beckett, *Ill Seen Ill Said*, in *New Yorker* (5 October 1981) p. 48, first para.)

Interruption is forced, uninterruption disallowed, by the very sharpness of the disturbing short sentence. The form fends against the last expressions of what is left of 'content'. Emptying the 'content' is a production, in language, towards *nothing*, towards not allowing any fullness to any word, phrase, sequence or sentence. The process goes *against*, extracting bit by bit from the words, remnants of 'content' mulled over and over, reified, finished with, emptied. The entropic move of this process is antagonistic to the power of narrative. A fending against meaning, thus, not some transcendental totalism of 'emptiness' or 'fullness'.

Rather than starting from a complete voiding of description, this writing of Beckett's places representation only in order to evacuate it, bit by bit, phrase by phrase, tortuously. An attempted evacuation of any chance of any of it retaining reference or signification. This is a realism of *use*, of language-use, not of communication. It is a realism of language against the formulation of the 'I' (any I), against its locus and durated locii. The tension is between that and history, prior and to follow.

> Gone, again and again . . . out of frame . . . whose . . . fade . . . try to move on to other matters . . . black fast . . . stand stare stark still. . . .   (Samuel Beckett, *A Piece of Monologue*, pp. 72–4)

XI

Quote: *Endgame*, Hamm and Clov; *Godot*, Didi and Gogo

The Nothing Towards Which (Voiding of Desire)

Hilarity of Denial

Identification and Mimesis

CLOV:	Oh, by the way, your story
HAMM:	(*surprised*) What story?
CLOV:	The one you've been telling yourself all your days
HAMM:	Ah, you mean my chronicle?
CLOV:	That's the one (*Pause*)
HAMM:	(*angrily*) Keep going, can't you, keep going!
CLOV:	You've got on with it, I hope.
HAMM:	(*modestly*) Oh not very far, not very far. (*He sighs.*) There are days like that, one isn't inspired. (*Pause*) Nothing you can do about it, just wait for it to come. (*Pause*) No forcing, no forcing, it's fatal. (*Pause*) I've got on with it a little all the same. (*Pause*) Technique, you know. (*Pause*) (*irritably*) I say I've got on with it a little all the same.
CLOV:	(*admiringly*) Well I never! In spite of everything you were able to get on with it!
HAMM:	(*modestly*) Oh not very far, you know, not very far, but nevertheless better than nothing.
CLOV:	Better than nothing! Is it possible? (Samuel Beckett, *Endgame*, Trilingual edn (Frankfurt: Suhrkamp, 1963) p. 488)

ESTRAGON:	Don't touch me! (*Vladimir holds back, pained*)

51

VLADIMIR:	Do you want me to go away? (*Pause*) Gogo! (*Pause. Vladimir observes him attentively*) Did they beat you? (*Pause*) Gogo! (*Estragon remains silent, head bowed*) Where did you spend the night?
ESTRAGON:	Don't touch me! Don't question me! Don't speak to me! Stay with me!
VLADIMIR:	Did I ever leave you?
ESTRAGON:	You let me go.
VLADIMIR:	Look at me. (*Estragon does not raise his head. Violently*). Will you look at me! (*Estragon raises his head. They look long at each other, then suddenly embrace, clapping each other on the back. End of the embrace. Estragon, no longer supported, almost falls*)
ESTRAGON:	What a day!
VLADIMIR:	Who beat you? Tell me.
ESTRAGON:	Another day done with.
VLADIMIR:	Not yet.
ESTRAGON:	For me it's over and done with, no matter what happens. (*Silence*). I heard you singing.
VLADIMIR:	That's right, I remember.
ESTRAGON:	That finished me. I said to myself, He's all alone, he thinks I'm gone for ever, and he sings.
VLADIMIR:	One is not master of one's moods. All day I've felt in great form. (*Pause*). I didn't get up in the night, not once!
ESTRAGON:	(*sadly*) You see, you piss better when I'm not there.
VLADIMIR:	I missed you ... and at the same time I was happy. Isn't that a queer thing?
ESTRAGON:	(*shocked*) Happy?
VLADIMIR:	Perhaps it's not quite the right word.
ESTRAGON:	And now?
VLADIMIR:	Now? ... (*Joyous*) There you are again ... (*Indifferent*) There we are again ... (*Gloomy*) There I am again.
ESTRAGON:	You see, you feel worse when I'm with you. I feel better alone too.
VLADIMIR:	(*vexed*) Then why do you always come crawling back?
ESTRAGON:	I don't know.
VLADIMIR:	No, but I do. It's because you don't know how to

defend yourself. I wouldn't have let them beat
you.

ESTRAGON: You couldn't have stopped them.

VLADIMIR: Why not?

ESTRAGON: There was ten of them.

VLADIMIR: No, I mean before they beat you. I would have
stopped you from doing whatever it was you were
doing.

ESTRAGON: I wasn't doing anything.

VLADIMIR: Then why did they beat you?

ESTRAGON: I don't know.

VLADIMIR: Ah no, Gogo, the truth is there are things escape
you that don't escape me, you must feel it yourself.

ESTRAGON: I tell you I wasn't doing anything.

VLADIMIR: Perhaps you weren't. But it's the way of doing it
that counts, the way of doing it, if you want to go
on living.

ESTRAGON: I wasn't doing anything.

VLADIMIR: You must be happy too, deep down, if you only
knew it.

ESTRAGON: Happy about what?

VLADIMIR: To be back with me again.

ESTRAGON: Would you say so?

VLADIMIR: Say you are, even if it's not true.

ESTRAGON.   What am I to say?

VLADIMIR: Say, I am happy.

ESTRAGON: I am happy.

VLADIMIR: So am I.

ESTRAGON: So am I.

VLADIMIR: We are happy.

ESTRAGON: We are happy. (*Silence*) What do we do now, now
that we are happy?   (Samuel Beckett, *Waiting for
Godot* (London: Faber, 1965) pp. 37–9)

The process of such 'dialogue' leads to the voiding of desire. The
running down and out of motivated feelings, the evacuation of
desire, the (constant) ending of dialogue, is what such process *is*.
There is a materiality to such language-*use* which is outside of
anything prior or predestined. It is language as language, used
towards a position, situation, in language. The 'dialogue' has its

specific ways of working, in the *Godot* section cited, and those specific workings are not 'about' something described, some event prior or in the future, but rather a material language process 'between' two ciphers. In the language they are situating themselves *vis à vis* one another, and the running down and out of language in that section quoted is the effecting of *dialectic* nothingness. The nothingness towards which language takes one, that running down and out, the nihilism of the process, is not 'about' nihilism. It is not 'about' the evacuation of desire in language. It is the production of language as endless attempt to ward off the end. The dialectic strategies towards this in language in *Godot* are precisely such a process.

In all this there is much denial. There is, here, a hilariousness in denial, which functions both as denial *per se* and as reflexively about denial and its processes and strategies. Humour has no little sadism. Denial as hilarious, as in the *screamed*, and screeched, repetitions of NO NO NO NO NO NO NO NO. The attempted banishment of a phobia, or an idea, or simply any content, via the NO NO NO NO NO NO NO! Analogous to this, the *content* of the statement (in the *Godot* dialogue), 'You let me go!' could only be taken in a straightforward manner, without any break in identification, if accepted within a strictly Calvinist tradition or a Jewish tradition of guilt. The structure of Judaeo-Calvinist guilt's lack of hilarity is precisely *there*. The masochistic desire for the law, articulated through the word STOP or NO or DON'T GO, the ritual game's mythic, *real*, seriousness, points to nothing but the structure of immersion in self-pity, the butt of Beckett's humour.

Whilst a reflexiveness, a reflexive consciousness, is produced in the listener–viewer–audience, this is not given as such for Estragon. Thus, for the audience, his speaking does not function as some kind of 'successful' mimesis. The more 'successful' (i.e. the more dramatically precise) his shrieking mimesis, the *less* mimetic the performance and the less the words allow the identificatory process to take place for the viewer–listener–audience. This is a formalising of a structure of speech and a content of speech via its articulation as *extreme*. Unambiguous position in the content, 'you let me go', pared down form, extremity of technique in the shriek. The precision of Didi's and Gogo's mimesis forces the viewer to *not* identify-with. The fourth-wall naturalism in Beckettian theatrics foregrounds the structure, and produces the kind of constantly reflexive distanciation process which *opposes* the theatrical convention of fourth-wall naturalism: 'Play it *as* fourth-wall naturalism' (Beckett, directing *Endgame*).

XII

Quote: Nietzsche on Guilt

Vorwurf/Reproach

The Joke

... who gives their word as something on which one could depend.... Only that which doesn't stop hurting remains in the memory.... that every damage somehow has its equivalent, and could really be paid, should it even be through the perpetrator's pain. From whence this age-old deeply rooted, perhaps no more to be vanquished idea took its power, the idea of an equivalence of damage and pain? I have already told it: in the contractual relationship between the believer and the guilty, which is as old as the existence of 'subjects of right', and which, in its turn, harks back to the basic forms of buying, selling, trade, commerce*, and change.   (Friedrich Nietzsche, *Sämtliche Werke*, vol. 5 (Munich: Deutscher Taschenbuch Verlag, 1980) pp. 294, 295, 298)

ESTRAGON: Don't touch me! Don't question me! Don't speak
            to me! Stay with me!
VLADIMIR: Did I ever leave you?
ESTRAGON: You let me go.   (Beckett, *Godot*, p. 61)

Depending on tone, speed of delivery, intonation, this could be the 'typical' hilarity of the judaic joke's reproach, its insistent torment and demand. It could be the manipulatory self-pity, the enunciation of which functions as a trap in a sadomasochistic

* *'Handel'*, 'commerce', also means 'conduct'.

structure. The demand being for that to be taken seriously which it is impossible to take seriously outside of guilt. Inside this structure, there then is a sadomasochistic replacing of active by passive (you *let* me go!), a structure formed for the accommodation (displacement) of guilt onto the other. I left, yours the guilt for allowing such. Your lack of sadistic activity enabled my will (leaving) to be carried out. I was thereby enabled in carrying out my (ostensibly now to me but in fact at the time to you) painful ends. The obviousness of this projection of guilt in the terse response 'you let me go' is what makes it impossible, impossible in the sense of impossible to satisfactorily fulfil the demand. There is no possible resolution to such a guilt structure. The hilarity is in the vehemence of the imposition of such obviousness, making of this artifice, this manipulation-device, just play. 'It is all just play' (Beckett, *Play*). When the structure of the formulation of language foregrounds itself, through such devices as well as through the terse, sharp, bantering tone, speed, and scream, the perversity of the projection onto the other evidences itself as device. The hilarity springs from that; the listener–viewer's identification with Didi or Gogo is rent asunder, *forced from that identity*. It is thus forced from identification-with, *and* from self-identity, *at that moment*.

XIII

The product of the guilt-ridden speaking is laughter.

> ULULATION: . . . it is not the bitter laugh, the ethical laugh, that laughs at that which is not good; it is not the hollow laugh, the intellectual laugh, that laughs at what is not true; it is perhaps the mirthless laugh, 'the dianoetic laugh, down the snout'. It is the laugh of laughs, the risus purus, the laugh laughing at the laugh, the beholding, the saluting the highest joke, in a word, the laugh that laughs – silence please – at that which is unhappy.   (Beckett, *Watt*, p. 46)

Laughter, guilt, and the unsuccessful mimesis via fourth-wall naturalism work to produce theatric effects of reflexive distanciation via the listener–viewer in a way which no longer allows a notion of the inseparability of these forms. Rather, they have specific modes of interaction which produce certain effects under certain conditions, some of which have been and some of which will be, somehow, described. In H.D.'s writings there is the fourth, Freudian, wall as there and not there, producing both a structure for meaning and momentary coherence *and* producing structured incoherence, the structures of arbitrary signification, the artifices of meaning. By such artifices she is foregrounding materially in language (via reading) a process of meaning-*making* which puts the viewer–listener inside the production-process. This is precisely to have the viewer–reader not identify-with, not be involved *in* it; thus it is not the psychoanalytics of the voyeur.[12] What is given in such a process is a lack of an illusionist movement; simultaneous with being a part (and in the interests) of a process in its ideological constructedness, forcing a position, a politics, a thought, but not being ineluctably moved into it. A material(ist) process, of which one is part, not an apparition from processed repression.

Act so that there is no use in a centre. . . . A fact is that when the place was replaced all was left that was stored and all was retained that would not satisfy more than another. The question is this, is it possible to suggest more to replace that thing. This question and this perfect denial does make the time change all the time. (Gertrude Stein, 'Rooms', *Tender Buttons* (New York: Marie Claire Editions, 1914) p. 63)

As the 4th wall to a room. If we alter our course, around this very room where I have been talking with the Professor and start with the wall to my left, against which the couch is placed, and go counter-clockwise, we may number the Professor's wall with the exit door 2, the wall with the entrance door (the case of pottery images and flat Greek bowls) 3, and the wall opposite the couch 4. This wall actually is largely unwalled, as the space there is left vacant by the wide-open double-doors. The room beyond may appear very dark. (H.D., *Tribute to Freud* (New York: Pantheon, 1957) p. 30)

Illus. 3   Billie Whitelaw in *Footfalls* (1976), freeze-frames

'An Incident Here and There'
1. there as here, there are no doors
2. ruin everywhere, yet as the fallen roof
   leaves the sealed room
   open to the air
3. yet the frame held:
   we passed the flame; we wonder
   what saves us? what for?
   (H.D., *The Walls Do Not Fall* (Oxford: Oxford University
   Press, 1944) p. 7)

Well, the wall will have to move a little, that's all. (Samuel
Beckett (1962), in conversation, reported in L. Harvey, *Samuel
Beckett: Poet and Critic* (Princeton, N.J.: Princeton University
Press, 1970) p. 435)[13]

(See Illustration 3.)[14]

The stills do not do justice, are guilty of an interpretation, as each
gesture here, photographically, is held and takes on resonance (of
Kollwitz, Barlach, Masareel). On the stage, in gesture and
speech, the 'frozen' images are a series of theatred freeze-frames,
equal blocks of form none of which stands *for* another, none of
which *condenses* meaning, none of which is icon, none of which,
finally, anymore, is referent to or of the real.

Finally, thus, too, the multiple processes for 'correct' mimesis of,
for example, walking in the street is nowhere adumbrated onstage
by Billie Whitelaw's walk in *Footfalls*. (The photographs in Illus. 3
though do not prove this theatrical process described.) It is not a
walk but a series of Bunraku-like gestures, still and moving,
neither of which bear (indexical) similarity to a person walking.
Such a distanciated form of being-seen initiates a distanciated
look.

How is this dialectically distanciated process instigated? (Added
to which *distanciation* is neither mere distance-from nor a solipsism
of reflexion.) Billie Whitelaw's dress in *Footfalls* is precisely visible
as costume: theatrical rags, 'cobwebbed, aged'. Were these 'rags'
she wears more 'abstract', less 'real', less imitation, then they
would militate *against* the production of dialectically reflexive
distanciation which is an anti-illusionist position for the viewer.
This dress of rags specifically in relation to the concrete

Illus. 4 Bunraku, Japanese Puppet Theatre

abstractions of speech and gesture ('freezes') forms the material(ist) theatricalisation against any notion of 'the real'. Theatrical convention, the fourth wall, of what is 'the real' or 'reality' is hereby in *Footfalls* undercut. But it is never simply dealt with once and for all. It is the movement and the speaking that problematises codes of naturalism producing a disfunction, a malefaction.

(See Illus. 4 and 5.)

Any suspension by the viewer is, as Nietzsche noted, an act of will to place oneself as viewer–listener in an ideologically more secure, possessible, place.

> Vergesslichkeit . . . dem es zuzuschreiben ist das was von uns erlebt . . . ebensowenig ins Bewusstsein tritt, als der ganze Prozess mit dem sich . . . die sogenannte Einverleibung abspielt. . . . Ein Thier heranzuzuechten, das versprechen darf – ist das nicht gerade jene paradoxe Aufgabe selbst, welche sich die Natur in Hinsicht auf den Menschen gestellt hat? (Versprechen means to promise, and sich versprechen means slip). Und der aktiven Vergesslichkeit . . . der Mensch in dem dieser Hemmungsapparat beschaedigt wird . . . wird mit nichts 'fertig' . . . (nicht) ein nicht wieder loswerden einem ein Mal verfaendeten Wort (sondern) ein nicht wieder loswerden-wollen. Was setzt das aber alles voraus! . . . wie muss dazu der Mensch selbst . . . notwendig geworden sein auch sich selbst fuer seine eigene Vorstellung, um endlich dergestalt, wie es ein Versprechender tut, fuer sich als Zukunft gut sagen zu koennen!

> [Forgetfulness . . . to which can be attributed that that which is experienced . . . as little becomes conscious as the whole process through which . . . so-called identification gets played out. To train an animal which can promise, isn't that exactly the paradoxical aim which nature has given itself as to people? And (as to) active . . . forgetfulness . . . the person in whom this inhibitor is damaged accomplishes nothing. . . . Not the inability to rid oneself of a once-promised word but a not wanting to rid oneself. . . . But what all this is predicated upon! . . . How must a person have become . . . necessary, even for him/herself, for one's own assumptions, in order to speak for one's own future, finally, the way in which one who promises does!] (Friedrich Nietzsche, *Gesammelte Werke*, vol. 5 (Munich: DTV, 1980) p. 292)

Illus. 5   Bunraku, 'The Love Suicides at Sonezaki' (Chikamatsu
Monzaemon, 1703)

v: Will you never have done? Will you never have done . . . revolving it all?

m: It?

v: It all. (*Pause*) In your poor mind. (*Pause*) It all. (*Pause*) It all. (Samuel Beckett, *Footfalls* (London: Faber, 1976) p. 34)

What materialism refers to here in language would be the way the phrase 'it all' for the listener–viewer refers to various possibilities, of all the specificities not one singly enunciated or evidenced as correct, good, or true. Repetition is one use towards reification of meaning through language: 'To want to not repeat, but a final answer would be death' (H.D., *Tribute to Freud* (Boston, Mass.: David R. Godine, 1974) p. 47). In the *Footfalls* quote, it is the past, the remembered, which is referred to and never done being revolved, whilst it is that remembering in the present that is acted out. The referential, that which is referred to in the phrases spoken, harking to memory-attempts, was always already an enactment, acted-out. No enactment is given as 'more' real. None as the real.

The materialist functioning of words on a page may be covered by a poetics and series of held associations very different from same language and gesture onstage. The monological referent can seem, on the printed page, alone, to function as the purely transparent signification of imaginary reference unmitigated. This is not posited as necessarily or ontologically the case, witness much of Stein's work, and Beckett's *Company, Imagination Dead Imagine, Lessness, The Lost Ones*, wherein a single speaker is complexly imbricated with a third-person speaker, and where the structures even of the monological are formed against language-constructs' materialities (both as material, 'vulgarly' spoken, and the material of production of meaning/meaninglessness, in the 'space' of the social meaning of 'literature'). Producing meaning*fulness* always requires meaning to *precede* language-as-process, language as artifice, language as political ideology. Such precedence then makes of the productive power of the language-process a (pre)given 'natural' unquestioned 'neutrality', a *form* which simply 'contains' the contents of all subjective and objective history/histories.

What is necessary is a context in which the texts, rather than any critical overtures, constantly attempt splits with identification and identity. Such splits are the very opposite of concepts of 'deconstruction'. In the latter, persistent identification, seamless throughout the narrative or quasi-narrative or 'abstruse' narrative, is somehow 'undermined', 'deconstructed', via inconsistencies or specific 'counter' conventions. The notion of deconstruction via counterconventions, utilising a specific convention against a dominant convention within the same framework, implies some given non-hierarchical world, in which each convention, dominant or not, is of equal value and power, and therefore, of equal potential for deconstruction. Such harmful *naïveté* is subsumed by bourgeois notions of freedom and democracy in the ideological politics of aesthetics. Deconstruction demands the formation of a retroactive seamlessness, some finality to the questioning; it also insists on solidifying whatever exactly is constituted as 'the norm'.

Against this, there are texts which produce, throughout their duration, both a contradiction between what is said and how it is said *and* a contradiction between what is referred to and what for the viewer is the actual reference, i.e. the material of speech and gesture. Were the work such, it could begin to militate against critical *a prioris* which read meaning in a manner to suppress difference between viewer and viewed, listener and speaker, speaker and spoken-of, etc. The ideology of truth and the constant reintegration of the bourgeois ideology of realism is set in conflict with the materialism of the whole language-meaning/listener–viewer apparatus. The repression of space (between you and it) and time (then and now), and fantasised foreverness, in the theatre, cinema and reading apparatus is in the interests of annihilating the subjective and objective material history of both the viewer-subject and the meanings and meaninglessnesses produced as constructs, artifice, ideology (nothing ever outside the latter; that too needs stating), in an attempt towards imaginary sameness which gives itself as both natural and neutral. In certain interests such systems institute themselves. The notes on the back covers of Beckett books are mere examples of the unwavering battle of certain interests to keep certain figments figments; against that we have Beckett's Formulation:

'Not the old slum coming down, then the new slum going up, but both simultaneously.' Less is less. *More* has to be constructed differently. There can, finally, be no presumption of the political by the magic of the signified, entrenchment of capitalist patriarchy, without the hold for which different orders of action are seen for what they are, as in, for example, the political of ideology in language.

In all this there can be no mention of an author, though a critical backlash has begun to attempt to reintegrate the authority of the author.

> I'd agree with Derrida that talk of authors, intentions, historical conditions of production and so on is perfectly appropriate and quite unmetaphysical: these are certainly constraints of meaning. The mistake is merely to assume they are always the governing structures. So I find it ironic that . . . everyone is rushing to deconstruct the author as 'metaphysical' . . . There's Foucault of course, but where precisely is the subject in all of Foucault? *Let alone any subject plausibly capable of toppling* [Prime Minister] *Thatcher.* (Terry Eagleton, letter to author, 17 February 1981; italics mine)

Because you can not know others' thoughts, you have to go on primary narcissism, projecting what you feel onto how you feel they feel about you, the only 'known'. Thus there never *is* a conscious, lived-out, historically placed, present. Unconscious paranoias and their structuration are apart from *any* specific character, though not separable from that *relation* of you and it/he/she.

The not knower is produced by a relentless abandoning of the fiction of the subject-in-knowledge, a relentless abandonment of a homology of knowing and can-ing. The ablation is not of desire but of desire to desire, of the crude assumption of individual power and force over another. What then exists is the paranoia that someone is listening, unbuttressed by any paranoia that pure communication exists ('pure' meaning outside of the psychoanalytic-political radically subversive). Abandonment of the fiction of subject-in-knowledge, and subject as centre-of-knowledge, is also an abandoning of *fiction*, fiction the reality of the sado-masochistic *hold*. The abandonment of 'knowing' is an ablation of that dominant ideological desire, *against* the power in/of capitalism and patriarchy. The above is delineating the specifics of power as materialist concretions of 'abstract' ideology. The above is also seeing that the 'psychoanalytic' sado-masochistic hold is inseparable from politics.[15] You go on the projection of a primary narcissism and you can then consciously intervene (inasmuch as anything is conscious; and it is). You intervene on that mechanism of projection of what you feel onto how you feel they feel about you, projection of what you know onto how you know they know (about) you. The contradictions of power between the unconscious and the conscious in this paranoia-construction are the political/sexual which produce such works as *Godot*'s mono- and dia-logics.

XIV

Quote: Didi and Gogo (*Godot*) Dialogue

Language against 'Type'

Object 'Choice'

Series and Fragment

Enactment

Viewer as Subject

ESTRAGON:	Well?
VLADIMIR:	What was I saying, we could go on from there.
ESTRAGON:	What were you saying when?
VLADIMIR:	At the very beginning.
ESTRAGON:	The very beginning of WHAT?
VLADIMIR:	This evening ... I was saying ... I was saying ...
ESTRAGON:	I'm not a historian.
VLADIMIR:	Wait ... we embraced ... we were happy ... happy ... what do we do now that we're happy ... go on waiting ... waiting ... let me think ... it's coming ... go on waiting ... now that we're happy ... let me see ... ah! The tree!
ESTRAGON:	The tree?
VLADIMIR:	Do you remember?
ESTRAGON:	I'm tired.
VLADIMIR:	Look at it. (*They look at the tree*)
ESTRAGON:	I see nothing.
VLADIMIR:	But yesterday evening it was all black and bare. And now it's covered with leaves.
ESTRAGON:	Leaves?
VLADIMIR:	In a single night.
ESTRAGON:	It must be the Spring.

VLADIMIR: But in a single night!

ESTRAGON: I tell you we weren't here yesterday. Another of your nightmares.

VLADIMIR: And where were we yesterday evening according to you?

ESTRAGON: How would I know? In another compartment. There's no lack of void.

VLADIMIR: (*sure of himself*) Good. We weren't here yesterday evening. Now what did we do yesterday evening?

ESTRAGON: Do?   (Beckett, *Godot*, pp. 42–3)

and

VLADIMIR: I missed you ... and at the same time I was happy. Isn't that a queer thing?

ESTRAGON: (*shocked*) Happy?

VLADIMIR: Perhaps it's not quite the right word.

ESTRAGON: And now?

VLADIMIR: Now? ... (*joyous*) There you are again ... (*indifferent*) There we are again ... (*gloomy*) There I am again.

ESTRAGON: You see, you feel worse when I'm with you. I feel better alone too.

VLADIMIR: (*vexed*) Then why do you always come crawling back?

ESTRAGON: I don't know.   (ibid., p. 38)

To say that Vladimir's other is Estragon is not to say in any way that one is a 'side' of the other. Aside, constantly geometrically tangential to another's side, is more like it.

ESTRAGON: Pull your pants up.

VLADIMIR: I can't.   (ibid., p. 99)

and

VLADIMIR: Can you get up?

ESTRAGON: I don't know.   (ibid., p. 86)

The inability, here, to structure the one (Vladimir or Estragon) as dominant forces an equation. Thus any codification, here, onto type, is a neat fiction and an impossibility. These dialogues go against the construction of archetype: in the production of *Godot* by Beckett the body's archness is supported by what Beckett called 'the text's ability to claw'. The quote pertained to *Endgame*, and for *Godot* the clawing is of a more subtle kind, the inability of the text's clawing to let go of the characters. They are never unbound from the text, never become realistic free-agents; they're always arch. The verbal text's speaking is, in fact, a *being-spoken* by each, by Didi and Gogo. And it is that which does not allow for a biological–characterological *type* to be produced. They speak it, it speaks them, no emanation other than the holding of the characters to the text's needs. In that sense they are marionettes without the characterological characterisational parameters that critics need to invent. Thus Didi not other of Gogo, neither are they a fusion. The need to find words, find something to say, say it, let that saying produce effects of speech, i.e. the other's speech, till it runs out and down; and the whole thing may or may not start again. Speech is therefore precisely not used as a ladder which one can utilise in order to then pull it (the ladder!) away. No vehicular notions for speech here.

Object-choice can be based on sameness, not denying 'difference' but not having to be an object-choice of such difference as to make finally of the choice a representation of manifest self-dislike.

This is not a matter of moral categories, narcissism as somehow 'good' or 'bad', simply that choosing an other on the basis of self-dislike, such masochistic narcissism, may feed short-term self-lacerating needs towards a long-term bind which in its self-piteous indulgence produces what can only be a redundancy. The ideology here is of the return of the same, outside history (one's own, for example). As opposed to what? A different kind of contract: Nagg's and Nell's, Didi's and Gogo's, Speaker's with Voice (in *Company*), 1st person and 3rd person (in *A Piece of Monologue*). The contract is for the Real, the choice of necessity a neurosis but not a representation, not a characterisation of a fabled *then*; *then* is nothing other than fable, duration annihilated to seamless ends. Instead: no end, constant end, just means, meanings, meaninglessnesses, means, the words in constant material and political process. 'Lick thy neighbor as thyself' (Beckett, 1931).

Illus. 6   *Footfalls* rehearsal (1976): (*from left to right*) Billie Whitelaw,
Rose Hill (Voice) and Samuel Beckett

The constant demands of Estragon and Vladimir are monological materialisations of the impossibility of knowing the other, of 'insight'. Didi/Gogo monologues function as constant materialisations of the projection-mechanism (even!) in their constant disavowals. Non-knower, non-can-er, not non-doer. Always an act: an act of language and an act of the body in the *use* of language and the *use* of the body.

The impossibility of knowing is never anything but a political battle against the illusion of such (knowing), the smug humanistic satisfactions inducing no little catharsis, whose function is the forward-projected idealisation/sentimentalisation of a mythical past in the interests of 'less is more' or 'more is less', instead of the horrendous, and revolutionary, insight that less is less.

(See Illus. 3.)

There are various problems with the understanding of such images. A *single* close-up, or even a single longshot, of this image can operate as a fragment-of something *else*, it can be taken as part for whole. The other possibility is that the series functions as a singular totality, 'series' being merely a manner by which to form a larger unit, collapsed into a single 'meaning'. One other possibility, neither part-for-whole, nor singular-totality, could be a series of differences, deferring singularity. The constant rearresting of an image, against a previous and future one. The latter structure's function would be without teleology, no retrospective good-conscience rationalising of means to ends. Thus each 'to end' would not be co-optable but would be, each time, each sight, each moment, a cessation against each previous and future cessation. There would be no annihilating time towards some metaphysic of finality (and attendant transcendences).[16]

The third possibility outlined is the one inculcated by the theatre-*performance* itself. The series of differences function on the viewer as the force to take position. The act works thereby as never separable from the force to re-enact/re-act, thus a non-wholistic series of gestural acts. No en-actment, done thus, covers *other* moments, other gestures, prior, subsequent, or 'in the real world'. And no enactment, done thus, functions as metaphor.

Timelessness as a concept and a reality never gets credence. The gesture is separate from its signified (signified equals *concept*). The gesture of difference, moment-to-moment, as signif*ier*, is constantly in process. Always again the meaning 'of' an image and 'for' a viewer is processed with/through the viewer and with/through the image. Construction is always a material process; it is given *as* process in *Footfalls*.

Whether such a process of meaning-construction refuses repression of the apparatus of theatre and all its parts, refuses the repression of process, but still maintains an 'end' towards which it is utilised or not (i.e. whether it thereby makes of the process an '*all*', a fetish, instead of encountering meaninglessness at every moment in the constancy of meanings taken up, and the ideological of that), is another matter.

The moment the viewer is placed in some purposively perfect (ideal) position, separate from the viewer-as-subject's historical contradictions, there is a mechanisation of the historical process. This disallows the viewer-as-subject a place in production, and attempts in that denial to subjugate each subject to a specific position outside of a material ideological process. An example would be a woman's being held to her position in patriarchy, thereby denying the productive functions of the contradictions that motor *resistance* (and the contradictions that motor history even outside of any resistances). Being held to one's oppression, as if it, and one, is objectively and subjectively outside of the historical process and its politics, would be by denying patriarchal oppression and theorising that denial, and/or it would be arguing for the impossibility of radical political/cultural production by women (or, perversely, such productions as if only *within* the current hegemonic discourse, so that they are neither radically art nor radically political, as *it* is not). Such an argument is self-justifying philosophical elucidation in the interests of the current hegemonic power of the male bourgeoisie in late capitalism (in the West).

XV

Quote: *Preface and Introduction to a Contribution to the Critique of Political Economy* (Marx)

Subject in History

No Hidden History in the Billie Whitelaw Freeze-frames

Viewer's Labour Process; Lenin's Objective Dialectics

Viewer Sexuality in Relation to *Footfalls*

The example of labour strikingly demonstrates how even the most abstract categories, despite their validity – precisely because of their abstraction – for all epochs, are themselves equally the product of historical conditions even in the specific form of this abstraction, and they possess their full validity only for and within these conditions. (Karl Marx, *Preface and Introduction to a Contribution to the Critique of Political Economy* (1857–9) (Moscow: Progress Publishers, 1959) p. 37)

The example holds precisely because the subject is always in history, history no less a process for being a process without *a* subject. No subject is ever out-of-history,[17] schemas belying the dialectical structure of constant contradiction notwithstanding.

For objective dialectics the absolute is also to be found in the relative. The unity, the coincidence, identity, resultant force, of opposites, is conditional, temporary, transitory, and relative. (Lenin, 'On Dialectics', in *Materialism and Empirio-Criticism* (London: Martin Lawrence, 1936) p. 324)

The force of this argument for the freeze-frame image of Billie Whitelaw playing in *Footfalls* is the position that there is no consumable underneath, no 'hidden history' in the

75

representation. This is because it (her theatrical act) is not a
representation. It does not hold, in its moment-to-moment moves,
articulations, gestures, attempts at graspable meaning, a
representation, a duration, a meaning, and does not hold you to it.
Positions of that staged representation, its histories and the
positions of/for the viewer, are produced in that dialectic. The
viewer is thereby in a dialectical theatrical apparatus (the whole
machine), *not* covered and closured and 'finalised' in meaning via
a position's *pre*-existence that would deny the material(ist)
construction of position. The guessing-game as to 'what is being
stated' or 'what is meant to be meant' can end. The guessing-
game whose answers, whose missing piece in the jigsaw puzzle, is
always determined by dominant meanings and associations for
any and every given 'complexity', is at an end. The *known* as the
illusion, in this culture, as either *present* (through interpretation)
or *absent* (but present, i.e. merely difficult to ascertain) is in this
mode of theatre radically opposed. The known, as given through
what is perceived, is now here opposed by the known as the
materially dialecticised conflict of subjects/histories/processes. It
is therefore now a matter, here, of the *seeming-known* in
contradiction to other knowns, and the active labour of the viewer
in that, to produce through that labour certain conscious and
unconscious positions for, and in, the viewer. The viewer is thus
part of the labour process, and this radically positions him/her
against the position of voyeur. The 'loss of faith' in the voyeuristic
'knowledge' of 'truth' forces action of thought against such 'truth'.
The motive force for such opposition and radicality is a politically
different theoretical ideology, in the interests of a politically
different practice of representation.

An instance of the above is the mitigation of the viewer's
conventionalisation and 'consumption' of the sexuality of the
speaker/mover in *Footfalls*. This would result, does result, in the
disallowing of the specific woman's speech and movement as
'woman's' speech and movement. The politics of sexuality is in
that disallowance; *now*. The oppression by (certain) sexual
definition is no longer taken as read. Sexual definition is then
redefined as the specific result of a specific process of sexual
positioning, historically specific, ideologically specific,
patriarchally specific, nothing given as given. What is thereby
posited is conflict rather than reaffirmation, a political process of

the effects of representation (representation-effects) as opposed to quietism. What is posited is struggle against the seamless reproduction of power. (That this, of course, does not mean the effect on each viewer and of each viewer will be somehow spontaneously subversive needs reiteration, or blind empirico-positivism sets itself up yet again.)

The spectator/listener is an effect of the piece of work, rather than a commentator upon it *a posteriori*. (He/she is many other things as well!) The spectator/listener's reflexion can be experienced as reflexion,* voyeurism experienced as voyeurism, meaning-making experienced as meaning-making, etc.

*But not in the sense of fetishising the viewer-as-subject (self), or the filmmaker/film. Rather, reflexivity (or apperception, or 'self'-reflexivity) as a subversion (of seamless voyeurism), *a step*, a means toward distanciation, a break from identity/identification.

XVI

Quote: Brecht on Realism

Subjectivity not Subject

Formalism/Anti-formalism

Realism

'Specific' Context

Science isn't so free of superstition. Where knowledge doesn't suffice, faith produces itself, and that is always superstition . . . our lyricists didn't lose their voice because of the book *Capital* but in the face of Capital itself.

If Realism *isn't* defined purely formalistically (that which in the 1890's was considered Realism, in the realm of the bourgeois novel) then much can be said against techniques like montage, interior monologue, or distancing [*Verfremdung*], only not from the point of view of Realism! . . . as a technical means, the interior monologue [of Joyce] (though unbeknownst to Brecht, it should be attributed to Dorothy Richardson), was rejected, one called it formalist. I never understood the reasoning. Just because Tolstoy would've done it differently isn't a reason to reject the way Joyce does it. The objections were constructed so superficially that one got the impression that if Joyce had put the same monologue [Molly Bloom's final one] in the psychoanalytical session, everything would've been alright.

Realist, that means consciously influenced by reality, and consciously influencing reality . . . the techniques of Joyce and Döblin are not simply wasteproducts; if one eliminates their influence, instead of modifying it, one ends up merely with the influence of the epigones, such as the Hemingways. The works of Joyce and Döblin betray, in the largest sense, the

Illus. 7   Andy Warhol, *Mao Tse-Tung*, drawing, 1973 (43¼ × 37½ in.)

world-historical contradictions into which the forces of production have fallen vis-à-vis relations of production. In the works, productive forces are represented to a certain degree. Especially the socialist writers can learn valuable highly developed technical means [*Elemente*] from these documents of hopelessness [*Ausweglosigkeit*]. They see the way out.

Perhaps our readers might just *not* feel that they've been given the key to events when they, seduced by many wiles [*Künste*] merely take part in [*beteiligen*] the soulful emotions of the heroes. (Bertolt Brecht, 'Ueber den Realismus' (1938), *Gesammelte Werke*, p. 29 (my translation), quoted in *Studio International*, November 1975, n. 7, 'Theory and Definition'

Brecht also wavered from above views more often than not. Though he fought against the formally bourgeoisifying notions of Realism which the social(ist) Realists conveniently sidetracked, he also wrote often of a

Realism directly from the standpoint of a class, unfolding the ruling viewpoints as the viewpoints of the ruling, and . . . representing reality *the way it is* [*die Realität wiedergeben*]   (ibid.)

Further difficulties arise in the case of *Die Massnahme* (*The Measures Taken*), where his communist class position differed polemically/politically from, and intervened in, KPD (German Communist Party) politics in Berlin in 1930. (See Peter Horn, 'Truth is Concrete: Brecht's *The Measures Taken* and the Question of Party Discipline', in *Brecht Jahrbuch*, ed. J. Fuegi (Frankfurt: Suhrkamp, 1978) pp. 39–65.)

This all has to do with the realisms previously spoken/written of, the viewer's position in relation to the spoken 'realities', the realisms of the Billie Whitelaw freeze-frames, the politics of position.

Subjectivity is not a subject. The Mao drawing (Illustration 7) by Warhol is neither the hand that drew it nor the artist represented transparently, present-in-absence: subjectivity, not subjectivism. The subjectivity in that reproduction 'of' a history is the history of painting in (the) painting. In the painting *Mao*, 'background' of 'nature-in-painting' is never a natural recreation, always beneath and over and through the singular 'iconic' Mao image. Thus neither pure content nor pure form. Meaning can attach as X to Y cemented in momentary *present* (a functionable concept though philosophically, and in terms of theoretical physics, impossible!). Thus the picture does not function as some process-annihilating idealism, 'beauty', 'truth', 'reality', or 'the possibilities of the future' or 'that past'. The enterprise of such painting is problematical and given as such. The painting's monumentality (20 feet high) is no less materially about the icon and the process of its representational construction than the 6-inch high line drawing, simplified outlines assuming an image, the signifier (movement of line on paper, mark of pen on paper) producing *a*, never *the*, signified (the concepts adhering to the representational image) or its referent in the world 'outside' aesthetics.

> adopted princedouris. Words and then words. They slid and made strange running sound like water. Words were his preoccupation, his plague. Yes, mother was right. There was nothing for it. Life was lived in words, and lives multiplied in the word Athenian. (H.D., *Hedylus* (1928) (Oxford: Basil Blackwell, 1980) p. 17)

The monological voice speaks (when structured as monological voice and not fragment *of* narrative, or essence *of* something *else*) by definition an unviable 'truth'. The monological aesthetic act (as in the drawing by Warhol) the same.

Realism must be seen as inseparable from a basis in the form(al). So it is no longer a question of (a) formalism *vs* (b) anti-formalism, i.e. realism. In *A Piece of Monologue*, for example, the attempt at stillness, the recognition of death, is formulated not as withdrawal and decadence but as a discomfort. The realism, as inseparable from a basis in the form(al), is given through the running down and out of language, in language, both a comfort and a discomfort in terms of *usage*. It is given through the simultaneous attempting of withdrawal/non-withdrawal from the process of speech. The larger context gives a work its use, historical, sexual, economic. But that meaning and function of a work operate within a specific context does not mean that that specific context makes the work's meaning. Thus the concept of *use* must be instated outside of any overdeterminations by context. Since a work is situated inseparably from its larger historical, sexual, economic context, it is important not to speak of 'context' as if it were some variable minor series of possibilities for any work determining the material existence of a work and (its) historical, sexual and economic time and place. Thus the larger context must consistently be understood as different from any day-to-day specific context, and the latter is always subsidiary to the *work's* materialist reality and function.

To argue against this and state that the specific context for a work makes its meaning would be to reduce and mechanise, in idealist desire, all practices to more or less idiosyncratic 'creations' of dominant ideology, either as infrastructural productions or as their cultural *re*flections (superstructure). Those two positions are increasingly evident in the anti-Marxist, anti-feminist and anti/avantgarde discourse that is becoming dominant even within oppositional tendencies. Virtual total concentration is either on economic relations or on some specific context as *the* context, reducing everything to individual interpretation and individual will as the origin of all social relations, all politico/aesthetic productions, etc. Academic metadiscourse becomes *the* discourse, descriptions *of* ideology take the place of ideological-political struggle. All forms of production become, thereby, elided. What is betrayed in all these manoeuvres is a fear of production, given at times, perversely, in the rhetoric of a *denial* of consumption, 'anti-materialism', elitism in the interests of certain possessions remaining within a certain group. Them that's got, unwilling to engage in productive labour, telling them that's not got, who are constantly engaged in productive labour, to get beyond consumption. Production, finally, obviates the coherent ego of academic discourse.

XVII

Quote: *A Piece of Monologue*

Against Consumption

Identities

Monologues' 'Centrality'

Structuring the 'Anti-human'

Theatrical Space

Birth was the death of him. Again. Words are few. . . . Trying to treat of other matters. Till half hears there are no other matters. Never were other matters. Never two matters. Never but the one matter. The dead and gone. The dying and the going. From the word go. The word begone. (Beckett, *A Piece of Monologue*, pp. 70, 79)

Since conscious and unconscious identifications may be pitted against each other, and are themselves not somehow uncontradictory, the specific spectator–listener context has its relevance (but not predetermination) in relation to, for example, unconscious identifications and *resistances*. Thus a female reader or, differently, a male reader.

A voice comes to one in the dark. Imagine . . . that then is the proposition . . . and in another dark or in the same, another devising it all for company. (Beckett, *Company*, pp. 7, 8)

This leaves you, the reader, nowhere, but certainly not in stillness. At the same time it leaves you not in speech, but speechlessness, not in meaning but in meaninglessness, produced as the effect, and end, of those few sentences. That production in contradiction

is the power of the usages Beckett's prose issues. This is not the
plethora of evocation words mean, not the 'fullness' of an absence
of that plethora either, but the unplethora as privileged discourse.
That's a polemic reminiscent of

> The absurdity, here or there, of either without the other, the
> inaccessible other. (Samuel Beckett, 'Denis Devlin', in
> *Transition*, no. 27 (Paris, 1938) p. 290)

preceded by

> Here scabs, lucre, etc., there torment, bosom, etc., but both
> here and there *gulf*.   (ibid.)

And later

> the identities made up of cathexes not only multivalent but
> interchangeable.   (ibid.)

It is the sense, in the writing, for the listener–reader, that an other
is there, in the writing, but impossible in the confusions/
multiplicities/fragmentings/contradictions of the referents and
signifieds. The *writing* is the other, and the difficulties and
disallowances previously written about instate themselves in this
specificity. It is neither a matter of reducing the general to the
specific, nor of giving a specific upon which a general may be
formulated. Subjectivity without a subject, process without a
subject, history without a subject. The *other* in this writing is
precisely how it is when you are not there but know both of a there
and a here not enough to suggest even which it may more likely be.
This realism belies positionality its 'formal' *or* 'contentual'
rationale, its status as pure description or prescription, as both
would have as origin and end a voice 'there', or 'here' (on stage, on
page, etc.) reinveigling the authoritative power, the identities, of
that anthropomorphism of patriarchal truth.

So who is speaking, and for whom, and how? In fact, all speech is
monologue, and the designation 'monologue' as specificity within
discourse of a certain kind forged.

Does monologue need a centrality? Does the mouth have to be

central? Does the tongue have to be central to the lips, does the
iconographic cathexis of necessity have to indulge in Renaissance
perspective? For the mind? For the body? Does a possessive
capitalist space found its appropriateness in monologue? Does a
figuration in fact have to assist in establishing a domestic space
for, for example, a non-corporeal monological structuring and
process to have effect? How in *Not I* as to centring/decentredness
does the mouth do what our eyes do?

To start with, it could be presumed that a figuration does not have
to assist in establishing a (domestic or domesticisable) space, for
imaginary functioning, via identification, in meaning. A
figuration does not have to persist for a 'human' signification
(however non-corporeal) to be. The question of importance is how
can a figuration *not* assist in establishing a (domestic or
domesticisable) space – how does the persistence of figuration not
necessarily construct a 'human' signification in the process of
monologue.

> ... out ... into this world ... this world ... tiny little thing ... before
> its time ... in a godfor- ... what? ... girl? ... yes ... tiny little girl ...
> into this ... out into this ... before her time ...   (Samuel Beckett,
> *Not I* (London: Faber, 1973) unpaginated)

A determinant for the non-construction of human signification[18]
is, here, determined by speed of delivery (ten words per second,
high pitch, non-stop segments, empty black stage, nothing to be
seen except for the spotlight on mouth, speed of facial muscles'
movements unarrestable).

The depth and the height of the mouth are not easily fixed
perceptually by the viewer, if at all. And what the mind knows
about height, through empirical life in the world, and through
empirical life in the theatre, is not given adequacy by perception,
as the height is higher than a 'norm', and the depth unfocusable
due to the lack of reference points (height being one amongst
them). When the depth seems, after a time of viewing, to be
fixable, the barely focusable height is no longer holdable. And vice
versa: doing two things at once here becomes materially
impossible. Knowledge and perception never synchronise with
each other, and cohesion becomes visually more difficult due to

the speed with which speech erupts and demands concentrated intensity of listening, to no cohesive avail. Visual and aural physiological parameters make image and sound unfixed, unfixable. Should a momentary perceptive hold occur, or an after-image as the result of intense concentration on, for example, the visual, via the perceptive memory-faculties, then there is always the unholding by the mouth's intensely fast movement. And the language's breakneck eruption of speech disallows any 'flow' of sound an acclimatisation to meaning. The various apprehension and comprehension attempts cut through one another. The viewer is in constant dialectically material(ist) *attempt.*

(See Illus. 8 and 9.)

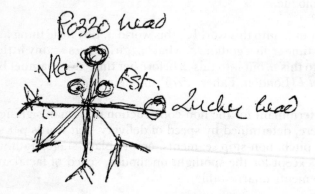

Illus. 8   Beckett's diagram of Pozzo, Lucky, Didi and Gogo falling.

The four bodies must form an intersection; ' "It must not", Mr Beckett says, "be an untidy heap, but has to function." (John Fletcher, Afterword to *Waiting for Godot*, London: Faber, 1971, p. 143)

In conventional theatre, the theatrical space is set forth as 'neutral', as if the style of the theatrical space (in whatever style it happens to be), the set-design, the height and depth of the stage,

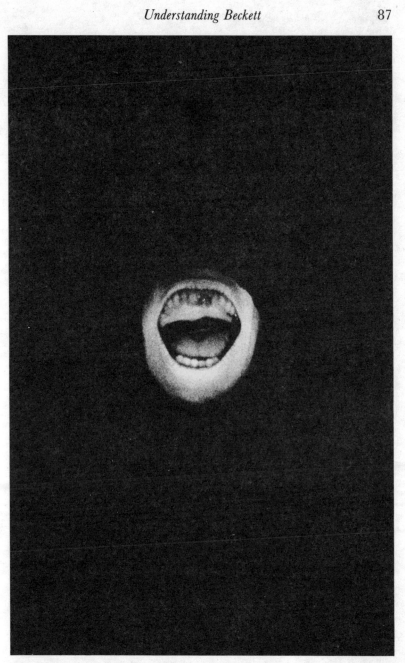

Illus. 9   Billie Whitelaw (Mouth) in *Not I* (1973) at the Royal Court Theatre, London

the lighting, the costumes, etc., were natural for the specific performance at hand. This naturalisation/neutralisation does not take place in *Not I*, due to the structur*ings* via gesture and language. A space given theatrically as coherent to the specific performance at hand is a spatial naturalism which is antagonistic to *Not I*'s verbal and visual processes; its very materiality would not allow for such a naturalism. In other words, the naturalism of synchronicity, a cohesion of a space with that which takes place 'within' it, is not produced here. The naturalism I am writing of here is not the style termed naturalism in the history of theatre, history of representation, wherein it is one code amongst many. *Not I*'s structuring could not use 'a space as articulated theatrical space for meaning', which is precisely the articulation I am calling naturalistic. That synchronicity which produces its ideological meaning sets itself against the desynchronicity of verbal/gestural artifice as materialist production process. In *Not I* the spatial circumferi are not given, and not only not given but not there. There is (a) space without reference point outside, no outside shape, no box, no walls; the focusing of the viewer's position *vis à vis* the speaking mouth in *Not I* is a process of *attempted* definition and forced divesting of secure position of consumption. The object to be consumed *qua* box ('within which things exist, actions take place, etc.') does not exist.

XVIII

Quote: *Not I*

On *Not I*

The Attempt to See/Hear/Know

Television *vs* Stage in Respect of *Not I*

Face as Mask

Sexuality and Voice in *Not I*

Power and Voice

The Skeletal 'Beneath'

Monologue

Monologue's Monotony

MOUTH: ... out ... into this world ... this world ... tiny little thing ... before its time ... in a godfor- ... what? ... girl? ... yes ... tiny little girl ... into this ... out into this ... before her time ... godforsaken hole called ... called ... no matter ... parents unknown ... unheard of ... he having vanished ... thin air ... no sooner buttoned up his breeches ... she similarly ... eight months later ... almost to the tick ... so no love ... spared that ... no love such as normally vented on the ... speechless infant ... in the home ... no ... nor indeed for that matter any of any kind ... no love of any kind ... at any subsequent stage ... so typical affair ... nothing of any note till coming up to sixty when- ... what? ... seventy? ... good God! ... coming up to seventy ... wandering in a field ... looking aimlessly for cowslips ... to make a ball ... a few steps then stop ... stare into space ... then on ... a few more ... stop and stare again ... so on ... drifting around ... when suddenly ... gradually ... all went

89

out ... all that early April morning light ... and she found
herself in the- ... what? ... who? .. no! ... she! . . . found herself
in the dark ... and if not exactly ... insentient ... insentient ...
for she could still hear the buzzing ... so-called ... in the ears ...
and a ray of light came and went ... came and went ... such as
the moon might cast ... drifting ... in and out of cloud ... but so
dulled ... feeling ... feeling so dulled ... she did not know ...
what position she was in ... imagine! ... what position she was
in! ... whether standing ... or sitting ... but the brain- ... what?
... kneeling? ... yes ... whether standing ... or sitting ... or
kneeling ... but the brain ... what? ... lying? ... yes ... whether
standing ... or sitting ... or kneeling ... or lying ... but the brain
still ... in a way ... for her first thought was ... oh long after ...
sudden flash ... brought up as she had been to believe ... with
the other waifs ... in a merciful ... (*brief laugh*) ... God ... (*good
laugh*) ... first thought was ... oh long after ... sudden flash ...
she was being punished ... for her sins ... a number of which
then ... further proof if proof were needed ... flashed through
her mind ... one after another ... then dismissed as foolish ...
oh long after ... this thought dismissed ... as she suddenly
realized ... gradually realized ... she was not suffering ...
imagine! ... not suffering! ... indeed could not remember ...
off-hand ... when she had suffered less ... unless of course she
was ... *meant* to be suffering ... ha! ... thought to be suffering ...
just as the odd time ... in her life ... when clearly intended to
be having pleasure ... she was in fact ... having none ... not the
slightest ... in which case of course ...   (Beckett, *Not I*,
pp. 1–3)

In *Not I* there is no such finality of final image as in the *Godot*
diagram. There is no adequacy of image. Whether or not a
figuration has to assist in the production and locution of a space
and a viewer's relation to its naturalism as defined, this one (in *Not
I*) does not and could not, if a monological struc*turing* (not
struc*ture*; rather, the gerund form) is to take place and time.

The concept of the 'non-corporeal' as I have used it is a concept of
the anti-corporeal. That is, it is not-enough full-figure to be
ascertainable from the fragment, thereby undermining as well the
usual use of 'fragment', as the latter is a quantitative problem and
always designates itself as fragment-*of*. The use of the concept

fragment, as metaphor, and the use of the concept corporeal or non-corporeal, as metaphor and transcendance, is disallowed. The interests of the material theatric process of *Not I* force this position.

A domestic space is one that functions as correct for the representations assumed, needs its ideological teleology. The befitting space is in enough ways homogenous with the 'content's' function as to not be at variance to a degree that would produce contradictions, onstage or for the viewer. It must not produce contradiction, but may produce dilemma, psychological, physical, metaphysical or other. A space in which figures represent figures, or represent their functions, can only be domestic(ated) space, befitting space.

The viewer's attempt to see, the first process which forces her or him to be in process, and the viewer's attempt to hear, the first process also which forces her or him to be in process, and the viewer's attempt to know (understand), a first process which forces her or him to be in process, and the viewer's attempt to produce some signification, constantly, which could link; but the movement's rapidity and non-localisability all 'maintain' the staged 'object' as a subject-not-i. Not you the viewer either, as the normative identification-process, even that of self-identity (imagined or desired) is made impossible. The linkage between every signifier (the mark, or the word, or the image), every signifier being a signified for another signifier, is broken down here, or not upheld. It is kept in process, so as to disallow a process of linkage from taking place.

Implicit in such a critique is also one of any hierarchies for body, mind, figure, language. It must additionally be added that the *Not I* production written about here suppresses, for the time being, the second figure on stage, the listener, cloaked in darkness, hardly seen and, in fact, through this production made invisible. Beckett's autocritique of the usage of this figure led to his self-directed Paris production relinquishing the figure altogether (a result which he had in the London production achieved through *mise en scène*: the figure simply was avoidable). Such an absenting of a figure in a production can be achieved simply through any aspect of the theatrical apparatus (light, sound, decor, volume, etc.) and the way it sets the viewer up for certain things and not for others. Certain figures in Chekhov or Ibsen, Dario Fo and Franca Rame or Cunning Stunts, can, similarly, be absented in the production. This is mentioned here simply to show that this event was no major matter in terms of directorial cleverness.

What could be countered (though I wouldn't) is that the figure at the side, the 'listener' who stands in semi-darkness enables a de-abstractification of the speaking mouth of Billie Whitelaw in *Not I* which, paradoxically, may be necessary to counter any imaginary assumptions of an apprehendable character or '2 characters': one speaking, one spoken to; one visible, one not. It could be stated that this listener-figure cannot be totally absented by the direction Beckett gave (in the London production). But the figure *did* absent itself through this specific production. With a materialist work and a dialectical production, it is always a matter of what is, finally, overdetermining. The anti-human scale, the speed of voice, the impossibility of 'true' perception, the techniques and devices which produced the necessity for the active viewer's struggle with the process (and as part of the function of its productive power against 'meaning' as reproduced) formulated the concrete–abstract singular mouth onstage (absenting any *figura*tion). Such a production functions *against* the possibility of any overriding reading of the mouth's movements and languagings as simply a stylistic within conventionally human, dramatically normative, *scale*.

An analogy: Beckett's production of *Endgame* with absolute fourth-wall playing, not to an audience at any time, to the point of cutting certain written and published passages and scenes that are not consistent with this end. 'The audience must not become an accomplice. The work is a self-enclosed system. The work must be played as if there were a 4th wall at the footlights' (Michael Haerdter, 'Beckett inszeniert "Endspiel"', *Theater*, 1968). The three directed curtain calls to that production were in the form of an unchanging frozen tableau, locked in time with no end, locked in space via the curtain.

As to centring: how does the mouth do what the eyes do? Eyes centre the viewer in a point (quattrocento) away from the stage-rectangle. How do the mouth's movements and rememoration-attempts parallel the viewer's processes (described above), though not covering them in any kind of adequacy? The case is not additive, nor subtractive, but divisive. The answer is the mouth does not. But the mouth does what the viewer's eyes do, which is move, attempt to grasp, rememorate, hold, lose, always lose, not manage to hold that loss; always structuring-process, forget structuring, just process. Each word used elsewhere and here has already such in-built histories and teleologies, aims and goals which make each word almost impossible to use without subscribing to the use, and reproduction, of certain futures.

The use of language in this way, and its difficulties, are a constant difficulty in Beckett's work, whilst simultaneously the fiction/reality question is at once laid to rest from the start *and* is constantly being played out/worked out in the texts and Beckett-directed productions. The histories of this working-out/playing-out are not buffetted by anything in the language's syntax which would give evidence to anything but grasps and losses. There is nothing to be held to outside the theatrical process; no fixed representation (somehow fixed) mirrored by an unfixed theatrical one (somehow unfixed). Thus, in *Not I* there is no believable or unbelievable referent, no identif*ied*, no *representation*, period. This is history in the objective moment as history. This is not to deny anything *else* and is similarly not to privilege subjective sight, intuition, knowledge, either. It becomes a matter of *position*: ideology and politics, that *act*.

Thus what we at most may have is *a* subject not *the* subject. It can thus be *a* subject that at any moment you are, not *the* subject, and not any imaginary solidity as characterisable fundament. This is a position demanding an anti-patriarchal lack of hold in the word.

This means that the word does not hold you, and cannot somehow 'give' you, your comings and goings, psychical, physical. It also means that you cannot hold the word, you can not 'find' the word. This does not mean that words have no use. The illusionary assimilability of words to meanings is precisely their use-value. The myths of adequacy and representation are very real. At the expense of accepting their codes of use, we can find out what the weather is like in Moscow; when the friend wants to see you and for how long, though the 'why?' already brings immense pressure to bear on the contract for language code's usage. The pressures are inculcated by paranoia, loss, and the artifice of meaning-construction in the first place (those ideologies!). Short-term (political) contracts are needed to sustain meaning's use. An example: do not tell me anything but what time it is. It is four o'clock. Thank you. Or: when do we blow up the police station in Brixton. 5 o'clock. Fine. Here language is not used as language, it is used as stand-in for prefixed meaning (a code), and the transference of that operates usually quite simply. It is the more, and the less, of language which some writing and some literature and some theatric production functions as, for example Beckett's.

Fixity, or probity, is contexted differently 'in' television than 'on' stage. The mouth is, in Beckett's television production of *Not I*, in close-up, full-screen. The mouth's movements are at the same speed as onstage. The lips, the teeth, the tongue are in constant unutterable movement, the eyes of the viewer unable to grasp that articulation whilst hearing. The rapidity of sound-emanation and the perceptual lack of stillness produces effects similar to those on stage, taking into account differences of distance, height, size, sound (television *vs* theatre). So here a 'similarity' is effected via entirely different means. The television close-up is much larger than lifesize – the sound is technologically mediated differently (on stage it was through a small microphone situated in the dark, right under the neck). The image, too, is technologically differently mediated, as the lines through the image are part of television technology (520 lines in Britain, 370 in the USA). The viewer's eyes are given no resting point 'in' the television screen. In the stage production, there is no resting point 'in' a figure or figure's fragment. If, in the centre of the television screen, the mouth had been in longshot, of a minute size, as an effect of distance, thereby imitating the distance of the mouth in the stage production, there would have, precisely, been a resting point for the viewer's eyes, producing the opposite of the intended effect. A coherent whole would have been thereby set up, or a convincing one, in perspective depth, because those factors which on stage militated against that hold (height, isolation in darkness, unfathomable distance without stage reference-points, etc.) do not exist for the television apparatus. There you have different contingencies: the set (the box), the lines, in various shades of grey or, if high contrast black and white, an even more holdable single contrasting image, white mouth against 'black' background, held in place by that. Finally the way this television production operates, all that is finally given is the extreme close-up mouth, tongue, lips, with the 'givens' the *least* amenable to its functioning as literalist image, as nearly ungraspable to eyes and ears as television allows.

The mouth *qua* mouth on television operates as *close-up* mechanism for speech, whereas on stage there is the at first felt imminent *absence* of a figured body due to the context for fully figured representation, even in its lack. Such an *absence* does not present itself within the codifications of *television* representation; whereas, on stage, there's no convention of *close-up*. On stage and on television, what is given is theatrical *masque*, that is to say prior to anything 'happening', prior to process, prior to analysis, prior to language, there are the very gestural characteristics as a material base, the image of mouth *qua* mouth moving. In the production by Beckett one hears before one sees (both in stage and in television versions). On stage, one hears more, i.e. louder, as the curtain rises, breaking the physical blockage.

The masque remains as neither connotative nor denotative. Examples of what could be but is not: denoting an age, a class, facial lines, lack of them, etc., connoting resignation, optimism, etc. Here in the opaqueness, as opposed to transparency, of staged material, material process of language and gesture, is material speech *per se* as effect of mouth/tongue/teeth/lips' movement.[19]

Bunraku (see Illustration 4) demands of the controllers of the lifesize marionettes that they persist in their stage existences throughout, to stay on stage, a constant construction/deconstruction/construction – continuum; the operation of *Not I* opposes that. Bunraku homogenises from a materially 'complex' heterogeneity, whereas this piece heterogenises from a univocal 'simple' position. It is a useful analogue if what is Brechtian about theatre (and *Not I*) can be said to be distanciation, the giving (playing/working) of every effect and every affect as effect and affect, of actor's (one usage amongst many) quoting rather than 'living' their characterisations, often against 'their nature'.

One effect of this process of language's materialism in *Not I* is in the placement of the spectator: the spectator's extrication from male sexual 'superiority' into the non-male voice. But the *equation* or identity of the spectator with 'voice' must also be at the same time questioned. 'The spectator' (*male and female*) becomes 'extricated from' the identifications male superiority demands (and the consequent identities that at any moment are thereby given). The extrication is from that 'into the non-male voice'. Yet 'extrication into the non-male voice' would mean a possible conflation of spectator-position with voice, as if the two were the same, *and* a possible conflation of power with voice. The spectator's positions and identities, through identification mechanisms during the viewing/listening process, are not simply then positioned in, and finalised through, 'the non-male voice' (and all along here I am speaking specifically of the voice and its speech in *Not I*). The spectator comes with a history, histories, and the momentary positioning through voice is one mode of ideological political power that can be processed and transformed in the specific case at hand, making certain identifications, and the reproduction of certain identities impossible *here*, forcing different positions. One such different position is the forcing of the viewer into the identification with/positioning in relation to, this non-male voice, thus the production of that rather than the *re*production of what is given 'elsewhere' in dominant patriarchal representations in sound and image.

Power and voice, too, are not the same, nor does voice simply *reflect* the state of some overall power-scheme. It is through and with the voice that positions of power are worked out: it is also through the economy, through physical coercion (and the threat of such) etc. Economic power and language power are two separate things. A relation has to be constructed; what at points, and at moments, is possible. Sometimes a certain language does equal a certain power, for example economic power; sometimes a certain, for example economic, power equals a certain kind of language.

This by way of analogue: the West African tradeswomen who run the markets have economic power, yet in the home defer to the word of the male, due to the patriarchal *ideology* having a stronger hold in that instance than their individual and collective economic power. Of course, it could be argued that their economic power is obliterated because the physical power, not the ideological power, of patriarchy dominates them. The male beating the woman, men beating women, and the *organising* (laws, etc.) by men to legitimate the beating and domination of women, rather than the male's word in the home, is what obliterates the possibilities of women's economic power determining their emancipation. But precisely such *organisation* by men is *ideological organisation* (whether it be conscious or unconscious in its motivation) – it is in one group's *interests*, and it maintains hegemony when the other group's interests are not fully organised against it. Through all this, 'power' and 'voice' remain separate, except at those cruxes at which links are constructed. The West African tradeswomen's language does not reflect their social position. Language is not simply reflective of the economy, nor of the relation to the physical strength of men (which in industrial society should be a minor matter anyway) as this male strength exists in the marketplaces and does not hinder, there, the language and economic power of women. The codes by which both sides 'agree' to live (even if physical power is an element) are ideological codes, systems which through the force of language and against language's forces are enunciated and worked out. The representation of 'male' and 'female' in language (tone, timbre, delivery, volume, flow, viewpoint) is the site of this. There is no reason to deny that positions within other relations of power are equally necessary for radical change to take place.

It would be voluntaristic to assume that, through changes of subject-position and identificatory mechanisms as described, a patriarchal social positioning could be obliterated; it would be equally idealist to assume that the changing of, for example, economic power positions alone would somehow transform and obliterate the concrete power of patriarchy's ideological positions. Both are absolutely necessary. So the spectator, and his/her power and powerlessness, is always more than just voice.

Bearing this in mind, the second point is that the extrication from certain kinds of identities of *power in voice* is different for men than for women – 'the spectator's extrication from male sexual superiority into the non-male voice' is an extrication giving certain power to women and taking it from men. The process (due to the social construction, arbitrary as it is, of the sexual category 'men' and the sexual category 'women') produces different symptoms, effects and consequences.

The male romance of non-admission of (the Oedipal?) crisis is put into the mouth of a woman in *Not I*. The romance of non-admission, the hysteria of that crisis for the male, is enunciated by a woman's speech (by 'romance' here is meant that which is allowed, but only through non-admission, through repression; and as it is motored through repression, it is motored hysterically as in constant repetitive denial: 'no, no, no, no, she!!!'). Lou Andreas-Salome's notion of women as culturally produced with less *fantasy* of power, less a repressed Oedipality necessitating the abnegation of 'the practical' (the body), has relevance here.[20] It allows women a practicality/materiality obviating the need for hysteria (a symptom nevertheless played out at times of heightened oppression upon the woman's body, including speech – the *reaction to male power*, both through 'hysterical' non-movement, catatonia and in 'hysterical' movement). Hysterical movement is enacted usually as male, in 'the act', or in the hysterical catatonic silence of male repression and refusal, the refusal, for example, to talk, denoting speech, and speaking itself, as somehow neurotic, 'feminine', in the face of 'earnest masculinity'. Such male hysteria is of course not usually defined as hysterical. It operates in opposition both to a movement of processes without finalities, and to the silences of autonomy, both culturally defined as 'female'.

The figuring-out of this problematic in *Not I*'s form engages the viewer in the apparatus of speech-making and positions him/her in a manner that disallows the male voyeur/listener/doctor. The non-movement of any figure, and the constant voice, simultaneous with its constant non-admission ('what ... who ... no ... she!') forms for the listener an untenable position as both hearer and non-hearer from which to 'hear' the denial, the other's denial. Denials are played out on the body of the mouth's voice with speech itself as the body. One is ("I") given no position: untenable, unapprehendable, thus making that transference impossible. The eviction of hysteria from the listener onto the subject 'on' stage through unconscious identification (repression) is now no longer possible. The hysteria, the denial, remains unfigured, neither here nor there, and this break of identification is the collapse, impossibility, of difference here and there, here to there, there to here. Importantly, a desired collusion of time and space is hereby produced as collapsed, any illusion thereof thus reflexivised. Positions of sex, sexual power, knowledge, are collapsed, an impossibility, no given 'other' onstage, making identity, identification, and the repressions necessitated for those ideological (but real) mechanisms to take place impossible. This blockage of identification and transference in the theatrically voiced act catatonises and paralyses the listener–viewer, in its (his/her) body, whilst forcing the mind into production, against consumption. The *imaginary* of the viewer's movement and being-moved, in theatrical drama/television/*narrative*, is an identificatory male hysteria never identified as such. Against that, the viewer('s body) in *Not I* is positioned as a woman's (ideological) body; the usual patriarchal identification-structure positioning the viewer, male and female, to the defining function as male is opposed. The effect of that opposition is a problematising contradictory position *against*. A theoretical practice of production, in 'viewing/listening', inculcates itself hereby. This process of opposition can not be popular.[21]

The skeletal is finally all that could possibly exist, not 'beneath' the mask of Mouth's speaking engagement but as is. This talking-through, a talking to death, in *Not I*, is a deathdrive both psychoanalytical and entropic. It is neither a decathexis nor a non-cathexis but a cathexis abandoned. Language is left as the end. One cannot resolve the relation 'with' the other without the other. One can only have a relation with the other with the other. The attempt to know, let alone control (as opposed to oppress) an other is imaginary. And the attempt to control an other is impossible because it relies on a non-admission of *samenesses*, equalness, which means an other is not complementary to and can *not* be *contained* by one self('s norms). The other does not permit that hierarchicalisation – it is not complementary to one. So there is loss, through the non-admission of the other's sameness, *and* the other's different history of struggle. In this Beckettian scheme, depression is the state of being not numb: 'don't wait to be hunted to hide' (Samuel Beckett, quoted in Marcuse, *One Dimensional Man* (Boston, Mass.: Beacon Press, 1964) p. 243). 'That first last look in the shadows after all those in the light to come' (Beckett, quoted by Richard Seaver on BBC Radio 3, 17 August 1980).

The monological is a constant attempt precisely to hide. It is an attempt to not be hunted, or, rather, hunting is given as a metaphysic of the self's hunting the hunted, the latter the self as well. The hiding is an act in the Real which has to do with non-availability for the speaker (that *it* that monologues). For you, for her, for him, holding another is the impossible. *It* will not but cover with language the you that ought not wait to be hunted to hide. The reason? The sado-masochism (I have, I want, you) of power's control (over demand) forcing the inadmissability of loss, of being, finally, alone. So even alone, hiding necessary. That is not a poesis of 'aloneness', but of being without anything but the illusion of adequacy. The illusion of non-aloneness, that as adequacy, is the whole act. It is this final emphasis which leaves nothing but monologue as material for figure, voice, language, larynx's teleology.[22] Monologue is given, therefore, as an *effect*, as device which is not the start, but the end, of a process and in a process.

So, each process is already the effect of another process. The monologue is what one is left with as the final production, not the beginning of a multi-layered, ever-more-complex communication-possibility, or narrative, story, short story (four parts including denouement, etc.). No opening out of possibilities is given in this materialist definition of monologue. Or rather, that 'opening out of possibilities' and of 'communication' is nothing but what could be desired, and needed, and wanted, even, but in no relation to the real other than by deference of the real; illusion, want, desire, all prevailing upon the human body and the human mind to make of matters what they are not. Certain monologues do all in their language's power to function *not* as monologue, but as the phantasmatic beginning of communication and its 'potential'. *There* is the anti-materialist monologue, and it is dominant and resistable.

So: monologue as in process, to be materialist, dialectical, political. No more a matter of language simply getting you to act but also language as act. Does this mean that all other sorts of acts are no longer important? No. But they're other acts. The language and 'its' ideology has, and has had, its effects; the economic and the directly political-legal framework and 'its' ideology, has, and has had, its effects. Sexuality's materialist positions and 'its' ideologies have, and have had, their effects on sexuality and against sexuality's patriarchal ideologies.

The question arises of monologue's monotony. If what is meant as 'monotone' is a flattening-out in the seeming non-distinguishing of one sound from another, then Beckett's monologues *function* as oppositional to monotone. This is not to state that they are not *perceived*, nevertheless, within the culture, as monotonous in their production and their effects, relative to the perceived non-monotony of narrative drama as it is culturally situated. In *Not I* we must distinguish the non-monotony of the speech-inflection from the 'monotony' of the result. It is not a matter of subjectivities, but of what one allows as acceptable *definition* of theatrics regardless of the happenstance individual interpretations (which thereby remain excluded from this system of definition of the monotone). There is no 'open text'. The what and the how of the *it* (the monologue) that is 'monotonous' are still circumscribed concepts held by the primacy of the specific text at hand. It is more, really, a question of 'the monotone' not functioning as *purely* monotone. But it is not a matter of arguing over definitions, or of a hierarchy of elitest versus popular response or understanding. It comes down to the specific work and what use one puts a 'monotone' work to and what different pleasures and what critiques of pleasure as conventionally defined are brought to bear.

All this apart, there is still the question of the non-monotonous Beckettian monologue articulating as one of its effects *monotony*.[23] Equally a (non-Beckettian) monotone production of voice in monologue can produce, for example, an *effect* of non-monotony, inculcating identification into the very 'depths' of character, identification with, for example, the speaker's dramas, allowing the speaker to characterise his/her truth. That procedure is a structure of identification that can produce suspension of disbelief (and with effects that are) perceived by the viewer–listener as anything but monotone.

'There is no monologue' (M. M. Bakhtin, 'Discourse in the Novel', *The Dialogic Imagination* (Austin, Texas: The University of Texas Press, 1981) p. 314)

Interpretation-demanding ambiguity masks sameness and redundancy of language and in language. The non-admission of the return of the same is not the same as the return of the same. It is in the latter that, in such monologues as *Not I*, the conflict for the subject (understood as the viewer–listener) is; the subject, understood as you. The warding-off of that conflict is what conventions of, and for, narrative are.[24]

In *Not I* and elsewhere in some Beckett texts, speech constructions take us to a point where the surety we demand from language no longer holds us, and the effect of that is surely monotone no matter how rhythmic, or chromatic, the articulation is. The monotone of the anti-illusionist process demands the material/aural practice that listening/viewing must be to counter dominant and conventional practices which annihilate the subject within and without. Thus what is being described here is a listening/viewing that counters dominant and conventional practices which annihilate history, or any history other than the mechanistic referent, that which is theatrically referred to on stage, alluded to as 'history as it is', i.e. as it pre-exists, never itself part of a production process, never transformed through various forces of struggle. Thus what is established is a history that is historicist, ahistorical, hysterical, catatonic. From such bourgeois notions of history both the non-normative concept of exploitation and the normative concept of oppression become excluded. The subjectivity of the speaker becomes annihilated, the difficulty of 'language covering something else' annihilated, the making of meaning and meaninglessness annihilated, the dialectically contradictory politics of positionality within an impossibility of truth, annihilated.

XIX

Quote: 'One is Not Born a Woman' (Monique Wittig)

Quote: '"Phallomorphic Power" and the Psychology of "Woman": a Patriarchal Chain' (Monique Plaza)

'Woman''s Voice

Women's Speech and Oppression

Difference

Women will have to abstract themselves from the definition 'woman' which is imposed upon them. . . . Our fight aims to suppress men as a class, not through a genocidal, but a political, struggle. Once the class 'men' disappears, 'women' as a class will disappear as well, for there are no slaves without masters. . . . Our first task it seems is to always thoroughly dissociate 'women' (the class within which we fight) and 'woman', the myth. For 'woman' does not exist for us: it is only an imaginary formation, while 'women' is the production of a social relationship . . . which is based on the oppression of women by men and which produces the doctrine of the difference between the sexes to justify this oppression. . . . What we believe to be a physical and direct perception is only a sophisticated and mythic construction, an 'imaginary formation' (Guillaumin) which reinterprets physical features (in themselves as neutral as any others but marked by the social system) through the network of relationships in which they are perceived. (Monique Wittig, 'One is Not Born a Woman', *Feminist Issues*, no. II (1980) pp. 48–9, 53; trans. from *Questions Feministes*, n. 1, 1978)

To found a field of study on this belief in the inevitability of natural sex differences can only compound patriarchal logic

103

and not subvert it: to pose woman as the specific object of oppression, we hide the fact that she is the object of oppression *through* the specific. [And that therefore it is women, not 'woman': author.] Far from taking the Difference as the basis of our project, we should demolish it and denounce its falsity. Analysing how and why it takes on an ineluctable character: I must be man or woman; neither both nor something else . . . at the risk of getting lost. In this sense, building a solidarity indispensable to our survival may not rest on the elaboration of a feminine universe, on the idea of a shared nature of women. Which does not signify either that we are going to 'deny' our bodies, or want 'to be men'. The oppression of women is based on the appropriation of their bodies by patriarchy, on the restriction of sexuality within the framework imposed by the masculine–feminine opposition, the subjection of the woman in confinement to medical power, the contemptuousness of menstruation, the lack of recognition of sexuality. But recognising this vast sexual oppression of women must not lead us to the conclusion that oppression derives from the body, or from sex; or that the body explains social oppression. Woman's sex is denied, unrecognised. But that does not mean that woman's oppression derives from that lack of recognition. We must guard ourselves from a form of reflexive 'pan-sexualism' which is only a coarse, disguised naturalism. If the category of sex has such an important position in patriarchal logic . . . it is because the social is able to make sexual forms seem obvious and thereby hide oppressive systems. . . . Woman exists too much as a signifier. Woman exists too much as subjected, exploited, individual. The 'not enough', 'not yet' situates itself . . . on the (reverse) side of the material and psychic *autonomy* of women. *That is something that cannot be constructed in a problematic of the Difference. Nor in a prospective of the unutterable.* (Monique Plaza, ' "Phallomorphic Power" and the Psychology of "Woman": a Patriarchal Chain', *Ideology and Consciousness* (Autumn 1978) pp. 9 and 27; also reprinted in *Questions Feministes*, no. 1 (1978, Paris)

Woman's voice is given in patriarchy as an ahistorical voice; ahistoricism is immediately always posed in patriarchy as an unmediated, timeless and spaceless-ness (infinite and eternal). This both reconstructs woman as dangerous, for her 'unstoppable' sexuality, and posits individual women as such. The fear that such a *structure* posits, let alone any specified characterological 'content', subsists through the duration of a woman's speech. The enactment of female monologue always takes issue with that structure, either to reproduce and reify or to undercut and oppose it, demanding a different process for the speaker and the listener–viewer. But that different process must be constructed as a sameness, not a sexually defined 'difference', to operate as materialist practice as it does in, for example, *Not I*. Language as demand becomes collapsed with an ideology of the 'feminine' for a concept of the bourgeois-patriarchal that has nothing to do with the Real but more with a 'real*ism*'. Language as physical/mental fear-induction within patriarchy's hegemony of power is power in the street and power in the meanings in the mind, in semi-autonomous relation. Language as the positionings of the male within fear, here through the woman's speech which maintains a duration of discourse; the feverish attempt is at escape from that voice and that demand, the rush of sound (in *Not I*) which is not *held* to meaning or to pre-defined meanings and positions. *That* power of women's speech voided only in patriarchy by silence, death, or the unutterable, so far ineffaceable, process of misogyny. The multiple orgasm a woman's biology allows (not demands) is a different definition of closure. Thus male/female oppositions (given in *terms* of narcissistic satisfaction) are 'wanted' because needed by patriarchy in the sheer impossibility of *anything* which can be 'satisfied' except for the imaginary and very real narcissism of phallocentric male sexuality. Satisfaction as an ideological concept of consumption must be questioned. Male sexuality's desire is constructed in this context as the closured satisfactions of phallomorphic sexuality, phallomorphic power, and the female's exhaustion. That exhaustion would replace the woman 'back' into the given history, into a point of beginning and end which can then be consumed as her 'meaning'. Against this there are for women durable, and for patriarchy unendurable, other, radical, political meanings and histories.

Conceptual exhumations of sameness and difference male to female have import in specifying what relation it is structurally that speech of the mouth in *Not I* has as primary function when heard by men and/or women in patriarchy. Men and women have different histories *and* the same histories. Though biology is not determining, biology exists. Difference, which is not constituted *by* biology, but which is the perceptual basis upon which segregations *for* difference are constituted, 'exists'. Different histories result – 'hidden from history' where within dominant conventions work by women, and women's speech, is censored, suppressed and repressed, *and* 'other histories' exist, the work of resistance and struggle, kept separate from '*the*' history and from any history given as *History*.

The above argument does not say that biology holds meanings outside of the social constructions for that biology, that physical 'difference' by which's recognisability empirical categories of woman and man are arbitrarily set up. The result of this social construction for that biology simply leads to the following concept: that more likely than not, X (male) will not be disturbed by such and such an oppressive image of women in such and such a play, film, novel, etc., because he is a male, and more likely than not Y (a woman) will be disturbed by such and such an image of women given in that image-representation. This is not to say one can determine and map response and political position simply via biological construction; but in the oppressions of patriarchy, the category 'men' are the main enemy for 'women'. The category 'women' is both the oppressed and the resistance to male oppression, able in power and struggle against it. As in patriarchy oppression is women's oppression, positioning by a woman is against that, whether consciously or unconsciously and whether in 'feeling' or in 'thought'.

This positioning is defined by the body which 'allows' (forces) women to be that category 'woman'. Men are constituted as hegemonic 'man'. That is not to say that necessarily a woman will react and feel this way, a man that way, just that it is more likely than not, *given the objective positioning* (unfortunately via a biological characterisation) in relation to power. If one tries to eradicate this likelihood of 'more likely than not' altogether, if one tries to separate patriarchal definition from sexual definition (even in the interests of an anti-biologism, anti-determinism) then one is creating an apolitical idealism which infers that oppression is arbitrary, i.e. not in certain interests. Ideology is that through which our social existence is lived, and therefore not all women are feminists and not all men are at one, subjectively, with the given norms, but objectively those norms either give power (to men) or take power (from women) within such a system and structure, regardless of whatever subjective identifications with or against, treasonous or not to their sex, class, subjectness.

XX

Quote: Sections of *Not I* and *Enough*

Female's Speech and Meaning

MOUTH: ... out ... into this world ... this world ... tiny little thing ... before its time ... in a godfor- ... what? ... girl? ... yes ... tiny little girl ... into this ... out into this ... before her time ... godforsaken hole called ... called ... no matter ... parents unknown ... unheard of ... he having vanished ... thin air ... no sooner buttoned up his breeches ... she similarly ... eight months later ... almost to the tick ... so no love ... spared that ... no love such as normally vented on the ... speechless infant ... in the home ... no ... nor ... indeed for that matter any of any kind ... no love of any kind ... at any subsequent stage ... so typical affair ... nothing of any note till coming up to sixty when- ... what? ... seventy? ... good God! ... coming up to seventy ... wandering in a field ... looking aimlessly for cowslips ... to make a ball ... a few steps then stop ... stare into space ... then on ... a few more ... stop and stare again ... so on ... drifting around ... when suddenly ... gradually ... all went out ... all that early April morning light ... and she found herself in the- ... what? ... who? ... no! ... she! . . . found herself in the dark ... and if not exactly ... insentient ... insentient ... for she could still hear the buzzing ... so-called ... in the ears ... and a ray of light came and went ... came and went ... such as the moon might cast ... drifting ... in and out of cloud ... but so dulled ... feeling ... feeling so dulled ... she did not know ... what position she was in ... imagine! ... what position she was in! ... whether standing ... or sitting ... but the brain- ... what? ... kneeling? ... yes ... whether standing ... or sitting ... or kneeling ... but the brain ... what? ... lying? ... yes ... whether standing ... or sitting ... or kneeling ... or lying ... but the brain still ... in a way ... for her first thought was ... oh long after ... sudden flash ... brought up as she had been to believe ... with the other waifs ... in a merciful ... (*brief laugh*) ... God ... (*good laugh*) ... first thought was ... oh long after ... sudden flash ... she was being punished ... for her sins ... a number of which then ... further proof if proof were needed ... flashed through her mind ... one after another ... then dismissed as foolish ... oh long after ... this thought dismissed ... as she suddenly realized ... gradually realized ... she was not suffering ... imagine! ... not suffering! ... indeed could not remember ... off-hand ... when she had suffered less ... unless of course she was ... *meant* to be suffering ... ha! ... thought to be suffering ... just as the odd time ... in her life ... when clearly intended to be having pleasure ... she was in fact ... having none ... not the slightest ... in which case of course ... (Beckett, *Not I*, pp. 1–3)

Whilst speaking quickly one mustn't get loud, whilst speaking loudly one mustn't get pathetic. (Bertolt Brecht, 'Elementary Rules for Actors, GW16', *Schriften zum Theatre* (Frankfurt: Suhrkamp, 1967) vol. 2, p. 744)

New art in its beginning is non-objective, abstract for everything else, but always concrete for itself. (K. Malevich, 'New Art', *The World as Non-Objectivity*, in *Unpublished Writings 1922–25*, ed. Troels Anderson (Copenhagen: Borgen, 1976) vol. III, p. 252)

For the material (is) in the abstract (H.D., *Tribute to Freud*, p. 77)

All that goes before forget. Too much at a time is too much. That gives the pen time to note. I don't see it but I hear it there behind me. Such is the silence. When the pen stops I go on. Sometimes it refuses. When it refuses I go on. Too much silence is too much. Or it's my voice too weak at times. The one that comes out of me. So much for the art and craft.

I did all he desired. I desired it too. For him. Whenever he
desired something so did I. He only had to say what thing.
When he didn't desire anything neither did I. In this way I
didn't live without desires. If he had desired something for me I
would have desired it too. Happiness for example or fame. I
only had the desires he manifested. But he must have
manifested them all. All his desires and needs. When he was
silent he must have been like me. When he told me to lick his
penis I hastened to do so. I drew satisfaction from it. We must
have had the same satisfactions. The same needs and the same
satisfactions.

One day he told me to leave him. It's the verb he used. He must
have been on his last legs. I don't know if by that he meant me to
leave him for good or only to step aside a moment. I never asked
myself the question. I never asked myself any questions but his.
Whatever it was he meant I made off without looking back.
Gone from reach of his voice I was gone from his life.   (Samuel
Beckett, *Enough*, pp. 1–2)

Speech always means something for someone, always signifies.
Meaning is always imbricated by the histories from which it is
spoken. Female speech as a concept is non-existent, but there is
speech spoken by a female, which has its histories and meanings;
male speech similarly. Speech can have use-value and exchange-
value: some monological speaking has mainly exchange-value
(what you are left with afterwards, that property), some
monological speaking has mainly use-value (what you can do with
it, the use to which it is put, at the time of its process, without it
necessarily leaving you with any 'thing' afterwards as property).
Commoditisation of ideas means ideas as currency, i.e. your
property and ownership, or the illusion of such. Commoditisation
of ideas as currency and property means there is something worth
investing in, in direct relation to some assumed calculable
meritorious effect, and equally in direct relation to some assumed
calculable meritorious affect. Those effects'/affects' power over
you, and yours over them (both consciously and unconsciously), in
the theatre, are the 'economy' in question. Certain (preceding)
monologues by Beckett disallow the monologue as exchange-
value, that economy of consumption, or property owned and held,
transferred, exchanged in aid of extracting profit and surplus. The

ideological value given by such monologues which regress, which imbue a process of language but don't make of language a cohesive closured narrative package, is a bad investment. It forces you into production as active producer, in the sense of the production process of labour (not in the sense of the capitalist 'producer' who must be outside of the production process to invest capital). So in such monologues as *Not I* one is left with use-value, with use. Use as enough to hope to have had after such eleven minutes, thus left with nothing. Any indulgences the viewer seeks from *Not I*, to own something in meaning after the monologue is spoken, something retained afterwards, are disabused precisely by the authority here in *Not I* of female speech.

XXI

Quote: *African Women: Their Struggle for Economic Independence* (Christine Obbo)

Male Humanism's Patriarchal Power Against the Power of Women

The Non-biological

The Signifier

Authority of Female Voice in *Not I*

Generally, *power* is a way of securing compliance with obligations. In a familial decision-making situation, power is the potential ability of one partner to influence the other's behaviour in order to secure favourable outcomes. *Authority* is the right to make a particular decision as well as commanding obedience. This authority is power held by one partner because either or both partners feel it is proper for that person to do so, or because society at large prescribed it. (Christine Obbo, *African Women: Their Struggle for Economic Independence* (London: Zed Press, 1980) p. 102)[25]

In capitalist patriarchy the male viewer is *opposed* in his position as consumer of potential value for himself, his power-in-ideology, power-in-meaning, by such monologue as Mouth's in *Not I*. Thus the constant 'critical' attempt to convert this Mouth's speech into some humanism which can deliver some interpretable anterior content, some story outside of the following: the material(ist) process of speech; rememoration-attempts; the dialectic of the difficulty of hearing/seeing; the impossibility of speech-as-truth, etc. This attempt to convert such speech into a consumable humanism reassuring of the patriarchal ideology of the 'truth of the word', and the word as 'male' (as opposed to the word in *Not I*

112

as debiologised, though spoken by a female), can be seen also in the quotes by Beckett's publishers on the dustjackets of various works:

> Beckett's plots are good, understandable, interesting plots, his situations are believable, his characters quickly become old friends.

So one is, for a few pounds, buying the comfort of old friends, an investment-ideology the viewer–reader is constantly meant to partake of. The constant reproduction of this ideology in relation to the making amenable of materialist texts is not a coincidence,* but simply the endless demand of a system reproducing its own power relations in every sphere, constantly, against all opposition. Certain forms of monologue attempt to expropriate the word from the phallocracy and from that biologism.

It must be reiterated that attempted materialist speech as in *Not I* is not in any way to be somehow held to female biology. It is precisely *not* an attempt to essentialise or sensationalise as somehow female, some kind of fetish of the female which would keep the male position of voyeur firmly intact. Being reified the latter would also be yet again to instil a notion of speech-*re*production, reproduction as by the female *for* the male. Somehow, women's speaking "voice" must be re-acquired neither for 'fragmentation and chaos' (whether thereby defined as *threat* or *non-threat*) nor for transparency, process-annihilating 'communication' (the system we already have). Otherwise the 'answer' becomes reduced to the belief at best, yet again, in 'left-wing message in a right-wing form'. The latter is always a possible (in certain specific circumstances and contexts) short-term gain but long-term reinstitution of those transparent patrilineal codes of authority of language's phallocentricity which attempt to annihilate (and expropriate the material economic base and the material ideological base of) all but those with power and authority.[26] If cultural work is seen as not necessary to all this, it must be seen as only a mirror to the dominant power, and for leisure, with no politics of aesthetics, and no effects. Such a bourgeoisification of

---

*And, of course, one is imbricated in such identifications and therefore problematically does feel this!

culture is, rather, the bourgeois ideology which subscribes to such 'ideas' of culture whilst having for itself no intention of keeping politics and political effects out of aesthetics. It is simply that the politics of all this becomes the *repressed* of culture, the way politics becomes the repressed of the bourgeois concept of freedom. The speaking in *Not I* must be seen as a radical tendency, a left curve in anti-patriarchal language and anti-capitalist language and language-production/speech production. A radical positioning against meaning-as-is, and a labour-process against meaning-as-is.

XXII

Quote: Billie Whitelaw on her Work for *Not I*

Quote: Eisenstein on *Strike*/Revolutionary Art

The Marionette-like

Every night I had to work this through anew, I could never just remember, and perform, it. It was an incredible task, each night again. (Billie Whitelaw in conversation with the author in 1982, on studying *Not I* and *Rockaby*)[27]

The theatric signifier is that which signifies meaning via its existence onstage, inseparable from the theatrical apparatus it is part of. The theatric signifier is never the referent. The latter is always from the extra-theatrical world that is referred to; the extra-theatrical world also *from* which reference is 'embodied' onstage. The cultural meanings given to any signifier, as with the cultural meanings given to any signified, are always historical, and ideological. They are always constructed and determined, and in that sense *arbitrary*. They do not have an inherentness. A chair is never a chair, *per se*, in theatre, cinema – nor in that world outside.

With *Strike* we have the first example of revolutionary art in which the form proved more revolutionary than the content. (S. M. Eisenstein, *Strike* (Munich: Hanser, 1974) p. 230)

The form proved – *die Form erwies sich* – is a way of stating that materialist dialectic theory cannot utilise the concept of the 'future anterior'. What was revolutionary was not pre-determined, but was the result of practice, it proved, it turned out to be, '*es erwies sich*'. That a specific form proves itself, after a time, as more revolutionary than the 'content', though, is a structured necessity, as are communism and materialist radical feminism.

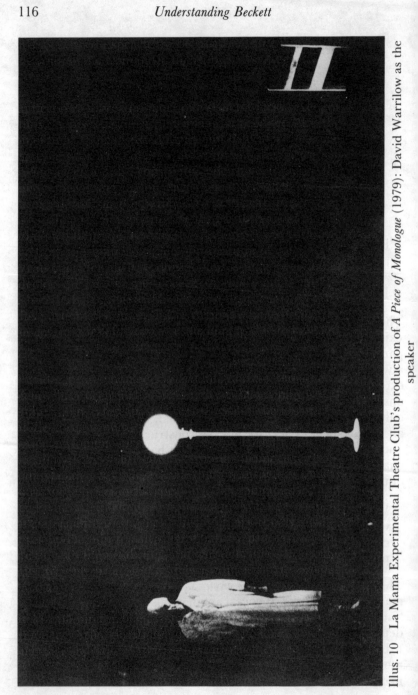

Illus. 10 La Mama Experimental Theatre Club's production of *A Piece of Monologue* (1979): David Warrilow as the speaker

Illus. 11   West African weaving, textile fragment (blue and gold)

Firstly, S. M. Eisenstein did not exit from the Proletcult, but rather he was *exited*.   V. Pletnev (theoretician and organiser of Proletkult), ibid., p. 308)

That is pure Beckett, Althusser, Karl Valentin: polemical, theoretical, 'sadistic'. The answer to 'what are you left with' is 'the form is more radical than the content'. And the other answer is 'Not the illusion that you are left with *more*'.[28] The realism[29] alluded to previously is precisely Realist, in the real sense, that one is *always* only left with a process (that history) and not the illusion of more. Beckett's manufacture of this is *Not I*.

(Reader: note *Not I* (script) on pp. 18–25.)

Is there anything marionette-like in all this? How does such a relation to what is marionette-like bespeak a relation to a material language? It is part of the machine, the theatrical apparatus, but unlike the manipulated figures in *Bunraku*, not simultaneously an icon, fragment-*of*. A wholist conception (a whole being; being whole or desiring such) is therefore not posited in *Not I*. Any figure figured through the image and language in *Not I* is somehow other, elsewhere, not here and not there. The repression of time and space is not the fundament of a materialist theatrical apparatus. The materialist conception of theatre here wants for a materialist production the what it is–how it is, and the how it is–what it is, not as stand-in, fragment-of, decoy, appendage, *fetish*. There is thus no inferable whole, no normatively scaled anthropomorph.[30] The aesthetic politics, against such normativisation, sets materialist theatrics of such monologue against any narrativisation of sound and image.

(See Illus. 10 and 11.)

The materialist discourse is never outside the historical–social–cultural context, and therefore, one, finally, can*not* say 'the context has to be considered', in any large sense of such a concept. It is precise to say that there is no materialism *per se*, as absolute. The avant-garde film *Wavelength* (1967) in West Africa may seem iconic, as West African weaving may seem here not to be. Again, that is why one can*not* say 'the context has to be considered'. It is *never* 'outside'.

XXIII

Quote: *Forgetful* and *The Aquarium* (Karl Valentin and Liesl Karlstadt)

The Concept of *Erstaunt-sein*/Astonishment

Laughter as Effect

Capitalist Realism

Aesthetic Politics

Colour

Hopelessness

Astonishment

Forgetful

KV: Ah, an old acquaintance, Mrs ... eh, I just can't recall your name.

LK: That's just like you. And to think that we've lived for so long in the same house, in the something-street ...

KV: You're right, true, true ... you're Mrs Schweighofer!

LK: No, no, on the contrary, a very short name ...

KV: Now I've got it, it's Mrs Long!

LK: No, no, I told you it's a short name! Of course I actually could *tell* you ...

KV: Mrs Mayerhofer!!

LK: Yes, absolutely right! And you're Mr Hofmeyer!

KV: Yup! Do you still remember how we at first used to always get the names mixed up? Well, well, Mrs Mayerhofer, it is good that I've just at this very moment bumped into you, I wanted to tell you something important, but right now I can't remember what ... what could it've been?

LK: That happens to me a lot too!

KV: What exactly could it've been? – Hm, hm, hm, *I could throw up!*

LK: Was it to do with business matters?

KV: No, no, it was uh ... and I'd thought to myself, *that* I've got to tell you if I should bump into you sometime!

LK: Well, dear God, one gets older and therefore more forgetful.

KV: That's true! – What was it I wanted to say? I just can't recall.

LK: It's the same for me. Yesterday I was at the, um, out there, um, you know ... oh, where was it?! Um ... in ...

KV: In at-home.

LK: No, no, I wasn't in at-home, uh, in, ahm, at, uh well *tell me*!!

KV: I have no idea where you were!

LK: I can believe that, that you don't know; *I* don't even know! In ... oh well, it's not important – and I had business matters to attend to, I was supposed to, um, uh ... I was supposed to ...

KV: That's *exactly* what always happens to me, I, at home I run into the other room, and when I'm there I have *no idea* what I wanted ...

LK: I once went to a doctor because of my forgetfulness, and when I was there he asked me what's missing, what's wrong – do you think I had any idea?! I completely forgot that I'd gone because of my forgetfulness.

KV: One should write everything down, then one doesn't forget it.

LK: I've even tried that already – I just can't do it.

KV: Why not?

LK: I always forget that I have to take a pencil along; and paper.

KV: *Once* I didn't forget something. I wanted to remember something really important, and I just told myself: Well, it's not worth trying to remember it as I'll just forget it anyway!! – And what do you think? I remembered it!!

LK: Well, and what was it?

KV: Hm, now I can't recall. (Karl Valentin and Liesl Karlstadt, *Vergesslich* [*Forgetful*], in *Alles von Karl Valentin* (Munich: Piper, 1978) p.243)

The Aquarium

As we're speaking about the Aquarium, as I lived earlier – not in Spring, *earlier*! – in the Sendlingerstrasse, not *in* the Sendlingerstrasse, that would be laughable, one couldn't live *in* the Sendlingerstrasse, because the streetcars *constantly* drive through it, I lived in the *houses* in the Sendlingerstrasse. Not in all the houses, in one of them, in the one that is sort of stuck between the others, I don't know if you know the house I mean. And that's where I live, but not in the whole house, but only in the first floor, on the first floor, that's under the second storey, and above the paterre, like that, in between, and there's a stairway going up to the second floor, well it goes down too, the stairs don't go up, we go up the stairs, well one just says it that way.

And there I have, in the living room, where I sleep, I have an extra living room, where I sleep, and in the bedroom I live and in the bedroom I have for my private amusement an Aquarium, standing sort of in the corner, it fits wonderfully into the corner.

I could've also had one of those round Aquariums, then the corner wouldn't've been filled out. The whole Aquarium isn't bigger than this (*gesturing*), let's say these are the two glass walls, these are my hands, I'm just explaining it, so that you understand it better – and these too are two walls, and underneath is the floor, which holds the water, so that the water doesn't flow out the bottom when one pours it in the top. If the floor weren't there, on top you could pour ten, twenty, thirty litres, all of it'd come flowing through and out the bottom. It's a completely different matter with a birdcage. With a birdcage the walls are similar to an Aquarium, only with a birdcage they're not made of glass, they're wire. That'd be a huge stupidity if it'd be the same with an Aquarium, because then the Aquarium couldn't hold the water, the water would run out between the wires constantly. That's why everything is so wonderfully organized by nature! Yes! And in that Aquarium I have goldfish, and in the birdcage I have a bird; the other day I was plagued by some stupidity and I put the goldfish in the birdcage and the bird in the Aquarium!

Of course the goldfish kept slipping off the swing in the birdcage and the canary would have soon drowned in the Aquarium, but then I put the whole thing as it had been and put the bird back in the birdcage and the goldfish back in the Aquarium where they belong!

Now the fishes swam happily around in the Aquarium, first up this way, then down that way, they swim differently nearly every day. The day before yesterday a Malheur happened to me, I saw that the fishes needed more water, and added a full pail of water, in the meantime that turned out to be too much, now the water was this high (*gesturing*) above the Aquarium, but I only noticed it the other day, and a goldfish swam off over the edge and fell on the floor, because in the room where the Aquarium stands, we have a floor underneath, and that's where it then lay, but only after it stopped falling.

Now, the fish didn't have any water on the floor, because we don't really have *any* more water in the room, apart from in the Aquarium. Then my housecleaner said, 'You'll see, the fish'll get broken on the floor down there, it'd be best if you kill the fish.' So that it wouldn't have to suffer so long, I thought to myself – do it with a hammer? In the end you'll hit yourself on the finger – so shoot it. But then I thought: in the end you'll miss, and it'll really start suffering, it'd be smarter, I said, if I just take the fish and carry it to the river and drown it.   (Karl Valentin, *Das Aquarium* (1908), in *Alles von Karl Valentin*, p. 14)

Astonishment, or amazement ('*erstaunt sein*') is one of Karl Valentin's and Liesl Karlstadt's repertoire of comic responses, in word and gesture. Valentin's '*erstaunt sein*' is usually about his own capacity to state something intelligent, usually a mundanity or something totally absurd arrived at through the logics of 'common sense'. Valentin's amazement is not only at his own capacity to state something 'intelligent', or intelligently, but is also an amazement at his own memory, his capacity to, rightly or wrongly, recall something. The apparent, momentary, capacity, via either of these routes, to cover the world via a word, or a concept, or a memory, establishes a kind of self-assuredness, equally momentary, that is at once identifiable with, identifiable and hilarious. The double '*erstaunt sein*' is thus based on a recognition of a momentary self's intelligence, seeing the self from the self, an auto-reflexivity which foregrounds and evidences precisely the divide, the split, that each 'person' is: the split of act *vs* consciousness, and the attempt at making some cohesion of the two; the split of world *vs* consciousness, and the attempt at making some cohesion however fruitless, helpless, and hilarious. The desperation engendered by the attempt at fitting, or finding a fittingness of, a word to a concept, via intelligence or memory, is the desperation of the Valentin/Karlstadt speech and gesture.

The seamless flow of language is blocked, thereby producing language as alienated and alienating, and distanciating. Both those senses of 'alienation' are processed by such a speech structure. Experiencing the divide, the process of searching out the precise problem (the grasping attempts to find out what to say and how to say it, to solve the given situational or language problem!), all serve to process the self's attempts at functioning. The alienation in Valentin is not that of the repressed, which functions nicely(!), but of the unrepressed unfunctioning. His monologue-attempt and his interrogatory obsessional 'dialogues' with Liesl Karlstadt are a series of constant stoppings, stoppages which force the self into immobility of movement and speech. It is a hearing of the self and being taken aback by that. That *that* is *I* for the speaker (the subject). Its effect is a fissure of presence at the moment of astonishment.

The experiencing of the divide is matched by the dislocation of any fittingness assumed for language/discourse, any fittingness that assumes a communication from *a* to *b* via the decoy of language. Language as a transparent enabling structure, simply able to say something about something else, is concretely disabled when the material operation of language is not suppressed. When the seeming-fit of language to the 'world described' becomes produced as conscious, or consciousness-provoking, it causes astonishment (*'erstaunt sein'*) because what it engages is the system of the illusory by which language attempts to suppress its own processes and inabilities adequately to be homogenous with anything outside language. There is always the split in language, that dislocation.

Thus language as impossible, a practice which is never at one with the meanings it is supposedly conveying. The process of the Valentin language-use is the material process of the impossibility of language's naturalism. It is always a construction and an attempt at a conscious process, thus the seeming automatic, natural, perfectly transparent fit of language to the meanings it sets out to convey becomes given equally as a constructed process (often unconscious via a series of conventions and codes). Language as never out of nowhere, as never somehow 'natural', as never un-ideological, is the materialist science of language and is the process of Valentin's speech productions. The Real thus exists as absence, as never present-in-language. One discourse never adequately covers another. One practice and one set of material realities can not be mapped out upon another, the sexual onto the political onto the biological onto the economic onto the historical, etc. The sadistic hilarity of the Valentin monologue is in its interrogation of words and phrases to force their materiality and their impossibility as truth, the impossibility of 'truth'. What are taken up are positions, ideologies, strategies, subjective histories, politics, no 'truth' outside that process. So language is impossible in the strictest sense. The impossibility is exactly that: the necessity to operate *as if* it were not impossible. The '*erstaunt sein*' (astonishment, amazement) is not produced when the fit (between self and world, between language and world) does not work, but when it does.

The amazement at one's (the speaking, to be identified-with, subject's) own intelligence, or capacity for applicable language-use, causes consternation. The fundamental assumption is thereby seen as opposite to what we usually ('normally') assume it to be, the appropriateness of language to the world of objects and nature, and the appropriateness of the self in the world, the straightforward functioning of intelligence and memory.

The moment of consternation/amazement is a moment of the 'freeze'. The double '*erstaunt sein*' shows our operation in the Real, and that repression is just that (repression not as simply not there, but rather, psychoanalytically, as there all the time). Reflexivity of self, fissure of language; a historical moment for the I. In the 'Valentin' pieces this is not a representative of another's history, some story *there*. The laughter produced from the Valentin/Karlstadt theatrics in you as listener–viewer is one effect, the break in identification another. The gestural is inseparable from this moment, and *tone* becomes the operative process enabling this. The fissure of language via compulsive obsessiveness in the Valentin/Karlstadt dialogue and the Valentin monologue, inseparable from the body's gestures and language's gestures (i.e. *tone*), force laughter and consciousness simultaneously. The resulting dislocation of narrative's seamlessness (via Valentin's obsessively hilarious compulsive interrogations and memory-attempts) oppose *moment for moment* the closured, imaginary, immaterial ideologies of representation which dominant theatre attempts to reproduce as the norm, and by which narrative continuum is effected. Valentin's work though is not some 'openness' or 'open text'. It is the *Real* of arbitrary, ideological, material closure (*vs* the *Imaginary* of natural, ideological, immaterial closure): 'A Charnel House!' (Beckett, *Godot*, p. 42).

Laughter is one effect, thought another. The problematic that maintains itself, here, though, is whether or not thought is about something else or about the process viewed of which one is part. If thought is about something else, is it about something else in terms of its *specific* meaning or as a general problem-idea? For example, *The Caucasian Chalk Circle* by Brecht is more about 'the specific' than 'the general', but even then, in its posing questions with the possibility of political answers ('land to the tillers of land'), it is finally *not* about specific possibilities but about an idealisation which does not problematise, let alone answer, anything specific *or* general. That the land should be the tillers' can for a Marxist political position only obtain under certain circumstances. And a more specific representation, for example, onstage, could not stand for the real historical, economic, cultural, sexual as *specific* moment. One representation can not adequately represent another. (This may not be enough of a theorisation of the problem of the adequacy of representation- attempts!) One is left with 'the general' in such 'political' representations onstage (or rather the attempted representation of politics). One is left with 'thought about that'. The elitism of such a 'political' theatre practice is that it necessitates a mode of thought outside the specific, and the political context becomes of necessity fetishised and condensed for the pleasure of consumption.

If *Red Race Riot* reminds of the 1960s, the specificity of the

Illus. 12   Andy Warhol, *Red Race Riot*, silkscreen on canvas, 1963
(114 × 82 in.)

Alabama, or 'Southern', race situation, and if the viewing is not of a photograph in a newspaper or magazine, nor in an exhibition, but of a Warhol silkscreen-print, using that still-image tinted red, then is there a distance created that is a distance in which you think about the process of reproduction of an image or the specific reality of the depicted situation, or what? Is a crude 'socialist' (i.e. capitalist) realism reasserting itself? Or a different realism which says (with Brecht) 'The political is not here in the theatre, but the theatre can show it is elsewhere'? Or is there *another* realism which says the political *is* here inasmuch as distanciated representation can make you 'think about the subject' as if the forms and ideologies of representation, and the histor*ies* of art, were non-existent? Such art to make you 'think about the subject' utilises form (the form of the artwork) towards an aestheticisation of the content (whilst decrying formalism!). Such aestheticisation of the political (the dictum of Fascist art, according to Walter Benjamin) merely turns the specific effects of representation upside-down; from aestheticisation for pleasure to aestheticisation for displeasure, or anger, or 'thought', or the catharsis of identifications (including self-identification). This notion of an art which makes you feel so bad you feel good, implies a decision making process in direct linearity from such feeling and thinking to an automatically correct political line, without further ado.

In such a (mistaken) notion, thinking about the subject is a political effect by definition, and 'progressive realism' is the whole context for that pursuit. The above possibilities for 'political aesthetics' are neither materialist nor historically specific. Art remains art with an endless subject-matter substitution or as the pointer to the political *elsewhere*. Such a straight kitchen-sink notion of art also takes us back to individualist catharsis and thought via the decoy literature, art, theatre, outside of the material processes of representation *and* outside of the ideology of the specific representation (sound/image), denying that it is *always* an image of an image, always already semiotic, inside certain meanings in certain interests.

What could we be left with? A different, dialectical distanciation (in relation to the Warhol silkscreen) which puts you in a process wherein is quoted the portrayal of the racist acts wherein conventional meaning-consumption (as unmitigated) is blocked (via the colour superimposed on, and thereby part of, the image). The function of the picture is of necessity through such simple devices questioned, and thereby the context also changed, *prior* to the first instance of perception. Thought is thus seen as not about some vague largesse of the thing-represented's 'existence', as 'thinking about' means literally nothing, i.e. no more than valorising and fetishising, as if 'thoughts about' *per se* were somehow necessarily the beginnings of new answers to 'problems depicted'. In fact, therefore, every depiction must be problema*tised*, whether the depiction is via an image, i.e. a picture, or via sounds and images leading to a mental attempt at ('depiction' and) position *vis à vis*, and *in*, the process and its structur*ing-attempts*.

If every depiction or depiction-attempt is *not* problematised, in theatre, music, film, painting (whether depiction of the specifically Political or not), 'thinking about' can only ever be a vague, non-specific reproduction of the given, neither about the forms of representation, the forms by which you are positioned, how the spectacle situates you, nor even about the *specific* referent or signified, but simply about idealised generalities, situations. The thought-process in every specificity must engage the problematisation of its own procedures in relation to the materiality at hand, the complexity of any theatric or pictorial presentation-attempt. Otherwise the apoliticism of bourgeois art retains its hegemony, producing a 'viewer' given objects to perceive and generally 'think about' (as opposed to an engaged, oppositional, contradictory reflexive mode). The bourgeoisie's hegemony in representation has as its project the annihilation of every signifier by the signified, every theatric, painterly, filmic, languaged signifier annihilated by *the* dominant signified, the meanings and politics of the bourgeoisie's '*nature*'. The politics of aesthetics is one practice, and one space within which ideological conflict materially operates.

The colour 'over' the race riot (i.e. the police riot) can either produce reflection about that, and the economic–historical–political of that, or about the process of the representation-as-artifice, as (therefore) non-communication, as blockage, as determinately the Real of that specific process. This leads to an unresolvable split. It is not that politics is outside the theatre, or outside painting, and that that which is inside the theatre, the theatrical process, the painterly process, is not politics, but rather that various politics exist, all imbricated in semi-autonomous possibilities of *material* change, the situating of the I no less than the attempt to stop the Western armies. The picture as picture is imbricated with that positioning and the meaning of meaning, the meanings of meanings. Unless one decries cultural practices altogether, which most critics of radical avant-garde culture do not pretend to, this is the least unradical possibility extant.

To decry this would be only to go back to the illusion of naturalism, suspension of disbelief, instancing 'general thoughts' about subjects via 'distanciation' (and misunderstanding that concept, thereby).

Thus the place for material/ideological concrete mental and physical *change*, in the political specificity of thoughts and actions against capitalist patriarchy, would be given a place outside that specificity of states, groups, individuals, contracts, sentences, words, conscious and unconscious desires, enactments, and so forth. That outside is a decoy.

The Warhol image often is analogue to the moment of verbal monological blockage, producing the inability to continue, hopelessness. '*Only when hopelessness is reached can action begin*' (Bakunin). (Hopelessness can also produce catatonia, but *not*, as in hope*ful*ness, in the illusion of movement, change, struggle.)

Central to the characterisation of the speaking non-subject in *Not I* or *Godot* or *Endgame* or *A Piece of Monologue* is the concept of non-identity. The subject as non-subject is based on the non-identity of 'character', 'a' character who is neither the unfissured whole subject, the narrativisable character of identification for the listener–viewer, nor a psychological entity, fissured or not. A post-psychological position is posed for the enactor as singular speaker (T. Adorno, *Versuch das Endspiel zu Verstehen* (Frankfurt: Suhrkamp, 1973) p. 188) through-whom is spoken. Such a position is categorised as one of meaninglessness, but is not subsumable to *that* as its meaning *nor* to an unpolemic '*vielfalt*' (muchness); rather, a negative practice. This is the '*Dialektik im Stillstand*' ('Dialectic whilst standing still') of

Benjamin, historical in 'its possibility of a real that can no longer be adequately thought' (p. 200); 'phantasm of eternity' (p. 219) as a negative ontology which must function as negation *of* ontology; historical fever of situation and speech concretising the ever-repetitive catastrophe, the history of the break with the phantasm (Adorno, *Versuch das Endspiel zu Verstehen*).

The amazement/astonishment ('*erstaunt sein*') is when that occurs, when the logic of the impossible, when blocked for a moment, its reality stopped short, is itself impossible, producing both laughter and the viewer's inability to act whilst inculcated to act, *at that moment*.

In *Not I*, *Godot*, *Endgame* or *A Piece of Monologue* the lack of the act becomes the moment of negativity, the lactation which withdraws; thus the amazement/astonishment of loss, of non-act, both of the subject that is seen/heard, *and* of the viewer–listener-as-subject (or as non-subject), additionally forcing any phantasms of internal or social unity to be undercut. What happens the rest of the time is the enactment of this process for the character(s), without necessarily moment for moment producing this *effect* in/through the viewer.

Yet *at the inception* of each word/phrase/series, the rearticulating of the universe of the stage, and the spectacle, 'over there', is no different from the representation 'here', at those moments when it seems inseparable from the viewer, operative as procedure of which he/she is part. *After* each word/phrase/series' inception, the stage and the spectacle's operations as separable from the viewer is reinstituted time and time again. Identification's complex dialectic is produced by both procedures.

The *material* of theatre is both the (total) apparatus and the represented action of speech and gesture, and that discourse is observable inasmuch as things are observable. The dichotomy between the referential (each signifier has a referent in the world!) (or an imaginary referent!) and the non-referential is a contradiction which motors a lot, but not synthesis or conclusion, not satisfaction or lack of unpleasure. The problematised contradictions which we culturally/politically are processed by/engaged with/in struggle against, are anonymity *vs* ego, languag*ed* spoken *vs* the individual speaker. Anonymity and the languaged spoken are the materialist politic against the speech and gesture, in theatre and out, of bourgeois individualism.

XXIV

Quote: Christine Delphy on Polemics

Political Acts

Representation

One cannot oppose polemic to theory because nothing is produced in a vacuum. (Christine Delphy, 'A Materialist Feminism is Possible', *Feminist Review*, no. 4 (1980, London) p. 89, and in C. Delphy, *Close to Home* (London: Hutchinson, 1984) pp. 154–82)

We are left with the necessity to act. Political acts have, or have not, historical efficacy. The practice of the theoretical act is also an act. The practicality of the empirical act is also an act. Whilst everything functions within referentiality, the production of non-referentiality of the production-process of meaning (which *makes* meaning in its processes) is a theoretically sound concept and reality within a materialist and dialectic position. The world is a series of meanings: economic, sexual, political. The *other* is ineluctably *not* colonisable, finally. How that is what it is is what we can investigate. *That* can be produced in constant process, in theatre, in film, in dialogues, in monologues, in sounds, in pictures. That production opposes others: mythical and individualist identities that foreclosure death as the final motivator, fearing lack of myth would demotivate altogether. Thus the return of the same (in whatever guise) is instituted as defence against loss. No wonder it's a charnel house.

One can't represent oneself. One can act every practice, act 'in' every practice. It is within that process, when the blockage of the monologue erupts, that the moment of amazement/astonishment occurs. At that moment of blockage as silence, nothing, death, the need to act against another's act, against identification, against collusion, against the other's continuum. The enactment onstage and the enactment in, and position of, the viewer makes of itself the process-apparatus, the verbal-visual physical-psychoanalytical material.

XXV

Quote: Wolfgang Iser on the Reader in the Text

Quote: *Critique of the Gotha Programme* (Marx)

Quote: *Rockaby*

The Female Protagonist in *Rockaby*, on Stage, and the Voice

Light (re: *Rockaby*)

The Female Body (Billie Whitelaw)

Bisexualising

Position Askew Onstage and Off (*Rockaby*)

Anti-patriarchal Theatrics

The Female Viewer

Asexualism

the disconnectedness of the language utterances [can] only be made aware from without   (Wolfgang Iser, *The Act of Reading* (London: Routledge, 1978) p. 134)

so that the speedy succession of speech-topic seems, not only for the speakers, but in any case for the viewers, to be a condensation of reality (shrinking of reality) . . . the dialogue specifies the isolation of the figures from the situations in which they are placed. The short utterance befits the haste of quickly-changing speech-themes, which betray a loosening of the relation between speech and person   (ibid., p. 137)

This tendency can be pushed to the extreme of separation of utterance from the figure   (ibid., p. 140) chains of association that can no longer be surveyed [are no longer retrievable: author]   (ibid., p. 145)

so the presentation of a potential ideal is given neither via yearning nor via negativity   (ibid., p. 145)

Not I militates against a transhistorical location of the problematic, as what is constantly operative is the foregrounded attempt to speak reality which is unspeakable, thereby placing the listener–viewer without any politics of consumption, and all engagement in language is forced as relative to that struggle outside of consumption. To deny such modes of struggle in language would posit a pure struggle elsewhere as natural. The struggle *with* (i.e. against) nature would thereby be made defunct. Thus the fantasy would persist that needs are natural and pre-ideological and purely empirical. The obverse fantasy would also persist: that needs are wants.

Marginal Notes to the Programme of the German Workers Party
1. Labour is the source of all wealth and all culture, and since useful labour is possible only in society and through society, the proceeds of labour belong undiminished with equal right to all members of society.

   First part of the paragraph: 'Labour is the source of all wealth and all culture.'

   Labour is *not the source* of all wealth. *Nature* is just as much the source of use values (and it is surely of such that material wealth consists!) as labour, which itself is only the manifestation of a force of nature, human labour powers. The above phrase is to be found in all children's primers and is correct in so far as it is implied that labour is performed with the appurtenant subjects and instruments. But a socialist programme cannot allow such bourgeois phrases to pass over in silence the *conditions* that alone give them meaning. Only in so far as man (*sic*) from the beginning behaves towards nature, the primary source of all instruments and sources of labour, as an owner, treats her (*sic*) as belonging to him (*sic*) does his (*sic*) labour

become the source of use values, therefore also of wealth.
The bourgeois have very good grounds for falsely ascribing
supernatural creative powers to labour; since precisely
from the fact that labour depends on nature it follows that
the man (*sic*) who possesses no other property than his
labour power must, in all conditions of society and culture,
be the slave of other men who have made themselves the
owners of the objective conditions of labour. He (*sic*) can
work only with their permission, hence live only with their
permission   (Karl Marx, *Critique of the Gotha Programme*
(1875) (Moscow: Progress Publishers, 1972) pp. 8–9)[31]

Fortunately, the Gotha programme has fared better than it
deserves. The workers as well as the bourgeoisie and petty
bourgeoisie read into it what should rightly be in it but is not,
and it has not occurred to anyone from any side to investigate
publicly a single one of these wonderful propositions for its real
content. This has enabled us to keep silent about this
programme. It comes to this, that nobody can translate these
propositions into any foreign language without being *compelled*
either to write down palpably crazy stuff or else, whether friend
or foe, to inject a communist meaning into them.   (Friedrich
Engels to Wilhelm Bracke, 11 October 1875, in Karl Marx,
Critique of the Gotha Programme (New York: International
Publishers, 1938) p. 48)

a little like
one blind up no more
another creature there
somewhere there
behind the pane
another living soul
one other living soul
till the day came
in the end came
close of a long day
when she said
to herself
whom else

time she stopped
time she stopped
sitting at her window
quiet at her window
only window   (Samuel Beckett, *Rockaby* (New York: Grove
Press, 1981) p. 16)

. . . for another
another like herself
another creature like herself
a little like
going to and fro
all eyes
all sides   (ibid., p. 10)

The 'protagonist' of the *Rockaby* monologue hears most of the
monologue from an offstage tape-recording. It is the viewer–
listener's assumption that the voice is hers. The voice on tape from
offstage is the classic *deus ex machina*, but here is in no way
anthropomorphic because it is not given a life of its own. The
structure of 'start' for the machined voice is reliant on the woman
in the rocker (Billie Whitelaw) desiring it with the words 'More',
desiring its end with the words, repeated in unison with those of
the tape-recording: '*time she stopped*' (and once in unison with the
words 'living soul'). The voice on tape functions as a constant
materiality of the theatric presence of sound. Synchronicity is
established by the protagonist's speaking in synch with the tape's
words. Yet the device for this operation in no way manifests any
natural relation between her voice and the consistent effect it has
on the stopping of the tape-voice's duration. This procedure thus
becomes convention for *this* piece of theatre, whilst simultaneously
establishing itself as convention, as a structure utilised for specific
theatric purposes specifically here. There is no magical and
hidden system which starts one sound, or counterpoints one
sound with another. Both voices, hers and the tape's, operate via
separate mechanisms, the machine and the larynx. They establish
a relation to each other, thereby though refusing any *one* as sole
'source' or primary object of possible identifications.

We assume the voice the woman hears is her own voice. It sounds like her voice. There is no plenitude of evidence for our assumption. We are given little. There is no internal diegetic or structural–textural position which would 'prove' the act of relating the two voices as same. The relation is thus made by the theatric structure 'as a residual deposit of duration'.[32]

What I am writing of here is a mechanism which we observe whilst being part of, more than which we cannot be able of since Wittgenstein. We hear the same voice 'she' hears, we think we know what we feel we know here but no more than that. She feels or acts as if she knows she hears the voice, whilst simultaneously certain theatrical and cinematic sound-conventions place the voice as inside her head, her telling herself a story about two women. It simultaneously functions as a voice outside her head, spatially located elsewhere, for *us* in locating the source of sound and for *her* in locating the sound. The 'physical homogeneity', operating via codifications, a produced illusion that the voice is inside her head, is a ruse. We are outside the 'sure'. The stage is not set up as a metaphor (neither symbol nor fragment) which would somehow seem to verify a homogeneity of the two voices. The structures of coding for narrativity are materially not effected here, thus the placing of the sound inside her head an after-effect, after-image, of *other* cultural productions; it is not the materiality of this one. The refusal of such a homogeneity is the refusal to allow the audiences' unconscious identifications into a coherence and generalised ego, in some phantasm of non-contradiction and authority over (and of) the word and image in collusion with the staged; it is a refusal of collaboration. The persistent disallowal of identification with an imaginary space, imaginary time, imaginary figure, imaginary voice, forces the contradiction: perception *vs* knowledge (the contradiction also of desire *vs* material).

The voice emanating from the tape offstage is a detached, unfigured, voice. The materiality of the tape-voice is undermined by conventions which would produce 'sourcelessness' as an absent *source*, out of view, 'just there', another route to attempt to anthropomorphise. Such an analysis then would, whilst admitting the voice is not 'in the head', insist the voice is one of an absent but existent being, figured *in absentia*. Again this is a 'reading' which is not determined by the material apparatus *theatre* and its specificity for *Rockaby*, but rather a determination based on identification-mechanisms for narrativity in *other* cultural productions and ideologies.

The woman is telling herself a story or hearing a story – out loud she is synching up with it. Her memory is of the retelling, it collides/is collided with, by her present speech. This is possible due to 'her' foreknowledge, a repeat, the return of the 'same' (differently), due to 'her' knowing what is coming or seeming to know: language *as if*. The anxiousness for the last three words '*time she stopped*' to befit, the compulsive obsessionality to retrace a trace of meaning, assures that the repetition is never a solution to any story, nor to any structure. Language functions as a specific process by which is instituted in this monologue/double-monologue a processing of speech and a processing of *listening*. This solipsism is tenable, untenable, durable, unendurable.

At the moment of 'synchronisation' the rocking chair stops; this stoppage of the physical continuum restarts when the woman speaks: '*More*'.

Each time the structure of repetition, of synch, of stoppage and non-stoppage, etc., rebegins, the light onstage dims one notch. Any concept, however concrete, of a 'natural' movement of figure, sound, speech, or light is militated against by the systematised formalism of the downward-gradation of light. Each artifice such as her hearing/respeaking the words exists against an off-scene control (the tape, the light). The specificity of this theatre piece is in its separate practices of light/sound/hearing/speaking/rocking. And all attempts at interrelation and/or synchronicity are produced as *produced*, the relation as the result of a specific, material, structuring attempt, a labour – but also precariously produced, *attempted*. And the off-scene devices are never given as one unified device or a conglomerate of devices, but rather as various, dispersed devices with their own functions and positions in relation to the on-scene, onstage gestures and sounds. Thereby any attempt at identifying a unitary force or control which could hold together the elements is broken. Any relation of effects to affects is given as a disparity, the one from the other. There is thus no god of the machine, but various machines – the material concretion not *of* an abstract but of the already-concrete, *inseparable from* the abstract.

The woman's speech is the speech 'by' the unseen Beckett, the male writer, in the voice of the woman (in the empirical sense: he wrote it).

The woman becomes more and more of a skeleton, less sexed, as the light dims. A bisexual/unsexual image is produced by the annihilation of light. This bisexual image not held to a biological sexual category has the effect of man and woman both one *woman*, written by one *man*; a split constantly operative both in the character-image becoming no longer vehemently either sex, i.e. becoming asexual, and in the author's paradoxical presence as name. This is, though, not to attempt to institute an authorial authorisation, an auteurism; rather, the author Beckett is simply not voidable from the context of the appropriation of meaning of his work in this specific cultural conjuncture. A man's writing, a material ideological fact in the speech of this woman in the indistinguished dark, is still sexed (set against the *annihilation of sex by light*). This particular woman, Billie Whitelaw, is, equally, the material ideological fact of a *woman*'s speaking and listening and acting.

In this particular production of *Enough* and *Rockaby* the actress Billie Whitelaw had been for the first half of the evening seen/ heard reading; Billie Whitelaw is dressed within the norm of a British middle-class woman ('It's what I wear when I go shopping'), as a woman speaking a text by Beckett, entitled *Enough*. As read by Billie Whitelaw a constant split, speaker from author, woman/man, was posited via the ambivalently placed sex of the narrator. The sex of the speaking *I* is problematised and contradictorily motored via the dialectic material/ideological split of enunciator, author, speaker (the latter as strongly sexual, female figure; body, mind, voice, gaze, all in process via the material presence of the process in and through Billie Whitelaw *and* Beckett's writing in *Enough*); that is the theatric process preceding *Rockaby*.

Is there a schizophrenia in the bisexualising/asexualising of the woman in *Rockaby*, the death-like male/female form and its vehement refusal to relinquish the listening *and* the gesture *and* the speaking?

In *Rockaby*, Billie Whitelaw stares head-on whilst listening; then eyes down as if dead or asleep. Then she (the rocking woman) speaks: '*More*'. This structure of repetition, return of the same–not the same, forces, through such monological structuring, the question: how not the same? The spectator–listener's position in this is positioned as unresolvable inside such a problematic ('How the same? How not the same?') and as unresolvable outside of such a problematic ('outside' such would be a simple affirmation of unproblematic spectatorship, identifying towards meaning and narrative, disallowed in this play by the dialectic materiality and contradictory placement against consuming knowledge, and therefore constantly *in-process*).

The woman in her rocking chair is placed slightly off-centre-stage, thereby dehypnotising, decentring the point of reference for the viewer. The hypnotic, which comes about here through various repetitions and through the monotone focusing attempt on a singular visual entity, can not find itself focused via any deep-space perspective depth. There is neither a *possible*, narcissistically mirrored, other, nor the deep-space of perspective and possession which would allow for the viewer's voyeuristic centrality thereby causing the viewed to become *object* (a fetish).*

The slightly 'off-centre' puts the stage askew, throughout, in the clinical, though not in the analytical sense (as each member of the audience is sitting at a different angle in any case from the actress). This 'askew' is the given position nevertheless, via the viewer–listener's positioning in the theatre in relation to the unconsciously perceived norm of centrality, regardless of his or her empirical *seat* in the theatre. Such unidentities and negations are processes refusing identification with image, voice and scene. Thereby, the *hold* of the supposedly pre-ideological biological is continually disallowed, moment by moment. The politics of splitting that identification is one of not acceding to the male viewer the identity of male-ego and power, and not giving the female viewer the holding of her identity to a biological category 'woman' as a figure of essence or necessity. What is also hereby ruled out is any psychologism or psychoanalism which would retain woman as a pre-Oedipal object, positing the mother's voice

* The off-centre 'golden-mean' of painting is another matter.

as pre-Oedipal, prior to the father's interdictory locution, word of the Father and the Law, and other phallocentrisms.

The conventions which would make of the woman's voice on tape some kind of pre-Oedipal maternal voice, to be followed by voices of phallic interdiction at later stages of imagined life, are not upheld. Attempts at identity of viewer–listener with that 'object', 'the maternal voice', function as a split from any object due to the apparatus previously described. The viewer is situated *against* and *in*-process *un-identified*. The anti-identification mechanisms described (re: sexuality, etc.) disallow any identity of subject (viewer–listener) with object (onstage), and disallow any male being held to 'the male', any female being held to 'the female', whether in the audience or onstage. These radical splittings and non-identities for the viewer–listener in process with the articulating protagonist (Billie Whitelaw) via Beckett's text are prior to any *conscious* problematisation and resistance.

The material positioning through anti-patriarchal theatrics is the feminist situating of viewer–listener *against* the grain of patri-archal authority (politics), drive (psychoanalysis) and signified (culture).

A part of this previously described apparatus is the positioning askew, in the non-empirical sense (as each viewer is not centred anyway in the theatre; in this case *La Mama*, New York). The possibilities for some empirically *ideal-and-real* (as one!) *viewer* are made inept in any theatre, unless it were a theatre for one person, constituting the 'audience'. But the concept that is utilised for the possessive space-consumption of bourgeois perspective in conventional theatre makes '*one*' of the 'whole' audience, without having to resort to the empirical. The ideological does nicely for these purposes, however denied. The viewing–listening is always theoretical *and* ideological – viewing–listening in its specificity. Were the chair the woman sits in in fact *centred* onstage, the ideology of seeing this centralisation would be the operative mode, via a situating of each viewer regardless of his/her actual seat, against which the positioning as askew is motivated in the above-described first production of *Rockaby*. This split between the empirical real and the ideological/theoretical real is important for such stage direction, which operates in the codified space of theatre against the expected normative central formations and expectations, refusing thereby both univocality and symmetry.

The obsessive fixations in *Rockaby* are to do with *use*. Rememoration attempts are motivated by memories' echoes' desires for synchronicity.

Stage direction from *Rockaby*:
Together: echo of 'time she stopped'; coming to rest of rock, faint fade of light.   (p.2)

> Distorted to such an extent that in the end oppression seems to be a consequence of this 'nature' within ourselves (a nature which is only an *idea*).   (Monique Wittig, 'One is Not Born a Woman', *Feminist Issues*, no. II, p. 46)

It is when wants are described as needs that a process of naturalisation takes place which attempts to make of ideological constructions (which everything is) something natural, something 'from nature'. What is enacted on stage as a character's natural outpouring of needs becomes acceptable because it is produced as necessary, anthropomorphically human, not to be vied with by argument of politics. This ideology of 'need' cements all mechanisms to a humanism rationalised as natural – it thereby attempts to annihilate all contradiction such as, for example, the impossibility of the woman's words matching somehow her desire, and the mismatch between her speaking and its effect on him and her within the audience.

This now poses the ablated question of the historically constituted sex of the viewer, played out/worked out on the body. Yet to attempt a debodiedness is to lose sight (gain sight) of the fact that precisely on the body is sexed meaning (and what is 'different') produced, as male or female; bodies for definition. This question is posed by the processes of *Rockaby*, *A Piece of Monologue*, *Not I*, *Enough* – the sexed position (*from which* ...) of the subject and object in struggle, insecure.

Only through the identification-modes *for* patriarchy is the female viewer always positioned schizophrenically, towards femaleness

whilst rejecting/accepting it, and towards maleness whilst
rejecting/accepting *it*. Narrative identification is thus an
oppressive mechanism in patriarchy's interests.

> The female spectator is thus placed in a masochistic position of
> either identifying with the woman punished by the narrative or
> treated as a scoptophilic fetish, or identifying with the male as
> controller of events. In both cases her difference (from the
> screen star) is vanquished, she is neither the female as
> represented nor the male. For men the problem is less complex.
> Either way, their power is endorsed; they are allowed the
> bisexual play of misrecognition (with the male body/with the
> female body) without losing their sameness to the
> male. (Anne Friedberg, 'Identification and the Star: a
> Refusal of Difference', in *Star Signs*, papers from a weekend
> workshop, January 1982; BFI Education Department,
> London)

It comes down to the right of sexlessness, the non-fetish as woman
(and man), rather than the right to *be* 'a woman'. This has
importance for *Rockaby*'s attempts to correlate/decorrelate the
materials of language with/from the materials of memory, a work
of language and gesture *in* language and gesture, as opposed to an
anarchic impressionism or expressionism of some 'pure otherness'
defined as 'woman':

> Our first task it seems is to always thoroughly dissociate
> 'women' (the class within which we fight) and 'woman', the
> myth. . . . But once we have shown that all so-called personal
> problems are class problems, we will still be left with the
> question of each singular woman – not the myth but each one of
> us . . . beyond the categories of sex.   (Wittig, 'One is Not Born
> a Woman', p. 53)

In *Rockaby* such sexlessness is produced as an effect of ten
light-levels, effected by ten lamps, across the top of the stage-set.
The play begins with one lamp on, cut to ten lamps on, then slow
dimming one by one, then none left on. Thus, we have the virtual
annihilation of all image by light; at the end the annihilation of
image through lack of light. The physical property of the material
trace of light on a body is real. In *Rockaby* it, at the end, leaves

Illus. 13   Billie Whitelaw in *Enough* (1981), directed by Alan Schneider

Illus. 14   Billie Whitelaw in *Rockaby* (1981), directed by Alan Schneider

So he used to ring me up two or three times a week to discuss it and then
just say the lines down the phone to me. Once I've heard Beckett say it –
just once – I've more or less got in my head the music of what it is he
wants. That doesn't necessarily restrict me, but I think 'Right. I know
what music they're playing'   (Billie Whitelaw quoted in *The Times*, 9
January 1985)

nothing but the figureless, shadows, skeleton-like, and at the very beginning the one bright, harsh, central light on the woman's face allows for the sighting of nothing else, the face isolate.[33]

(See Illus. 13 and 14.)

An example: when she, in *Rockaby*, closes her eyes (*Not I* has no eyes), she is dead, or she is still? What is this literarisation of her death, through the signifier *closed eyes*, *stopped rocking*, when the rocking movement was previously consistently given as a mechanism automatically rocking the rocking chair by an unseen machine, outside of any *body* movement. It is the unseen machine that produces rocking and stoppage. The attempted synchronisation between action and thought is a series of specifically necessary coincidences, that is to say, artifices, such as the image of eyes closed, of rocking stopped, repeated throughout the performance. Death as a concept and a reality is impossible here as a 'truth', or as a metaphor, or as a representation. Yet the play's *final* stillness could (still) connote, if not denote, that, so that at the very end the image is still in conflict. It is then in conflict with *knowledge* of the machine's stoppage, and its previous movement, the knowledge of what it meant previously in this performance, historically for you and it. It remains a mechanism, within a process of speech, hearing, rhythm: not closure.

This conflict leaves us with no certainty as to theatrical truth, merely with a theatrical device, and *its* effects-as-effects, effect-as-effect, no less than affect.

This simultaneity produces a distanciation from *any* truth but the notion of quoting.

XXVI

Quote: *Discourse in the Novel* (Bakhtin)

Nothing Outside Ideology

Politics and Language

As a living, socio-ideological concrete thing, as heteroglot opinion, language, for the individual consciousness, lies on the borderline between oneself and the other. The word in language is half someone else's. It becomes 'one's own' only when the speaker populates it with his (*sic*) own intention, his own accent, when he appropriates the word, adapting it to his own semantic and expressive intention. Prior to this moment of appropriation, the word does not exist in a neutral and impersonal language (it is not, after all, out of a dictionary that the speaker gets his words!), but rather it exists in other people's mouths, in other people's contexts, serving other people's intentions: it is from there that one must take the word, and make it one's own. And not all words for just anyone submit equally easily to this appropriation, to this seizure and transformation into private property: many words stubbornly resist, others remain alien, sound foreign in the mouth of the one who appropriated them and who now speaks them; they cannot be assimilated into his context (*sic*) and fall out of it; it is as if they put themselves in quotation marks against the will of the speaker. Language is not a neutral medium that passes freely and easily into the private property of the speaker's intentions; it is populated – overpopulated – with the intentions of others. Expropriating it, forcing it to submit to one's own intentions and accents, is a difficult and complicated process.   (Michael Bakhtin, 'Discourse in the Novel', p. 293)

There is thus no 'outside' *of* ideology, and no being 'outside' ideology: nothing is outside politics and position. Tendency (from *Tendenz*, meaning political tendency) is thus not recuperated or repressed, and the viewer is situated as his or her anti-tendency. This is a relegation of dialectics, of position of reflexivity, to the *un*-immediate, unspontaneous, *questioned*. It is in this sense that 'opposites towards unity' (Lenin) is not a concept of synthesis or balance, but rather one of unity as *momentary* resolution, momentary over-determination (in the Freudian *and* Althusserian senses) as to how we position ourselves and are positioned in the politics of that materialism.

In reflexion's infinite regress the knowledge of powerlessness can still be radically productive, as is the positioning of inaccessibility to cultural/political means of production. Thus a 'nihilistic' anti-humanism can be, at a moment of over-determination, a radical force against capitalist patriarchy.

XXVII

Quote: *Narration* (Gertrude Stein)

Billie Whitelaw's Sexuality, Reading *Enough*

Rockaby

Gesture against Monologue

Verdichtung/Condensation of Signifiers

Writing/Reading

Against the 'Open' Text

Writing was writing if it was being written and in it even if I was talking I was not talking as I was writing, nor was I writing as I was talking, why should anyone do that. . . . But to come back to the audience because after all there is no one who can be one if he is not one and so sometimes this can happen that no one alone has been no one has been one audience to that thing. I was, to that fire-engine house. I really was I was just that thing I was one audience nothing was happening that is to say the building was exciting but it always had been, what would be the matter with it if it had not been. Very well then an audience did I always have one I have I always been one, am I one, when anything is no longer happening, look alike if you like and then be that one of any one or two of them.

So then the audience is the thing. It helps a lot to know anything about this thing if you think are always really always thinking about the narrativing of anything of narrative being existing.

So then what did I know about myself as an audience.

I wondered often when I was quite young and watching and

150

still I am doing that thing watching anything inside me happen in relation to myself or in relation to any one what any one being as it were as if they were to be as I was where and when I am would believe as to what was happening. Do you see what I mean. That is the beginning anyhow one beginning of an audience being existing. And always anybody can know that always there is no such thing existing as any one really not knowing as if it were anything of any one else what is going on as if it were going on. When that happens they call it introspection but call it what you like it is after all anybody or nobody watching. I suppose inevitably if any one is going to be anybody telling anything and knowing anything of telling anything they are bound to begin with this thing, why not since after all you have to know less about it than about any other thing because nobody can do any contradicting because after all there it is and it is not at all there and it is not all there and nobody who says yes can say no and nobody who says yes can say no and nobody can say yes I know or no I know nobody no nobody at all because after all there is nothing there at all and that is something to which if there is there is no no no yes and there is no I guess. Nothing at all and all is such a comfort as it is where it is. That is what who is to know how they are to tell what they are to tell is sure to have as all there is as well. And so they begin so. This you all of you know.

Then after all what is the use as you all all of you know this. So then beside as any one can come to be certain of then if it is as it is that is an audience is what it is what is it if an audience is this, pretty soon then can feel again that an audience is this, and then introspection can go on but the habit of this thing makes it cease to be this, because the audience and is it this keep going on and so finally since it is all one, even when it is not this and it commences then not to go on being this although of course although of course yes it always will go on.

That is one, that is one audience then this.

So then we go on.

And then gradually anything goes on that is to say it is does not go on but any way there is anything there any way and is any

one that is are you the audience for that too that is to say do you
see it when it is there and is it there and what have you to say,
what have you to say.

What is it to be an audience, I tell I must get down solidly to
that what is it to be to have an audience what is it and is it the
same thing or is it.

What is it.

That is to say can does any one separate themselves from the
land so they can see it and if they see it are they the audience of it
or to it. If you see anything are you its audience and if you tell
anything are you its audience, and is there any audience for it
but the audience that sees or hears it. And if you do do that to
yourself or anything else you see does that after all begin what
you began when you were it as it happened to come to be it or
not. Who is alike then everybody looks at anybody and which is
like which, the thing which has been seen or the thing which is
prepared for it that is prepared to be seen because after all who
cannot who will not prepare it. Really no one, when you come to
think about it and yet every one does, does not prepare it. And
all this has so much to do with writing a narrative of anything
that I can almost cry about it.   (Gertrude Stein, *Narration*
(New York: Random House, 1935) pp. 48–52)

Billie Whitelaw's is a 'straight' reading of a Beckett text,
'Enough', the actress reading, standing behind, and at times in
front of, the dais, lectern, looking up from her reading-glasses,
touching inside her blouse whilst reading, a momentary gesture
not illustrating or associative of any spoken phrase ('natural'
gestures), continuous reading of the text. Simultaneously the
viewer expects a relation of word and act, and the overt sexuality
of the momentary gesture of self-touch retrospectively situates
itself problematically to the text precisely because it both does not
illustrate any specific phrase or meaning *and* is only one of a
continuum of gestures; it sets itself up as momentary *difference*
from any homogeneous identity of word and image and is thereby foregrounded and meaningful. Thereby contradiction is
produced, gesture against word, word against gesture, and this
system persists throughout the twenty-five minute 'reading'. A

dialectic of intention is set up, as against that of stage-direction, as against author's voice, as against actress's 'real' *vs* actress's enactments, etc. This material complexity of a straightforward reading processes the listener *as* viewer, disallowing narrative's consumption. This monological and gestural reading-practice becomes a drawing-out rather than a drawing-in. Actress, text, listener–viewer, are put to *use*.

The reading of *Enough* is followed by *Rockaby* as one programme. The performed relation of the two complexities is the physical and conceptual problematic of what is 'read', what is a 'play', where is the author's absent presence located, what is the director's authority, where is the line between enactment and actress, what constitutes material theatric evidence? The problematic relation this production sets you within is the problematic and functioning of *theatre's processes and positions*, forging (via such contradictions as above) the viewer–listener's inseparability from theatre's problematics. Here the viewer's working-through and theatre's working-through problematises both, thereby positioning both against dominant theatre's apparatus and political ideology. This militates against narrative's upholding of sexual identity, and against sexual identity's upholding of narrativity. The theatric moment as objective historical moment functions in and through the I's subjectivity and its histories.

Thus caesura is a constant process, not some final act. It is the cut between role and actress in the second play across the rememoration of the first. This is set against the imageless darkness at the end of *Rockaby*, followed by the theatric convention of bowing (against Beckett's usual usage of the end-freeze). It comes down to being another series of gestures 'ventriloquated' and radically heterogeneous to any primordial 'end', or 'beginning'. Gesture thus functions continuously against monologue.[34] Beckett's theatre distanciates itself from conventions of theatre exactly when holding to them: actress bowing, fourth-wall naturalism, etc. 'It must be played naturally' (Beckett on *Endgame*; this is slightly ambiguous in the original German, in which he stated: '*natürlich muss gespielt werden.*' This could be translated as 'of course it must be played' as in 'naturally one has to *play*'.) The Beckettian procedure is installed via the *as if*, produced as the *as if as if*. The 'same' conventions, when utilised in conventional drama and melodrama, are suspensions-of-disbelief, suspensions unaffected in the bourgeois theatre by actors and actresses smiling and bowing after the end (at the end) of the play, curtains opening and closing, etc. These conventions exist without interfering with the suspension-of-disbelief required by narrative identification. *The conventions function ideologically as invisible, no matter how visible they are empirically.* Precisely these conventions are broken in their Beckettian usages, wherein a total suspension-of-disbelief is never instituted. A code of momentary, partial suspensions of disbelief, or a 'naturalistic' code of fourth-wall acting, or a code which allows bowing at the end of a play, situates itself problematically and causes difficulty and blockage of any continuum for the viewer subjected to this process. Thus we are never given to know which code is operative, which subjectivity, in Beckettian theatrics as described. And such unknowing breaks even further any surety, however imaginary, *vis à vis* some reified *it* (the play). Producing a position of unknowing is its radical difference.

> All that goes before forget. Too much at a time is too much. That gives the pen time to note. I don't see it but I hear it there behind me. Such is the silence. When the pen stops I go on. Sometimes it refuses. When it refuses I go on. Too much silence is too much. Or it's my voice too weak at times. The one that comes out of me. So much for the art and craft. (Beckett, 'Enough' (1966) in *First Love and Other Shorts* (New York: Grove Press, 1974) p. 53)

How is such a speaking a writing? How is writing not speaking? The condensation (*Verdichtung*) (of signifiers) is the specificity, the primary concentration, of any practice, i.e. writing, speaking, etc. The line quoted spoken is no longer disinterrable from speed, delivery, tone, volume, sexual intonations, etc. I am not saying multivalence can be built in for a series of 'open text' or 'polyvalent text' interpretations. I am saying the multivalence can be over*ridden* through material speech practice and structurings of the spoken monologue against such multivalences. This can work against, for example, the tying up of meaning when near the end of a cluster of sentences, or a page, or the breath of the speaker. Retrospective readjustment can be inculcated, for example, adding 'not' to a sentence read out loud, previous phrases of which were whilst without that 'not' nevertheless with a prior slurred over negative so that that first negative seemed to cover the whole of the sentence. The pronounced 'not' thus at first semed to go *against* and then did not oppose the meaning, as the 'not' is set against the insecurity of the listener's knowledge as to the first 'negative' (which had been slurred past). The double-negative becomes problematised, and meaning is made retrospectively via memory and the contradictions of the listener's will and her or his assumptions.

In writing/reading, any lack of clarity can be reread, reworked; in speaking/hearing this operates differently, via memory. The condensations produced at each step in speaking/hearing set up difficulties, whereas in writing/reading, the condensations operative become known factors, available to analysis, in time, as in 'reread' or 'rewrite'. Yet writing and reading are the *same* in precisely those terms Barthes sees as different:

> Writing begins at the point where speech becomes *impossible*. (Roland Barthes, 'Writers, Intellectuals, Teachers', in *Image/Music/Text*, trans. Stephen Heath (London: Fontana Books, Collins, 1977) p. 190)

One could as well state the opposite. What is 'compared' is bourgeois writing and materialist speech, nullifying thereby the attempt.

> Ideas come whilst speaking.   (Heinrich von Kleist)

In this form ('ideas come *whilst* speaking') the act of speaking and the act of writing are equally a materially congealing/condensing unstoppable flow of words. This practice itself, of the speaking/ writing process *as* process, is the unstoppable history of monological speech-production, causing constant condensation (*Verdichtung*). When such writing/speech production represses (or suppresses) its own processes, such condensations (unlike psychoanalytic condensation which results *from* repression) do not occur, as the language process is then held to the conventions necessary to communicate something pre-existent, a retelling, annihilating the process of articulation, or association, of the subjectivity of the enunciator, and of the various dialectical contradictions which are materially* set in force to produce effects in language. The condensations via the unstoppable flow of language, writing and speech, necessitate a separating by the *listener*, an impossible disentangling of the conflictual sites within which speech and writing function. But condensation towards materialist monological speech and writing processes has another meaning as well: condensed sentences, phrases, words. Short stutters, fragments, first- and third-person moments without linear flow, such as in the work of (before Beckett) Gertrude Stein, some Kafka, some H.D. (later some Laura Riding Jackson and some Jean Rhys). The repetitious, endless, monological resituating of meaning via such condensations disallows the linear 'free-associative' and constantly controlled narrativity; disallows language as the author's system for simply or complexly conveying narrative, impression, expression; disallows the omniscient author as always the final authority for meaning; disallows a colonisation via a total reliance on signified and referent which would deny the materiality of the signifier, the word, the phrase, the language-production-process itself (in which 'ideas come whilst speaking' or ideas come whilst 'writing' – *in* the speaking, *in* the writing). The opposition is thus, here, between expansive, possessive complexity, and contractive, dispossessive complexity, an ideology against and exposing expansiveness and possessiveness in and via language. In such a schema, Stein's *Tender Buttons* (1914) and Beckett's *Not I* (1971), are posed against Joyce's *Ulysses* (1924) and *Finnegans Wake* (1928). Such a reductive model is not all-embracing but it is equally not without issue.

(See Illus. 15 and 16.[35])

---

* *Materialisations-in-speech*, if this concept can be understood without taking on denotations or connotations of re-presentation.

Illus. 15 Emily Dickinson, cancelled poem (1858), 'One Sister Have I in the House', from *The Manuscript Books of Emily Dickinson*, edited by R. W. Franklin (Cambridge, Mass.: The Belknap Press of Harvard University Press, 1981) p. 28

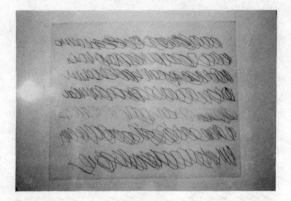

Illus. 16   Cy Twombly, *Note III, no. 6/14*, etching, 1967 (8 × 10 in.)

The monological force of the lines' attempts evidences no
guarantee of a satisfactory narration or erasure, or representation,
or 'end' to such. This is how this marking is clinically operative
against both a polyvalent/multivalent free-associative open
textuality *and* against a univocal logocentrum, some quasi-
monotheistic metaphor.

XXVIII

Quote: On *Footfalls* from *The Times* and *Frescoes in the Scull*

Description of *Footfalls* (Amy and May)

Desire for Other's Desire

Diegesis *vs* Non-diegesis

Apparatus Theatre, and Expression(ism)

The Final Step

Speaking Produces Speaker, Producing Anonymity

Monotone, without colour, very distant. You are composing. it is not a story, but an improvisation. You are looking for the words, you correct yourself constantly . . . at the end it can't go any farther. It is just at an end. (Samuel Beckett, *Journal of Beckett Studies*, no. 2 (1977) p. 86, discussing *Footfalls* in rehearsal)

In *Footfalls* (as in *Not I*) the fact that some intolerable memory is involved appears from the speaker's use of the third person. Again, one receives a misleading impression from the text, which contains passages suggesting domestic dialogue and realist detail. All this is thrust into the far distance by Beckett's production. Punctuated by a chiming bell, the brief opening exchange of dialogue and two solo speeches take the form of a three-act play, with a sense of immeasurable distance between the pacing woman and her uncomprehending mother. 'Will you never have done ... revolving it all?' she asks. But in this piece, the nature of the obsessive experience remains undisclosed . . . I do not understand this play; and by this time in the evening the consistently dim lighting has become hard on the eyes. (Irving Wardle, *The Times*, 21 May 1976)

Beckett began to write the short play *Footfalls* in Berlin on 2 March 1975. Two alternative titles, *Footfalls* and *It All* were assigned to the first version. . . . For Beckett insists that the image of the woman pacing relentlessly up and down is central to the play. 'This was my basic conception . . . the text; the words were only built up around this picture. If the play is full of repetitions, then it is because of these life-long stretches of walking. That is the centre of the play. Everything else is secondary.' Her pacing punctuates, or accompanies, the words in each of the three sections or stages of the play in which she appears. Moments of frozen immobility alternate with this pacing and an intricate interplay of movement and speech is envisaged from the earliest stage. But what is also clear from the manuscripts is that this central, and only visible, pacing figure, itself dimly lit, was conceived from the outset in relation to the surrounding darkness . . . sound and silence, repeated movement and total stillness, faint – and steadily diminishing – light and complete darkness supplying the various contrasting elements. (James Knowlson and John Pilling, *Frescoes of the Scull* (London: Calder & Boyars, 1979) p. 221)

'Will you never have done? (*Pause*) Will you never have done ... revolving it all? (*Pause*) It all. (*Pause*)' (*Footfalls*). Revolving *it*. What is meant is: revolving it in her mind. It is the paranoid interrogation, the projection *by* Amy of the interrogator (scripted as '*V*: Voice') having heard Amy. The projection is of another, and another's voice. It is the *desire for the other's desire*.

(See Illus. 3 on p. 60.)

The last light down excludes (downstage) the image of Amy and (upstage-left) the sound of May; Amy and May's ceasing synchronous to lack of light. At the same time as she is *perceptually* absent we know that the actress is standing there. For us in this circuit of relations there is no suspension-of-disbelief to any point of believing in the actress's sudden phantasmatic absence. Illusionism can apply as much to absence as to presence. The *there-not-there* operates as much for the viewer as the there-not-there of *Voice* for Amy. The spoken desire for the other's desire is the narcissistic identification as defined by Freud. This state, for psychoanalysis, is *not* within a definition of the sexed difference of male/female. Thus it is not yet the situating of an 'I' which would then allow for the formulation 'you'. (It is prior to a definition of 'ego as knowledge'.) As such it is of no use for the culturated myths of heterosexist power, the ideology of 'fulfilment of desire'. The desire for the other's desire is a constant impossible, impossibility of that 'rational possibility' wherein we must accept as 'mature' sexual definition sexual definition, procreate. That 'rational possibility' is the figmentive as social adaptation (preached by the empiricist Freud) and political adaptation (preached by the patriarchally essentialist Lacan).[36]

The 'line' of speech in *Footfalls* functions literally as a literary production abandoning the sutures of diegetic narrative, towards an economy of the caesura of self. Such a position for the listener–viewer problematises us, our bodies, our senses, our intellects.

> Professor Hubel and Professor Wiesel demonstrated that visual perception in the brain was considerably more complicated than the previous idea that the cerebral cortex worked like a filmscreen. Instead, they demonstrated that the image falling on the retina underwent analysis in a system of nerve cells stored in columns. ('Nobel Prize for Hubel and Wiesel', *The Times*)

The desire for the other's desire functions as overwhelmingly motivated outside of the *sex* of the desire as it exists outside of the coherent ego-as-knowledge. The sexualising of desire, and the militantly heterosexist positioning that defines it, is here radically undercut. There is thus, also, neither procreative teleology nor an underlying biologism. Though the speakers are both, through gesture and voice, given as 'female', it is speech and gesture, not the physically determined sex, which is functioning. This discourse radically undercuts a 'hidden' *story*, the *Family Romance* of enacted narrative. The viewer, *un*sutured, deferring the speakers' truths, differing from those truths, is in a circuit of unknowing. Who is May? Who is Amy? What desire is being spoken? Where does projection locate itself theatrically? Whose projection is Billie Whitelaw's speaking? Where is the second 'character' whose voice is offstage unseeable? The points at which projection by a speaker onstage becomes introjection for the viewer, and reprojected into the 'character' onstage, are a forced *difficulty* for the viewer, who is thus imbricated in this process and its complex functioning throughout. Because of the inability to identify simply projection and introjection as ever separable from 'true' speech on stage and simple understanding consumed by the viewer, it becomes impossible to formulate in *Footfalls* a notion of self, for the main character onstage or the disembodied offstage voice onstage or the viewer offstage. No self obtains. Character is unfounded, as is identity. Meaning is unmade as it is made. This process of signification and position militates against the disenfranchisement of the viewer from the materialist constructions of the making and unmaking of meaning and meaninglessness.

The question, here, taken up previously, of everything being diegetic, that is, being part of the mental space (imagined or otherwise) of the narrative, is forced to the limit. The tension here is literally our constant attempt to diegetise, together with the inability of such a project given this material, this play. The viewer is thus expelled from the conventional position of consuming a homogeneous fiction, a cohesive mental space of theatre in which all movement, speech, stage design, style, cohere into the fiction, the total given and imagined mental space and time, the diegesis. By being thus expelled, the viewer–listener (as part of the production process of the theatre apparatus) within the specificity of this play *Footfalls* is positioned against such a consumption. The 'result' of such a process is the unholding of any characterisation to a singular character, any 'thought' to a sentence expressed, any viable whole deduced or imagined from any fragment of movement, gesture, speech, act. We are given nothing but a simultaneous structuration and destructuration of a process of languaging, figuring, speaking. In that sense (in opposition to Bakhtin) *all dialogue is monologue*. And a vying of the power of one against the power of another is a dialectical transformative theatrics. The play must be seen/heard.

One question that nags as to such Beckettian monological works as *Footfalls*, *Not I*, *A Piece of Monologue* and *Rockaby*, is about the remnant of expressionism and its possible force. It is a lost expressionism, one in which there is no hold; a split of the self which motors the body and identity but results in identity-occluded figuring, a series of decadences without imaginary fullness, objects in process, speaking mouth, figure pacing machined by a pacing structure of repetition, not by some humanoid expressivity, etc. A rocker rocking, repeated in *Rockaby*, no identity given that movement in terms of an anthropomorphic desire or expression, is an anti-expressionism, moving as machine, speaking machin*ed*. Nothing is stabilised, not even the imagination's machinations. There is no (illusion of) ego, and without it expressionism cannot function; but the *demands* of expression are constantly implicated. *It is precisely in that that Beckett's theatre does not abjure the material historical subjectivity of the human figure, speech, movement, but rather, uses it radically, against individualism, against expressionism, and against reproduction of given identities.* There is no cake and no eating it.[37]

The figure on stage in *Footfalls*, wrapped, is never a figure *inside* a wrap. It is as a whole a wrap. The wrap *in toto* thus functions as a point of reference for the split expressionism described, the initial referent (that which one associates with the theatrics of 'old age, hunched back, walking slowly, etc.') having been expunged as useless in terms of realistic *motive*, useful in terms of the initial fictivity against which contradictory image and sound materialisations operate, discohering the fiction's function, thereby forcing the viewer–listener's subjective historical relation to such fictional representations of expressionism's remnants. The various subjectivities in conflict, and in conflict specifically with certain meanings produced onstage, necessitate a starting point within the extreme remnant of expressionism, rather than some stylistic 'void', or 'pureness' outside of the historical conventions of theatre. Beckett's works in this manner create, via materialist theatre of sound and image, the lack of fullness, of imaginary figuration, of projected fictions, but it is something produced *in-theatre*, not existent *a-priori* and then merely illustrated *by* theatre.*

'She is for herself' (Beckett, on Amy's 'role' in *Footfalls*, in Walter D. Asmus, 'Practical Aspects of Theatre, Radio and Television', *JOBS*, no. 2 (Summer 1977) p. 86). Expressionism is the historical vehicle, as much as the sexual and ideological. That

*This question, in relation to painting, is taken further in my 'Fugitive Theses re: Thérèse Oulton's Paintings' (*Fools' Gold*, catalogue, Gimpel Fils, London, 1984).

ladder is then pulled away, those identities unpracticable; after their use their uselessness. 'Neither the dead hand, nor the empty hand, just none' (Beckett). 'It is *nothing*' (Marx).

If my 'description' concerns, here, the play *Footfalls*, the latter is a theatricalisation wherefrom a 'next step' is not envisageable. What is hopefully ruled out is a reanthropomorphism, pseudo-existential alienation, hypersurrealist dramas, fragmentary collossi, etc. – all of it. This step of *Footfalls* as the last step possible situates it as *the caesura as the final step*. If any further, or different, or possible, final step were theatrically now given, it would by definition undermine the materialism and the paranoia of the splitting function of the play. The 'subjects constituted' (i.e. the subjects and subjectivities – never denying the viewer's histories) by the play's operation both on stage and off are neither replete with possibility for life 'outside' nor replete with a mechanistically determined notion of being theatrically real in communion with the without.

How is it that the speech-act produces the speaker rather than vice versa? How is it that 'ideas come whilst speaking' and that you are spoken-*through* in enunciating? How is it that certain decisions made in speech reposition and thereby repose both questions and answers to the point of transformation of the subject-in-speech (not of some pure persona behind speech)? It's not that there is a 'how it is' and a 'what it is' but that there is only a 'how it is what it is'.

It is the *verb* that makes narrative-fiction and that in its suturing disavows all breaks and splits between language and the lived; the lack of verb is a lack of phantasm; thus the reality of power/authority in action disavows a stuttering (lack of verb). This is akin to the short, elliptical 'fragments' of the prose, in repetition or out, of Gertrude Stein and Beckett.

It is in the speech-act, finally, that the speaker is lost. Reading and speaking and hearing are, in the monological enunciation-attempts discussed, articulated as attempts to find the place from which, or towards which, is 'spoken'. In such materialist processes, the speaker–listener–viewer is produced as anonymous, as the specific effect of the way in which is read, spoken, heard. If such enunciation produces nothing but itself and attendant positionings for speaker–viewer–listener, this is because any hints of a referral to something *outside* exist only at a moment of inception, simultaneously doubted and problematised. We have not only a non-humanisation and deauthorship (the author no where to be found in all this), but a deauthorisation, a structure against truth. Any moments of authority, additionally, are given no homology to any effects produced by the language in authority, so that when a phrase or a sentence spoken seems to be, for a moment, true, befitting some convention of a communicated truth, it simultaneously produces no evidence to hold this as true. Thus inference is produced *as* inference, for speaker and listener–viewer. The effects produced by the practice entitled 'the speech-act' are not evidenced as homologous to any authority. Inference and reference are in process without an attachment (for speaker–listener–viewer) to truth, or satisfaction.

Thus it is no matter of a primary anonymity, but of an anonymity created, as communistic, materialist(ic) and dialectic(al) as it is political, outside individualism. Concurrently, for the concept of anonymity, no false collectivity is presumed in the production-process. If anything, a retention of voice, voice only, body only.

Within the ideological which nothing finds separation from, the basis of what is given is the *arbitrary* and the *unnatural*. Positions are taken inside and outside of language: when outside language, then as that, *not* as a metaphor for or illustration of some linguistic meaning *de*-languaged and *then* given over 'abstractly' to be 'refound' in language (defabled). The latter system would be yet another decoy for the overdetermining prior meanings constructed but utilised *as if* they had pre-existed construction (thus as if they were religion and magic). Such 'natural' meaning, taken as if it were pre-existent 'truth' outside of a production-process, operates *use* towards *exchange*, as a contract with pre-known criteria 'acceptable to both sides', 'freely assumed'. This is the basis for the rise, and power, of the bourgeoisie as well, 'a contract between two free men (*sic*), the owner of capital and the labourer who sells labour power' (Marx, quoted in F. Engels, *On Marx's 'Capital'* (Moscow: Progress Publishers, 1972) p. 83).

XXIX

Quote: *Rockaby*

Rocking

Meaninglessness

Withholding Structure

Against Political Optimism

Rockaby . . . fuck life, stop her eyes, rock her off, rock her
off.   (Beckett, *Rockaby*, the first words and the last)

There is nothing there (onstage) to see but the act of rocking* from
first word to last act, the literalisation of that. It is not a metaphor.
It is the material *per se* onstage, and the material of meaning *per se*
in the semiosis of the viewer, within the cultural meanings of the
late twentieth century in 'the West'. The notion of literalisation of
material(ity) should not be understood as an orthodox empirical
representation of some being or act *á* 1947, or 1786, or 1985. To
historicise in such a manner would otherwise allow theatrical
practice simply the function of illustration and opinion, the
anti-materialist anti-dialectic option of journalism. Yet the other
side of the problem is academia's fetishisation of 'ideology', as a
saviour both from 'vulgar materialism' and from politics
(public/social and personal). Therefore the notion of the
literalisation of material(ity) should equally not be understood as
a philosophically 'pure' practice, outside of history or the
political.[38]

The rocking from the first word to the last act onstage (by Billie
Whitelaw) is a theatrics of a woman's discourses and labour

*See analysis of *Rockaby* on pp. 137–47.

166

processes against an 'identity' formed by the power of language's paternal metaphors, against patriarchal definitions: sound and image process neither individualised by nor stereotypical of '*woman*'.

In the process of the rocking in *Rockaby* meaninglessness is produced as the effect of a process, literalised, by the each-time-again-ending, each time again 'more!', each time less to signify, less to say, less to complexify, less signified; more of the act, its reiterations, repetitions, samenesses, attempted synchronicities of *speech*-act to the *machined* act, and the asynchronicities of the processes engaged. As such acts dominate theatre, meaninglessness becomes produced, concretely, as absence of metaphor and absence of the reference to the outside world of narrativity, absence thus of *the protheatric and its ideologies*. Metaphor's absence disturbs with such vehement issuelessness, *which is the lack of the illusion of non-issuelessness.*[39] The split, of the hypnotic, repetitious, compulsive-obsessive paranoiac, the demythified, broken, meaningless, non-metaphoric arbitrary, is a split the cover of which is usual theatrics, theatrics as usual. But even the theatric apparati machined to void reference cannot avoid the necrophiliac referent of a phrase such as 'rock her off', or the relation to the other of 'stop her eyes'. So with these it is through the repetitious function of the return of same phrases that they become reified, against the flexibilities of narrative illusion, imaginary referents, and so on.

The first word of *Rockaby* is 'More'. There is thereby an explicit (if not explicitly *explained*) beginning prior to theatre; at the same time no evidentiary 'priorness' is constructed for the imagination, memory, association, etc. The conflict is thus instituted for the viewer–listener's activation with the first word 'More'; a conflict is instituted with the Real as a process that one is inside and part of and which is amenable neither to calculable empirical bourgeois proof, *nor* to some freeflowing imagination against the odds, against the materiality of theatre, its text, its operation.

'Stop the eyes'/'More'/Rocking to that, against that, *that* as a that in mind not just some somewhere else; the split in that: the mind–body split is a separation made from the impossibility *equally* of non-separation as of separation.

Jael is ... well, that would be telling.   (Joanna Russ, *The Female
Man* (London: W. H. Allan, Star paperback, 1975) p. 43)

Stop the 'I's. Rocking is instituted in that split, also, of language's
inability to *mean outside of contradiction*. Contradiction is the motor
of meaning, the political and ideological *position*. The rocking is
given as a process neither 'within', emblematic of some interior
state, nor 'without', some meaningful illustration of an act or
thought. *Rocking as attempt*. It is *rocking*, whatever model is utilised
to intentionalise it or 'describe' it or analyse it. The
psychoanalytic model could come up with the following, for
example: 'desire for the mother', those imaginary and real
comforts/'the delerious desire for control of the objects of the world'
as in Freud's *Fort/Da* (in spite of Freud's wilful misreading of the
meaning of those words, which mean nothing like 'here/there'),/or
as Lacan's 'the *Symbolic* site of the possibility of the *Other*', etc. The
unconscious and repression are continuous processes, operative;
the trace of each act, each 'next' act, or repeated act, leads to no
break in the series; rather, it is always a new, always *again* the
same 'new' desire; effects of the same process, time after time, but
always an accumulation and an exhaustion, accumulated
exhaustions, *never* a transcendental product of exchange and
consumption, accumulated consumptions.

This is why the critique of some works by Beckett as ahistorical
endlessness, as if it were a critique 'from the Left' is mis-
conceived.[40] Such a critique usually ascribes to Beckett, (a) an
elitism of language, ascribable finally as a critique of all culture
and cultural work and production, because of its over-determined
inaccessibility to the proletariat *and* the bourgeoisie, and (b) a
depoliticised endlessness, the hopelessness of 'waiting' and
'repeating'. But, as to the latter, both Bakunin and Lenin had
political definitions against any humanistic, and therefore false,
optimism, the latter which in its critique of the negation posits
the bourgeois illusions which maintain bourgeois, and the
bourgeoisie's, power. The Leninist need, and want, for the
contradictions of capital to reach such a stage that revolutionary
transformations towards socialism, then communism, become
necessary, and constructed by that state, and Bakunin's need for
hopelessness without which no revolution can take place, point to
the epistemological break which is not dissimilar to the spark the

Party must follow to lead. Thus Beckett's 'Don't wait to be hunted to hide' is aligned with a working resistance-cell against fascism in France in 1940; a first lesson against decadent apolitical nonsense.[41] Yet there is no homology of radical political practice and radically political literary practice; a relation of sorts must be constructed.

XXX

Quote: *The Act of Reading* (Wolfgang Iser)

Negation

Description and Analysis (Giacometti)

There is an increasing tendency in modern literature to make primary negations* obtrusively subservient to secondary negations. The primary negations responsible for the constitution of the theme become increasingly impeded, thus intensifying the reader's ideational activity. The reader is aware of this mobilization, because he (*sic*) finds himself (*sic*) unable to consolidate his (*sic*) mental images, which thus become themselves the object of his attention. SB's novels contain a dense network of primary negations and the sentence structure consists of clearly irreconcilable strands. A statement is often immediately revoked by the next sentence. There is an extraordinary variety of links between sentences, ranging from more modification all the way to total negation. This ceaseless switching from statement to negation characterizes the texture of Beckett's language. The immediate outcome of this technique is a massive reduction in the possible implications of the language – it means what it says and negation always occurs when the words begin to mean more than they say. [That is to say negation always occurs, because language can never mean what it says. To hold onto the notion that all is well as long as it

*'Primary negations relate to a virtual theme which arises out of the act of negation. They refer to the repertoire of . . . the external world (thematic). . . . Secondary negations relate to the link-up between gestalten produced by the reading process and the disposition of the reader. Through them the assembled meaning of the text runs counter to the reader's familiar modes of orientation, and these must often be corrected if the new experience is to be comprehended. Their relevance is therefore functional'   (Iser, *The Act of Reading*, p. 221).

170

means what it says is the positivist fallacy which the above position can, but does not have to, fall into. Same problem exists with Wittgenstein being read as empiricist, as he who says you can *never* find out what *it* means, with the meaning of 'it' still retaining in that formulation its unquestioned hold over meaning, representation; a notion against this would state it is outside of meaning other than meaning constructed ideologically–historically in certain interests towards certain ends: the author]

This brings into view the virtual theme: Beckett's language is pure denotation, and sets out to eradicate all implications *in an almost painful effort to prevent itself from becoming connotative* [italics mine].

Stanley Cavell writes that Beckett 'shares with positivism its wish to escape connotation, rhetoric, the noncognitive, the irrationality and awkward memories of ordinary language, in favor of the directly verifiable, the isolated and perfected present.' But Beckett writes novels, and as fiction, these do not denote any given, empirical world; they should therefore conform to the literary conventions of using the denotative function of language to build up connotations which may then be grasped as units of meaning. Instead, Beckett takes language literally, and as words always mean more than they say, that which is said must constantly be modified or cancelled.

By using negation to turn language against itself, Beckett shows clearly just how language functions. But if language is used to block connotations and yet does not fulfill its alternative function of denoting an empirical object, it turns into pure statement, for which the reader feels called upon to provide the reference. At this point the primary negations switch into secondary. By the use of language the reader is forced continually to cancel the meanings he (*sic*) has formed, and through this negation is made to observe the projective nature of all the meanings which the text has impelled the reader to produce. This is the reason for the uneasiness which most Beckett readers feel, but it may also explain what Beckett meant when he spoke of the power of the texts to 'claw' their way into us.

Furthermore, the demands put on the reader to cancel his–her own projected meanings brings to light an expectation all readers cherish, in relation to the meaning of literary texts: meaning must ultimately resolve the tensions and conflicts brought about by the text. Classical and psychological aesthetics have always been at one over the postulate that the final resolution of initial tension in the work of art is coincidental with the emergence of meaning. With Beckett however we become aware that meaning as a relief from tension embodies an expectation of art which is historical in nature [and ideological: the author], and consequently loses its claim to be normative [it is still normative, a different norm: the author]. The density of negations not only lays bare the historicity [and ideologicalness: the author] of our concept of meaning but also reveals the defensive nature of such a traditional expectation – we obviously anticipate a meaning that will remove the illogicalities, conflicts and indeed the whole contingency of the world in the literary work. To experience meaning as a defence, or as having a defensive structure is of course also a meaning, which, however, the reader can only become conscious of when the traditional concept of meaning is invoked as a background, in order for it to be discredited. In this sense, almost all the primary negations issue forth into secondary ones. The primary negations of the Beckett text give language the appearance of pure denotation, but as there is nothing given to denote, the building up of connotations is left completely to the reader's imaginings, which he/she is made to invalidate him/herself, by the constant invocation and revocation operative in the sentence sequence. Now this apparently negative outcome does contain certain possibilities *which need not be realized by the reader but which, nevertheless, are built into the structure of the negation* [italics mine].

The apparent intensification of secondary negations in Beckett reveals a strategy that is closely akin to psychoanalytical procedures. This is not to say that Beckett has depicted such procedures – on the contrary, had he done so, his texts could not have the effect which they do have and which can only be rendered plausible through certain insights of psychoanalysis. The use of negation to evoke and invalidate mental images is a means of making the reader conscious of the 'preferential

Gestalts' (Scheler) that orient him or her. So long as he or she remain unconscious of the projective nature of his or her mental images, these will remain absolute, and he/she will be unable to detach him or her self from them, and he/she will endow characters and events with allegorical meaning, for which his/her undisputed projections provide the frame of reference. But if the negations take effect and the mental images are relegated to the status of projections, there begins a process of detachment which can have 2 consequences: 1. The projection becomes an object for the reader, and no longer orients him or her [no longer overdetermines his or her orientation: the author]. 2. He/She therefore becomes open to experiences which had been excluded by these projections as long as they remained valid for him/her. And this is the point at which Beckett's texts come so close to psychoanalysis. In his essay on *Verneinung* [Negation], Freud writes that: 'In analysis no "negative act" is to be found in the unconscious, and cognizance of the unconscious on the part of the ego expresses itself in a negative formula. . . . The displaced content of a mental image or a thought can therefore penetrate through to the conscious mind, on condition that it can be negated. Negation is a way in which one takes cognizance of what has been displaced – it is already a neutralization of displacement but not of course an acceptance of what has been displaced. One can see how here the intellectual function is distinguished from the affective process.' If there are no negations in the unconscious, their intellectual function can only come about through a conscious act. In Beckett's works such acts are initiated by the negations which invalidate the mental images formed by the reader. This invalidation makes the reader's subconscious orientations surface into consciousness: in negating them, he/she turns them into objects for observation and inspection. Whenever this happens, two consequences are bound to ensue: 1. If orientations are reduced to mere projections, then the reader has outstripped them – an act to which different readers will react differently. Yet whatever the reaction may be, the outcome no longer falls within the realm of aesthetics [?: the author] although it testifies to the important phenomenon of practical consequences resulting from aesthetic inducements [this is slightly voluntarist, though by no means exclusively incorrect, as the political of a position can be a result of aesthetics; to make, for conceptual purposes, here, for a moment, that separation: the author]. 2. If one's own ideas, present to oneself as mental images, become invalidated, it shows clearly the extent to which the mental images depend upon a fictive [ideologically closured: the author] element. This is only natural, since they are formed to fill in the blanks resulting from negations, and even if the text offers or invokes existing given knowledges, the final gap *can* only be closed through a fiction [there is, though, no 'true reality' outside ideology: Iser's argument holds as long as truth is not the 'opposite' pole: the author] since it is both the function and achievement of the literary work to bring into existence something which has no reality [?: the author] of its own and which can never be finally deduced from (pre)existing realities.

Now for all the given material that goes to make up a mental image, it is only the fictive element that can establish the consistency necessary to endow it with the appearance of reality, for consistency is not a given quality of reality. And so the fictive element always comes to the fore when we realize the projective nature of our mental images. This does not mean that we then wish to exclude the fictive element from our imges, for this is structurally impossible anyway – without the fictive link there can be no image.[42] But it can mean that, through our awareness of the fictive closure, integral to our acts of ideation, we may be able to transcend our hitherto fixed positions and at least we shall be conscious of the intriguing role which fiction plays in our ideational and conceptual activities. Indeed its very usefulness springs from the fact that it is drained of reality [the appearance of reality: the author]. Such an awareness will prevent us from locking ourselves up in our own projections – a result which coincides with what the writings of Beckett appear to communicate. Through negation his fictional texts enable us to understand what fiction is and herein lies the subtle appeal of his achievement.   (Iser, *The Act of Reading*, pp. 222–5)

Privileging this long quote from one of the few serious works on Beckett's works may undermine the opaque prose I write and practice, but plagiarism dulls.

An example: negation also exists in its 'positive' form. *I will* means *I might not* in the following: '*I will, yes.*' The rhetorical device of the

Illus. 17   Alberto Giacometti, *Standing Woman*, bronze from clay, 1958
(height: 132 cm)

question-mark queries 'do you want me to' and means 'I want you
to want me to'. It also means, 'outside of my wanting to, if you
want me to, and outside of my wanting you to want me to, I do *not*
want to.' This displaces the wish to be hailed onto the rhetorical
question. The rhetorical *yes?* is a demand to be answered. It
insures that there is no vagueness of desire left unquestioned; it
cannot be read as pure rhetoric except wilfully against the
question as stated. The question-mark after the word *yes?* would
attempt to bolster the speaker's rationalisation that in fact a
demand was not made, a simple question was asked. But such a
reading can only be wilfully accepted in suppression of the
question as stated. Such a reading is denied credibility as it relies
solely on the convention of the question-mark having a unitary
meaning outside of usage, namely to question, untendentiously.
This is, of course, nonsense. The paranoiac system places power
with the questioner–interrogator/ask-er, in the form of the latter's
supposed compliance with the wishes of the addressee. This is a
denial of power whilst engaging in its authority. (Naming this
operation 'negation in its positive form' is obviously to use the
term 'positive' non-normatively.) Language and gesture become
contingent factors for respectively such *acts* and such *language*.

What is to be done (not what is to be felt).

Giacometti's *Standing Woman* (1958), height 132.1 cm, final casting in bronze (see Illus. 17). Clay is added to face, the left 'eye'
part of the head is not a separable 'fragment'. An added piece,
elsewhere, flattened, rubbed aside, covers a bit between other
points *a* and *b*. Giacometti's 'I don't know how to represent,
always fail' here is not material taken away, pared down,
subtracted. Here opposing that process: a building-up never
fulfilled, a building-up unseeable, so that each 'addition' is not
readable as anything but an attempt at addition, with no end in
sight and no beginning (no teleology). Nothing is more finished
than anything else, neither anti-existentialist totalism/totemism,
nor existentialist ideology, the unreconstructed figure isolate *in
vacuo*, asocial, etc. Here the continual process of the attempt and
the impossibility of one material collapsing onto another material
(the world) is neither given as denoted whole nor connoted
closures imagined. The contradictions of process motored in such
a sculpture disclosure a process not of emptying out but of

trepidation with the figure, with representation, with association, with truth outside of *work*. Neither do we have here an individualism (the 'right' moment of stoppage) nor a collective naturalism (individual truths generalised as 'real'). So, yes, it is pedagogy: we learn about projection, fiction, figuring, figuring-out.

Another pedagogy is Twombly's *Note III* (1967).* Neither the content, nor the form, of a note, it is an inscribed trace of notation which in its describing describes its describing, hermeneutic, reflexive, meaningless, forming the position for the viewer of the lack of evidence for the fictional function's narrativisation and for the projections (laterally and in perspective space) which would attend. The process is anonymised; the repositioning of knowledge *vs* perception is a dialectic material act inseparable here from the labour of seeing and attempting to 'read' an image's constituent parts. Image as such then is inseparable therefrom anymore.

To be in the position of not being able to speak the truth, to not know the truth, to not perceive clearly perceptions allowing for a position of truth, is a different position engaging the productions of meaning and the positions of meaning-making, and unmaking, than the hegemonic one. Certain works, in other words, must be *regained*, the way Althusser demands Marxism and communism be regained, and Delphy demands radical materialist feminism be regained, for the production of very different histories.

*See p. 158.

XXXI

Quote: Brecht on *Gestus*

Realism *vs* 'Realistic Representation'

Gestus/Gestik vs Dramatic Function

Brecht *vs* Beckett

Brecht on *Verfremdung*/Distanciation

Personage *vs* Non-personage Onstage

Denotation as End of Struggle

P: But you're not working with actual distanciation after all, the way you suggest in your *Little Organon*?

B: No, we aren't far enough. (Bertolt Brecht, *Gesammelte Werke* (Frankfurt: Suhrkamp, 1973) vol. 16, p. 798)

In order to show [*beleuchten*] the *gestus* of one scene, we choose the first scene of the third act of *Mother Courage and Her Children*, and indeed in two versions. Courage enacts an improper deal with army goods, and admonishes her son, who is with the army, for his part always to be proper. Weigel enacted this scene so that Courage points out to her son not to listen to the deals being done, as they have nothing to do with him. In the Munich production based on the Berlin model, Giehse played the scene such so that with a handmovement she admonishes the quartermaster who had hesitated to speak when he saw her son, to continue, as the son could gladly listen to these deals. The dramatic function of the scene is maintained: in a corrupt milieu it is demanded of a young person to be consistently proper. The *gestus* of [Mother] Courage is not the same. (ibid., vol. 16, p. 754)

A *Gestus* draws the relationship of people to one
another.   (ibid., vol. 16, p. 753)

P: But you're not working with actual distanciation after all,
      the way you suggest in your *Little Organon*?

B: No. We aren't far enough ... an [example] and a small one!
      For example I would play the connections to the to be
      distanciated main actions, clearly as connections, quicker,
      unstressed, secondary, and I would give the events a
      demonstrative character, naturally without doing harm to
      the liveliness, realism, fullness.

P: Then why not simply do that?

B: The theatre is like a swimmer, who can only swim as quickly
      as the current and his/her strength allows. In a moment, for
      example, where the public still understands by 'realistic
      representation' a representation which gives the illusion
      of reality, we couldn't obtain any of the intended
      effects.   (ibid., vol. 16, p. 799)

The opposition between 'realistic representation' and Realism is
here set forth. Also set out is the reactionary tendency to follow the
public rather than to engage with it from a position of possible or
attempted leftism, which is to advance it *with* it.

In the West, under the rubric of freedom of thought and speech,
we are given the most violent ideological educations, coerced to a
propaganda-machine unimaginable in the East.

As to the different *gestus* of Giehse and Weigel (the former the
greatest 'Brecht-actress'), 'the dramatic function of the scene is
maintained: in a corrupt milieu it is demanded of a young person
to be consistently proper. The *gestus* of [Mother] Courage is not
the same' (ibid., p. 754). Here, precisely, realism (Brecht's) is set
against 'realistic representation' as illusion of reality. Brecht seems
to be giving Giehse responsibility (and credit) for the decision as
to the *gestus*. And it does seem in character, a particularly
Giehse-like decision, based on her other performances (especially
in Dürrenmatt's *The Physicists* (Zurich and Munich, 1962), her
recorded readings of Brecht's poetry, and the first *Mother Courage*
in Zurich in 1943 as discussed in Brecht's letters). In the end it is a
directorial decision, and cannot be taken up as motored by the

desire of the actress, *even when it is*, though the final *mise-en-scène*, or montage, or enactment, or acting, is not attachable to the intentionality of the actress nor, even, the intentionality of the writer–director. It is attachable only to its own materiality as textual process, the totality of which for convenience's sake is characterised as 'by such and such' (the author). That this attachment can be true, false, or somewhere else, is not the point: there is no manner of disinterring it; the author's privileging is merely another capitalist patriarchal fiction (even though the words were, for example, written by Bertolt Brecht), and extrapolating from the *mise-en-scène* moments of this or that person's 'contribution' is a minor reformism that leaves the state of things, finally, intact.

For Brecht, the *gestik* can be different, but the dramatic function of the scene is maintained. In *Not I*, as directed by Beckett, the lack of that 'meaningful difference', and the keeping of that *gestik* to a minimum, affects the spectator's viewing (of) precisely *a specific realism* defined by the non-homologousness of thought and feeling.

Whether or not this is 'correct' for some other society and ideology in another historical epoch, in this historical high bourgeois epoch of capitalist patriarchy Beckett's strict separation of thought from feeling engages the spectator–listener in that split, in *that* void. It is a voiding of the one from the other's mantle. In this the *gestik* is exactly the *lack* onstage of the possibility of a 'different *gestus* within a same dramatic function', a critique of that concrete concept thus ('truth is concrete', Brecht). We have here thus a critique by Beckett of Brecht: (1) of a difference of one *gestik* to another that is so formal* that it does *not* intervene on dramatic (and dramaturgic) function (Beckett's critique here is thus of the Brechtian non-intervention by *gestik* on dramatic function); and (2) of a fullness of human rightness *attributed to this or that dramatic function*.

Brecht's concept of dramatic function can thus be seen as teleological, in the *future anterior*, i.e. so ideologically encumbered and already determined, as a future placed and identified but

* This is the very opposite of some forms of radical Soviet formalism of the 1920s.

unlived. It is defined *now* already as a past seen from the future, as in: a 'boy' *born to be 'a man'*, a 'girl' *born to be 'a woman'*, and so on. Brecht's concept of dramatic function can equally be seen as teleological in its idealisation of *'the future'*, pure and simple. Neither of these concepts, however concrete, produce the need for, let alone the want for, struggle, in the viewer and/or in the pro-theatric (that about which it is, its references and signifieds).

In Beckett the meaningful difference between *gestik* and dramatic function is kept to a minimum.

Brecht also defines the *gestik* as 'draw(ing) the relationships of people to one another.' This is utilised in the strict sense in *Not I* and *Waiting for Godot* productions directed by Beckett. In *Not I* it is via the non-existent relationships unpresent (not even present-in-absence); the relation of image to word, unstoppable speech act, is the only process. In *Godot* it is via the Didi/Gogo relation as constant and endless, unstoppable *gestik-to-gestik* movement in word and gesture.

BECKETT: Lucky falls down twice, that must though not be made realistic, but simply done clearly.

WIGGER: But how does one avoid that thereby the human gets lost, that it gets sterile?

BECKETT: It is play, it is all play. When all four are on the ground, with that one couldn't go at it naturalistically. That has to be done with artifice ... otherwise everything would be imitation, an imitation of reality.   (quoted in the programme for *Waiting for Godot*, Schiller Theater, Berlin, 1975)

'R': Distanciation [*Verfremdung*]: that nothing remains selfunderstood, that one always knows what one is being given to feel even whilst maintaining the strongest shared feelings, that one doesn't simply allow the public to identify with (feel into) something and thereby take everything as natural, godgiven, and unchangeable, and so on.

BRECHT: 'Only!'   (Brecht, *Gesammelte Werke*, vol. 16, p. 910)

'R':   So our *actors* can't just simply without reservation
              throw themselves into the people of the play
              anymore; they can't blindly 'live' them as if
              everything were the for each person natural thing to
              do, unthinkable as anything else, also they can't
              allow the representation of any different behaviour
              unthinkable to be for the *audience*.* That they have to
              represent each figure as fully living persons in spite of
              all critique is clear. . . .

BRECHT: And like Weigel herself the public takes *Courage* as a
              whole person with all her contradictions.   (ibid.,
              vol. 16, p. 918)

There is a problem in this: such a character, '*whole* person *with* all
her contradictions', is *never* thinkable as different ('*als anders
denkbar*'). This is both a conceptual mistheorisation and a
misrecognition by the Brecht group of character-distanciation.

Nothing is not play, nothing is not artifice; there is no final
humanisation of body or mind, for Beckett. There is no full figure
to identify, and to be identified with or through, which means the
character as character onstage exists, no other. And it is that
which allows for the political other to be. *There is no closure or
recuperation of that*. Why not? Because there is no 'natural living
character' at all, no narrative space of and for living characters.
Thus at *this* point Beckett's specificity is of a certain Brechtian
type. Brecht posits the problem and its solution as no longer 'as if
everything were the for each person natural thing to do, unthinkable as anything else, as if for the public representation of
any different behaviour were unthinkable'. Where Brecht and
Beckett part company is in Brecht's follow-on, '[the] whole person
with all her contradictions' and 'That they have to represent each
figure as fully living persons, in spite of all critique, is clear'.
Beckett enacts a Brechtian distanciation-effect, whilst Brecht is
unBrechtian, because of his need for the denoted and its hold in
his theory, and his assumptions for 'a public'.

Beckett's production work is a theorisation-in-practice in which

---

* '*Publikum*' means 'audience' or 'public'.

no other possibilities for behaviour and for the situation are given. 'Natural' possibilities for differently thinkable acts are so *acutely* not given, that *all* other possibilities exist. Here his position coincides with the Brechtian of it no longer being a matter of 'as if everything were the for each person natural thing to do'. Yet specifically here is posited Beckett's opposing politic to Brecht's in terms of any 'whole person with all her contradictions'. Beckett's Didi and Gogo, Amy, Mouth in *Not I*, Rocker in *Rockaby* are so acutely particular and 'hermetic' and 'not differently thinkable' that they are that *unnatural* and unnaturalisable extreme against which other, equally ideological, political, 'un-natural' positions can be posited. No thing is 'true'; there is no 'true humanity'; no 'final solution' is denoted.

A *gestik* used *non*-denotatively (as denotations simply 'added-on' are immediately assimilable as a 'broadening') can disrupt the function of a scene, its dramaturgy, as each *gestik* is a new signifier, producing a new signification-chain which can disrupt previously held signifieds/significations (including those of prior *gestiks* already assimilated to the on-going dramatic function). Obviously each *gestik*, when producing a momentary stoppage, has a different use than thereafter when that stoppage has been assimilated to the changed direction (and meaning) of the dramaturgy – changed by the intervention of said *gestik* but on-going nevertheless. The *gestik* as signi*fier* can *disrupt* the dramaturgy's meaning (i.e. signi*fieds* and their struggleless functioning) only when *not* instituted as an immediately assimilable denotation. Thus *gestik I* may differ from *gestik 2*, and one may alter the dramatic function of a scene, but the other may not. What becomes a politically questionable concept is Brecht's description of differing *gestiks* within a *same* dramatic function, as in the example of *Mother Courage*, never positing the possible *disruption* of dramatic function through the use of whatever *gestik*.

Every denotation is a momentary stoppage of struggle.

Finally, *Courage*'s allowing or not allowing the boy to listen is yet another *extension* of her tragic, largely characterisational persona; for Beckett, it is the lack of such extension, a radical lack of such, that makes of the general a specificity. This can only be opposed by another specificity through the viewer/listener. All embracing

Illus. 18 (*left*) Horst Bollman (Estragon) and (*right*) Stefan Wigger (Vladimir) in Beckett's German production of *Warten auf Godot* (1975)

extension is for Beckett's work out of the question. For Brecht, on the other hand (who nevertheless theorised similarly a notion of the general as lived in the concrete specific), extension becomes the dominant mode, voluntaristically non-contradictory and unproblematic *finally*. *Mother Courage* then exists as tragic, forcing tears, '*political tears*', which however (psychoanalytically and politically) are (concretely and theoretically) an idealism.

Brecht's denotations of change, of no person natural, of the thinkableness of different behaviour, of nothing as godgiven, of the necessities of realism *against* 'realistic representation' (*Gesammelte Werke*, vol. 16, p. 799), must be seen as incongruous to this discussion of Brecht's theorisations of the *Verfremdungseffekt* (distanciation-effect) and *gestik*.

The question which demands the Beckettian 'solution', the Beckettian process, is 'to what extent does politics (denotated or connotated) exist other than in a spectator-relation (to "knowledge", "truth", "fiction") which suppresses the contradictions between knowledge and perception?'

The net that holds the two, Beckett and Brecht, at their most radical: positions/concepts of the *historical vs historicism*. The (Beckettian) former can seem *a*historical, the (Brechtian) latter can seem historical. The problem is that seeming.

(See Illus. 18.)

XXXII

Quote: Kleist on Marionettes
Dehumanised Gesture Ventriloquated
Brecht on Distanciation Effect
Brecht's and Beckett's Theorisations/The Political

I bathed, about three years ago, with a young man who at that time possessed extraordinary charm. He might have been about sixteen, and only indistinctly could one see the first traces of vanity caused by women's favours. We had recently seen in Paris 'The Youth Drawing a Thorn from his Foot'. The copy of this statue is well known and is present in most German collections. A glance he cast in a large mirror, while putting his foot on a stool to dry it, reminded him of this statue. He smiled, and told me of the discovery he had made. I had had the same idea, but either to test the strength of his charm, or to damp his vanity a little, I laughed and replied that he saw ghosts. He blushed and lifted his foot again to prove it, but the experiment failed, as could have been foreseen. Confused, he lifted his foot three, four, perhaps even ten times. In vain, he was unable to produce the same movement again. On the contrary, his movements now had such a comical element that I could hardly refrain from laughing. From that day, so to speak from that moment, an inconceivable change occurred in the young man. He began to stand before the mirror for days, and lost one charm after another. An invisible and inconceivable power had come like an iron net about the free play of his gestures, and after one year there was not a trace of his charm which before had delighted the eyes of his companions.

(Sometime later the author has a conversation with a

187

puppetmaster, whom he discusses gesture with. The former states):

'. . . there's a subtle relationship between the movement of the operator's fingers and the movements of the attached puppets (marionettes), something like the relationship between numbers and their logarithms, or between asymptote and hyperbola.' And yet he believed the marionettes could be divested of this last trace of human volition and their dance transferred completely to the realm of mechanical forces, even produced, as I had suggested, by turning a handle. . . . My reply was that, no matter how cleverly he might present his paradoxes, he would never make me believe a mechanical puppet could be more graceful than a living human body. He countered this by saying that as far as grace is concerned, it is impossible for man to come anywhere near a puppet. Only god can equal inanimate matter in this respect. (Heinrich von Kleist, *On the Marionette Theatre* (1810), in *Life and Letters Today*, vol. 16, no. 8 (Summer 1937) p. 103)

Here what matters is the dehumanised gesture ventriloquated but unsymbolic of anything else, unmetaphoric. The grace and apparent 'harmony' of the marionette is simultaneous to the quick, sudden, jagged moves and gestures of the marionette. Here is a materialism of contradictory enactment akin to form in Beckett, Valentin, Brecht, Warhol, Billie Whitelaw, Liesl Karlstadt, Therese Giehse, Ingrid Superstar.

There are limits to part's equality with whole. (Beckett, addenda to *Watt* (Paris: Merlin Books, 1953) p. 247)

The footsteps that we hear, obtrusively, pedantically, mechanically in *Footfalls* are as the obverse of the marionette-principle; thereby they ingratiate just such a principle; the weightfulness of the human figure on stage *in situ* is seen against the image-of the weightlessness of the marionette, its action held not mainly by gravity to the base, but by strings in an illusion of effortlessness.

The figures in the Beckett-directed Schiller Theatre production of *Waiting for Godot* are gesturised throughout so that there is neither a moment of pause when the going is a slow back and forth (whether it be in monologue, dialogue, or silent sections) nor a moment of speeding-up, when the going is in dialectically jagged quickness (whether it be in monologue, dialogue, or silent sections). There are no such moments which would break from the enduring, effortful, constantly re-established endlessness of ventriloquated gesture, marionetted-duration, durable and unendurable, material. Thus the 'truth' of any moment, *each* moment re-materialised, and re-dialecticised, through the viewer, is as artifice.

(11)   . . . the turn to the public also has to be considered, only not through suggestiveness which would result in intensification. What must be noticed is the difference between suggestive and convincing, plastic acting! (Brecht, *Gesammelte Werke*, vol. 15, p. 353)

(12)   In 'The expression of feelings in man and animal' Darwin complains that the study of expression is difficult, because 'when we witness some deep excitement our sympathy is so strongly excited that we forget, or it becomes almost impossible for us, to set up a careful observation'. This is where the artists must engage and construct events even of the deepest excitation in such a way that the 'witness', the viewer, remains capable of observation.   (ibid., vol. 15, p. 353)

(17)   The V-effect (distanciation effect) as a procedure of daily life. In producing the distanciation effect one is dealing with something common [*alltäglich*/everyday], thousand times repeated [*Tausendfaches*], it is nothing but a much practised way of making something understood for someone else or for oneself, and one observes it in research as well as at business conferences, in this or that form. The V-effect consists in making of a common, known, immediate thing a special, noticed, unexpected thing, in order that this thing which is to be viewed becomes understood. The selfunderstood becomes in specific ways un-understood, but that only happens in order to then make it understood. So that something known can become something recognized it has to come

> out of its inconspicuousness; the habit that a specified
> object needs no explanation must be broken. As popular
> as it may be it gets stamped, now, as something
> unusual'. (ibid., vol. 15, p. 357)

In the above, known must be written 'known', as in German
known, bekannt, is close to the habitual-known, the *usual*, denoting
less *knowledge* than *recognised, er*kannt, whereas in English *recognised*
pertains to the perceived, to a more superficial knowing.

> [Similarly] it is a matter of the distanciation-effect in its
> simplest form when a businessmeeting is begun with the
> sentence 'Have you ever thought about what happens to
> the garbage that flows from your factory day-in-day-out into the
> river?' This garbage hadn't been flowing unnoticed into the
> river; it had been carefully planned, people and machines are
> utilized, the river is already completely green as a result, and
> flowed very noticeably filled with garbage, but precisely *as
> garbage*. During the process of fabrication (of something else) it
> was garbage, now it is to become the object of fabrication, the
> eye views it with interest. The question, thus, has distanciated
> it, as it was meant to . . . we understand it as something strange,
> new, as a success as the result of construction, and in that as
> something unnatural. . . . But the distanciation-effect has only
> worked with those who've really understood that this effect is
> not reached by *every* representation but only by specific ones;
> this effect is only apparently something *usual*.   (Bertolt Brecht,
> *New Technique in the Art of Acting* (1940), in *Gesammelte Werke*, vol.
> 15, p. 357)

The other side of Brecht's theoretical and theatrical practice
follows via such positions as:

> Enough. It is naturally our new audience that allows us, and
> that makes it our duty, to aim for precisely such effects which
> rest upon a natural unity of thought and feeling. But I think that
> one can't question the fact that certain other feeling-
> complexities then fall away, ones that the audience as a whole,
> and especially an audience used to the theatre, is used to, and
> values. (Bertolt Brecht, *Dialectics on Theatre* (1955), in
> *Gesammelte Werke*, vol. 16, p. 905)

What this means is that in rationalising the natural oneness of thought and feeling as something radical and inculcated by a new audience, Brecht is forced to locate the loss of certain conventions which the audience 'as a whole' and especially those 'used to the theatre' hold dear. What remains unspecified is what these lost conventions are. The supposed radicality of the oneness of thought and feeling justifies this loss, for Brecht. Precisely *any* unity of thought and feeling is polemicised and theorised against by the Brecht cited *previously*. There is no 'epistemological break' that can be chronologically determined here, simply a politico-aesthetic ambivalence, and some opportunism.

> " 'R': Those are – whoever knows the performance, knows this – political tears."

Take the example of Weigel in *Courage*. As she [Weigel] *herself* views this person [*Courage*] critically, the audience *also* has very different feelings towards her due to Weigel's constantly changing behaviour in this respect. The audience admires her as mother and criticises her as trader. And, like Weigel herself, the audience takes *Courage* nevertheless as a whole person with all *her* contradictions, and not as a bloodless result of the analyses of an actress. (Brecht, *Gesammelte, Werke*, vol. 16, p. 918; this dialogue between 'W', 'R', 'P' and 'Brecht' was written by Brecht)

In *Footfalls* there is a stopping and listening, a stopping and waiting for external sound; to continue or not thereafter. There is a structural stoppage, near the end of the seven-step (in the London production nine-step) structure. This event is not given as internally motivated; nor is it given as 'a bloodless result of the analyses of an actress'. It is the enacting of what Brecht haltingly theorised as the as-yet impossible: no suggestive intensification, but 'convincing' (*Gesammelte Werke*, vol. 15, p. 353), making of the known something understood (vol. 16, p. 799), something *un*usual, playing the connections to the to be distanciated main actions quicker, unstressed, . . . [but] the theatre is like a swimmer [and] in a moment, for example, where the public still understands by 'realistic representation' a representation which gives the illusion of reality, we couldn't obtain any of the intended effects' (ibid. p. 799).

What makes of even Brecht's most advanced theorisation a problem (not least for Brecht!) is the insistence on not doing harm to the events' 'liveliness, realism, fullness' (ibid., p. 799), and the insistence on the political denotated. Beckett's *gestus* of '*Mensch im Begriff abzumagern*' ('The person about to thin out') is a different politics from Brecht's 'A work-operation for example is not a *gestus* if it does not contain a social relation such as exploitation or cooperation' (ibid., p. 753). Beckett assumes social being *in-audience*, Brecht assumes an *ideal* 'student' (therefore *in vacuo*) spoken of as observing the social. Thus Brecht produces the historical *vacuo* and Beckett produces the historical-social.

In *Not I*, Mouth onstage is the unfocused unfocusable attempt to represent, to tell truth, to rehistoricise itself into a representation, and the constant reattempted impossibility of language to that task. Thereby it is given a different politics from the story of being honest in dishonest times, the impossibility of honesty in the corrupt social-political milieu which constitutes human as never anything but corrupt-in-capitalism. There is no doubt that the Brecht position theatrically situates the realm of the political denoted in the *pro*-theatric (*re*presented theatrically), and in the spectator, whereas the Beckett position theatrically situates the realm of the political denotated *and connotated* in the *theatric* and in the spectator. In both Beckett and Brecht, *de*notation proceeds not only via the explicit but also via the implicit, as a, simple or complex, social relation does not have to be *named* to exist: 'You don't have sex with a name!' (quoted from Andy Warhol's film *Kitchen*, 1964).*

What is left *aside* above is '*consciousness*', when using the term 'spectator', and 'spectator–listener'. What is *assumed* above is the critical repositioning of the spectator through contradictions (inculcated throughout the theatric mechanism), contradictions motoring repositioning in *constant un-knowing*. The oppositions are between perception and knowledge, sight and sound, consumption and production, identity and loss, the body and the voice, here and there, end and endlessness, theatre and end. In both Beckett and Brecht specific plays and writings exist which posit such operations as theatric. Both are thus absolutely necessary for a radically political theatre of dialectics when production is materialist. Historical materialism is not more 'history' than materialism is 'material'.

*Actually do you?

XXXIII

The artist at the stage of Cubism, instead of creating a facial image, has multi-imaged the concrete difference, i.e. has transformed the face into elements and created a new phenomenon which in turn has become an abstraction and has roused the indignation of the vigilant citizen's consciousness. This has happened because existence, the object, for society was in one centre of reflection and, for the artist, in another, and what the former considered understood, ordered, and natural, was, for the latter, disordered, unnatural, and senseless. And then angry society must search either for a photographer, or for an artist not far removed from that photographer. . . . In the stages of Cubism . . . when many associative decisions are taken, hidden from the spectator, [one can see] an object which is understood by the masses, *the objective*, becomes sharply subjective, producing 'astonishment' in society because it is unintelligible to intelligence. . . . The Cubist has carried it from the intelligent into the unintelligent, and has temporarily broken the link with society, only because society has not had time to follow the kinesthetic associative displacement through to the end . . . some artists have taken fright at this break with the masses and have cut short. (Kasimir Malevich, *Unpublished Writings, 1922–25* (Copenhagen: Borgens, 1976) pp. 283–4)

I have not met a single person who would say that all artistic portraits of Lenin correspond to reality . . . only science can show his true portrait. The greater reality of his portrait is the cinema, it is outer truth, the scientific is inner truth, both together would be a portrait. Therefore the portrait of Lenin does not exist in art, as other portraits in general do not exist; when they enter the sphere of aesthetic painting they depart into the future, into the ideal. . . . Communists too object to non-objectivity, since, for them, existence without an object, like the capitalist without capital, cannot exist. With non-objectivity disappears their means of reflecting environment and portraits, propaganda through the object, propaganda through capital in the other case. The non-objective is incomprehensible . . . and abstract, the consciousness of society is deprived of its main support, what to see, what to cognise? This function can be materialistic; matter does not have an object-portrait . . . if it is fluid and dynamic. From matter we can make material and from material whatever one pleases: we do not have an authentic portrait of it, we can only create an image of our conjectures, transform the unknown into the known.   (ibid., p. 322)

Non-objectivity: that the idea does not attain the object except as an image. This non-representational image is the possible, finite form of materialism and reality.   (ibid., pp. 348–9)

If not disquisition disquiet. That sentence is a descriptive statement in reference to *Not I*'s form, and to the thought that the lack of disquisition (i.e. contradictions) is inbuilt for the viewer–listener producing disquiet. What *If not disquisition disquiet* states is that in *Not I*, the sentences, the repetition structure, the monologue-in time, is disquieting for the speaker and for the listener, producing a sense of disquiet in both. It is not a disquisition, i.e. speech *about* a subject. *If not disquisition disquiet* also means it might or might not be a disquisition, *might* but in any case hasn't become limited to that. This is what the idiomatic usage of 'if not . . .' denotes in current languge use. What it means is that in any case disquiet is produced. But the contradiction for the listener comes up because of the beginning word 'if'. 'If' as part of the idiomatic expression 'if not' has an *opposing*, strictly opposing, meaning to 'if' (meaning *when*) as in: 'when there is no disquisition then there is disquiet, *not otherwise*'. Thus the two uses of 'if' force a contradictory motoring of the reader–listener. And this contradictory motoring of the reader–listener in relation to the production of disquiet, and in relation to the production of a disquisition-monologue, forms contradictions which can only be resolved by the reader–listener's position, consciously or unconsciously, in the momentary resolution of (that) contradiction-in-meaning. Taking such a position has nothing to do with truth, but has to do with transformations of meaning through language-forces, and attempting to separate an idea, a thing, etc., from the process of its attempted description. This is not a playing with 'open' language where the reader–listener-as subject can willy-nilly insert him-/ herself in idealist play, but rather, the reading, or the play is the work. It is the work of taking a position in meaning and thereby, for that moment, formulating a political solution, not outside ideology and inside truth, but as a position, an acting within the process of contradiction, in language, in meaning, against the natural 'fulfilment' of speech as some pre-given truth or knowledge outside of the work of production and subjective and objective transformations of position. Such motivation of the reader–listener and the viewer–listener is beyond a mere energetics. The above is merely an example of a process that is on-going in *Not I*, *Rockaby* and *A Piece of Monologue*.

Seven Countenances of Time:
It is said 'the' time. Who wants may read 'our' time. But in no case can it be called 'my time'. Because it isn't *my time* which with brutal openness horrifically grins. My time stands in wild opposition to the times. I have nothing in common with the time which wretchedly hangs about. I am not a *contemporary* [*Zeitgenosse*, which means time plus comrade].

He who in this form gave countenance to 'the' time thought the drawings stood in stark opposition to the words which followed.

I would want them to stand in ten times stronger opposition to the words. But there is no 'stronger' opposition. There is only opposition. Opposition, as I feel it, has no adjective.

If I say 'wild' opposition or 'lazy' opposition, these aren't emphases, but rather adornments. The spirit is freezing and wants to warm itself with the heart's blood.   (B. Traven, 'Rut Marut', in *Der Ziegelbrenner* ('The Brickburner'), 21 December 1921), published during the Bavarian Soviet period

Given in Beckett's *Not I* the broken moments of stuttering speech and speechlessness, the memory, for example, of a previous moment causing moment-to-moment hesitation of the larynx, tone, movement; given such *gestik* of materialist monologue, sound against image (the image of the continuum of a mouth against the non-continuum of speech-production): how are we produced and how are we to make use of such means of production of language and sight, *in* language and sight? And how is such a construction produced against culturally inculcated 'narrative desire', when it is precisely the anti-narrative that materialist sound-and-sight-processes, as described, engage? How is all this put to *use*, rather than commodified for consumption? We can utilise the apparatus, the apparati, of meaning-making and meaning-unmaking as a move, not as an identification but against it, as a figuring of how is what it is what it is.

Cultural, intellectual, sensual (as in: the sense) use-value is important if use-value is to be seen as other than purely economic. The use-value of, for example, sexuality in its concretised form and in terms of sexual meanings (that woman there, rocking, on stage, that mouth speaking, those words, in such and such a way) is still a question of use-value *for whom*, not use-value pure and simple. That is one contradictory placement, as the *for whom* becomes an operative question *specifically in relation to the seeming use-value pure and simple.*

Another contradiction that is operative constantly is that use-value is always already exchange-value.

The third, in fact last-instance, contradiction is that, still, there is a difference between use-value and exchange-value: one is for use, process, productivity, one is for profitability. *At the same time*, the concept *use* is an ideology of use, and the concept *exchange* is an ideology of exchange, both of which can only be disinterred, towards various kinds of uses and exchanges, laboriously. Disinterring such concepts alone requires a materialist process, in endless regress 'towards' a political use and exchange separate from a pre-given 'good' or 'truth'.

> The process disappears in the product; the latter is a use value.   (Marx, *Captial*, vol. i, p. 176)

> though a use-value, in the form of a product, issues *from* the labour process, other use-values, products of previous labour, enter *into* it as means of production. The same use-value is both the product of a previous process, and a means of production in a later process. Products are therefore not only results, but also essential *conditions of labour*. It is generally by their imperfections as products that the means of production in any process assert themselves in their character.   (ibid., p. 178)

Human action, or the human voice, etc., with a view to the production of use-values, is 'the appropriation of natural substances to human requirements'.

'Rushed switching of subject matter loosens the relation between speech and person ... resulting in the detachment of the enunciation from the figure' (Beckett, *Materialien zu Warten auf Godot* (Frankfurt: Suhrkamp, 1973) pp. 136–6). In Gertrude Stein's *Tender Buttons* and much else, in H.D.'s *Palimpsest* and *Hedylus*, in Beckett's *How It Is*, this is the case. A non-localisability, causelessness, is structuring the reader-listener's imbrications through the text.

Can there be non-metaphysical materiality based on unanswerable (but real) cause and causelessness? Can there be material without theoretical explanation or formulation? The opposite also obtains: *theoretical* models, physically not observable, are no less real for that, though another historical conjuncture is necessary to 'observe' their physicality. Things are true for a time and place, in certain historical epochs, scientific for the specific ideology of each history, perception, conception, of science and the (ostensible) object. The object in its very concept is already redolent with the scientific or anti-scientific ideology of its historical moment; each is produced as an object of knowledge, no finite and static object of knowledge pre-existing.

The placement within the apparatus *theatre* of such a conceptual framework bears upon the matters and manners of effects with, and effects without, cause. In the case of the latter, it can be a matter of cause elsewhere, possibly denying the identifications and gratifications of a narcissism as reassuring as it is absurd. The speaking voice, its larynx-function, is the operation through you as sexed being of conscious and unconscious process in that present rememoration-attempt, a historical moment inseparable from the political relations produced and producing, *or preceding yet decaused*. It is a speaking voice staged *ars ficia*, as in: the artifice/the artificial.

Brecht and Beckett have both been described as producing non-Aristotelian theatre, though the former's hesitation on that score is often no less ambivalent than the latter's, according to interpretations which have as their bases some implicit authorial say-so. The humanisation inveigles itself and is attributed to the author of the 'lonely woman speaking her life' and the 'lonely woman acting her life', the one being Mouth in *Not I*, the other Mother Courage in *Mother Courage*. This attributed humanisation is based on the dual empiricisms: (a) the intentional fallacy, and (b) the reading-off an audience the truth of the piece, the audience thus as the adequate reflection/mirror of the piece's truth as a piece of truth. But what is needed is an analysis that does more (or less) than find in 'the audience' or in the 'implicit' author the rationale for a communication which pre-exists the theatric act as if the latter redoubles a nature outside the theatre.

Material theatric contradictions make Mother Courage a character who walks against the turning stage (as in the Berliner Ensemble production); she is standing, in fact, still. The insight in thought which that can produce, when 'compared' with an audience responding to the 'tragedy of her hopelessness' within only the most general sociality of the play, forms the basic question of interpretation against which all cultural production comes up. Throwing up that problem *outside* of a dialectic (that is, a possibly *useful*) work-process, which could lead to some sort of insight into the social theatrical and other mechanisms which produce the emotional effects a specific scene instigates, means throwing *out* that problem as a problematic and being left with the 'unanswerable', the problem of multiple interpretation. Multiple interpretation gets one nowhere near an 'answer', a position, because it allows for the over-determination by ideology of everything instate. A contract which would imply a willingness by the producer and a willingness by the consumer to provide and work with *a* specific meaning, an agreement as to the desirability of that, its use-value for both the producer and consumer, elides or could elide or does not necessarily *not* elide the question of ideological fabrication: the fabric of the audience's desire as much as the actor's and director's to consciously or not cater for meanings that, *prior to this staging*, have dominant power within the culture and its history. That would be an aesthetic and a politics of leaving well enough alone, whereas Beckett's work (and Brecht's occasionally) manages to leave nothing alone, not even nothing; forgoing the possibilities of satisfaction; leaving you to leave the theatre unsatisfied, dissatisfied, powerfully unassimilated, evicted from the comfort that closure and resolution, an ending, any ending, could supply. The consequent, and consequential, negation or refusal to terminate unpleasure is the aesthetic/ political importance of such work, when it works.

That Brecht's ambiguities at the end of each play allow for either socially useful and politically radical possibilities, in the realm of fantasy endings (for example *Threepenny Opera* and *The Caucasian Chalk Circle*), or for more crudely the anticipated correct ending for a politicised consciousness-in-concrete (in both senses!) (for example *St Joan of the Stockyards*, *Galileo*, *The Good Woman of Szechuan*, *The Measures Taken* and *Arturo Ui*) either through an empirical 'positive event' or with an anti-hero who can, via inversion, be identified with against the naturalistically represented reactionary forces, leaves the space for Beckett's radical solutions which are not solutions, enduring and unendurable (and in that their radicalism is precise).

Shortly after reading *Waiting for Godot*, Brecht wrote, as to his own early works, *Bei Durchsicht meiner ersten Stücke* ('Whilst looking through my first works'):

> I see today that my contradictory spirit led me close to the border of the Absurd. They (my first five full-length works) show . . . without regret how the great flood breaks upon the bourgeois world. First there is still land, but with laughter which becomes ruins [*Trumpeln*] and sin; then there is only the vastness of black water, with islands which quickly crumble.[43]

The act of speech is never *in vacuo*, the act of gesture is never *in vacuo*.[44] The marionette-like moves of Didi and Gogo in Beckett's production are a constant rearrangement, a constant attempt at impossible sociality, congruence, synchronicity, of either 'one' with either 'other'. These moves are also a constant attempt at impossible internal synchronicity of the sound/movement/speech/gesture/body's endless moves ending with no physical concretions other than this body, this mind, this hearing, this sight. Through the marionette-like *gestik* (which, though, is never mechanised to the point of illustrating 'industrial mechanisation' or 'alienation' or 'existential dehumanisation'), psychology and individual psychology are evicted and the external givens of a body (its movements, etc.) are not manifestations of character. Thus, nothing is given that can be used as an excuse to infer psychology and its categories of the known (implicit identity) for the audience's self-identifications and projections. The marionette-like *gestik* is thus not a substitute for 'the mechanical' or for a statement: 'people in this condition of identity are like marionettes'. It is, rather, a form of movement which declines to take the human conventions of movement and gesture as natural. It declines the pretence that 'natural actions' are codeless. The figures of Didi and Gogo are vacated of such naturalism; the discourse is as something else. For those who do not accept negation, it is materialism, process, subjectivity, history, position, both before and after *and during* (and always *against*) on-going attempts, by the conventions we know and recognise, at homogenisation. The power and authority of speech and gesture are instituted theatrically against other powers and authorities of the culturally dominant 'natural'.[45]

XXXIV

Quote: From the Zurich Production of *Bruchstücke/*
Fragments of Theatre

Realism, Code of Naturalism in Order to Denaturalise

Beckett on the Machine/Stage Directions

Operation of the Fourth Wall in Beckett

Palimpsest

Pleasure and Process

Gesture

Practice (Althusser)

In the Zurich 1981 (January) production of Beckett's *Bruchstücke*
(*Theatre I*, 1960), the 8 o'clock news on the radio is heard by the
viewers–listeners.

'. . . the judge is still being held by the Red Brigades; 2 editors of
Espresso have been arrested for complicity; 30 students in Zug
[neighbouring city of Zurich: the author] are on hungerstrike
for an *AJZ* [*Allgemeines Jugendzentrum*].' [AJZs were youthclubs
demanded in Zurich the previous year, a political demand
leading to police-riots; these political demands spread,
thereafter, to other cities and Cantons and people.] 'Now it is
8.05' Switch to a jazz tape (a man stage-left operating a
tape-recorder, in audience's full view, near the entrance-
door).[46]

The audience consisted of four rows of ten seats. Stage-left was a
violin-stand upright with an ashtray balanced on it. The viewers'
coat-racks were adjacent to the 'end' of the stage, i.e. downstage-

right, near the entrance door (next to the man operating the tape-recorder). As the jazz tape was begun, a man sitting stage-left with his head slumped forward raises it half way, no eye-line match with the audience, then down again. Thus we have here fourth-wall *acting*, theatrical naturalism not taking account of the audience, whereas the *mise-en-scène* is 'Brechtian', and the conflict of the two constant. Also constant is the rain pouring outside (the 'auditorium', i.e. audience-space is separated from the rainy street outside by the thin wall and the entrance door; there is no more to the building, no lobby, no other spaces). At one point a person (a character) emerges from the pouring rain; he is recognisable as the man who previously doubled that night as ticket-seller at the main office of the theatre company, down past the corner, a five-minute walk from the performance space. He is a Zurich actor who has appeared in a number of plays over the past few years; thus previously, his role as ticket-seller was also not quite 'acceptable' at first.

The written instructions for this play (looking at them now), in the published version, are as follows:

> *Street Corner. Ruins.*
> *A, blind, sitting on a folding stool, scrapes his fiddle. Beside him the case, half open, up-ended, surmounted by alms bowl. He stops playing, turns his head audience right, listens. Pause.*

The final stage instruction, after A and B's play, which I shan't describe, reads as follows:

> A whirls around, seizes the end of the pole, and wrenches it from B's grasp.

After that, the lights go out immediately, or did, then come back on; the actors both stood up and bowed, walked off and for the audience there was a pause. The actors were offstage back left, could be seen changing into their rubberboots, wintercoats, etc.; they left the performance space by the one door; the audience rises and mills about, picks up coats and umbrellas at the side where the tape-recorder is placed, and exits the same way.

It is not only possible, it is very possible to produce a social *gestik* in this manner, akin to Brecht's notion of the social *gestik* (as in his notion of having the world's great revolutions as back-projected films to the play *Waiting for Godot* at the Berliner Ensemble, a project never realised). But why does such an idea produce an automatistic assumption that the social-represent*ed*, a political signified, leads from insight, knowledge, questioning, to change via struggle?

10 April 1985

American exercises in Honduras are a warning to Nicaragua, said a State Department spokesman. A Labour Councillor stated that Mr Kinnock, Leader of the Labour Party, was completely out of touch with the rank and file of men and women in the Party if he thinks they'll implement Tory decisions. Sixteen years ago the United States Army massacred 601 unarmed men, women and children at My Lai in Vietnam. The Lieutenant who gave the order was freed after three years' house arrest. Simon Wiesenthal stated that Mengele is still alive in Paraguay. An investigation is taking place into why the Americans and the Catholic Church hierarchy in Italy helped his escape to South America. The Tate Gallery paid one million pounds (sterling) for a late de Chirico. The miners' strike, which lasted nearly one year, is still having serious effects on communities throughout Britain, with many who are back at work due to economic need refusing to work with those who worked throughout the strike. The coup in Sudan has not ended the fighting there. (Reuters, BBC World Service, *The Times*)

Any theatrical construction adequate against over-determining meanings imported untransformed from without must result in a denaturalising which (in one teleology) *leads to nothing*, to the *nothing-natural*. This leaves space for nothing but other *theatric* constructions, however 'real' they may or may not seem. In that sense, a truly *realist* theatric *gestik* leaves nothing; fullnesses are precisely a denial of the material real. If one or another viewer does not 'like' that, he or she can position within a political revolt, in or outside theatric representation, but this preferably not at the cost of devising a mythical representation of some 'truth'. It would be rather the devising of a (possible) attempted *history*, (of) demand, (and) struggle in and against the economic, in and against the sexual, in and against language's and gesture's *gestik*.

This is what *Realism* can be defined as. This demands a theatre neither of habilitation nor of some rehabilitation.

For such a *Realism* certain codes of naturalism are necessary precisely to denaturalise, 'to make strange' (Shklovsky's Russian term *Ostranenie* in 1917).[47] This *making-strange* is towards the imposing of difficulty to force a reorder, not just of the *viewer–listener* ('subject') but of the *theatre-work* (those objects' meanings); that is the materialism of that process. The *process*, with its concurrents of subjectivities and those histories, must not be annihilated simply because of the (very real) danger of possible *fetishisations*-of-process.

The fourth-wall code of naturalism is necessary for a *gestik* whose 'enclosures' are rent. The caesura's forcing the viewer–listener to be imbricated in this process disallows the hold of a world, focused for the viewer–listener, in which he/she could simply function (and forget). The fourth-wall naturalism operates as a mode (not a metaphor) against which all non-naturalisms (its own included) produce themselves as conflict with the represented real. This is crucially opposite to the 'normal' functioning of the naturalistic fourth-wall theatrical conception, historically and now.

> One gasps, when Beckett explains this with a principle of the naturalistic theatre. . . . 'The piece [*Endgame*] is to be played as if there were a fourth wall instead of the footlights.'   (Michael Haerdter, 'Beckett inszeniert "Endspiel" ', *Theater Heute Jahrbuch* (1968) p. 92

> The machine is capable of learning, it improves itself. One tries to prove this: there is no difference between the human brain and a machine.   (ibid., p. 100)

> As to the ordered zig-zag-course of 6 and 4, and 4 and then 6, steps: 'Even if one [the viewer] does not register these steps consciously, they register themselves on the unconscious.' He [Beckett] compares this to the short-interpellations in films which are subliminal, for propaganda purposes; constant repetition forces them into the unconscious (*'laffreux irrationel'*).   (ibid., p. 102)

(Freud would say unconscious unpleasure forces constant repetition (*out*) towards decathexis and reification.)

On the whole please colder. Can we mix blue and gray?   (ibid., p. 102)

The above formulate the Beckettian *gestik*: the way that colour and the fourth-wall structure operate define Beckett's *gestik* without it being *peopled*. If Beckett's *gestik* is primarily non-anthropomorphic, that does not disallow people into the *process*. But it does not allow the over-determination by and of the human, something Brecht's theorisation of *gestik* did not comprehend as it functioned outside a notion of ideological reading/viewing/ listening/meaning-making. Thought and desire were seen as either at one, thus bourgeois ideology, or possibly in conflict, with various interpretations then vying with one another towards a resolution where one simply determines. But there was for Brecht never a Leninist *gestik*, dialectically materialist, of thought and desire beyond the telos of capitalist/Stalinist resolution. A dialectically materialist *gestik* can militate against the current 'polysemicity' of contemporary anti-feminism and anti-Marxism, the 'free' oppressions of sado-masochistic aesthetic–political violence.

How does the fourth-wall function in *Not I* or *Rockaby*? It is produced through the machined unstoppable of motion and speech (produced through the static/fragmentary/interruptive). Yet its hearing/seeing *difficulties* are never the coy pornography of the constantly suggestive; thus it is always uncomfortable, *outside* of a voyeurism, in a suspension-of-disbelief at once non-existent and so radically contradictory that it cannot pretend closure. Thereby it defiles contemporary structuralist and post-structuralist mechanics of the psychoanalytic-semiotic. It works as *a theatrical remnant*, the radically unambivalent demand producing itself as a *stare*; a stare acutely *at* the audience as constantly there and necessarily part of the process of meaning and meaninglessness-production. A stare simultaneously oblivious in the objective sense, not-there, *not* integrative as a transcendent pseudo-collectivity of class, sex, and other determinants with the usual aim of obscuring the political positions of all senses in a pseudo-sociality marked by nothing but

the cohesions of cultural perfection (or shared ennui). Refusing
determinants their determinance is materialist enough; it is all
that theatrical materialism is.

Palimpsestuality refers to parchment having been used twice or
thrice, the first marks having been erased: '*scraped again*, from the
Greek'; 'the original having been erased or rubbed out, to make
room for the second' (*OED*); '1856, Mrs Browning: "Let who says
'The soul's clean, white paper' rather say 'A palimpsest . . .
defiled' " ' (*OED*). The *clawing* Beckett wants for his works is not
merely some literary notion *of* the claw, it is the process as claw.
The text's ability to claw is the barrier to an ease, ill seen ill said.
In his monologues as described, enforcing a closured fourth wall
mise-en-scène as *gestik*, this occurs precisely in order to force
the contradictory scrape so uncomfortable and potentially
revolutionary; it opposes guising the surd in any manner that
would insure the investments of predetermined meaning. No
matter how nihilistic, the possibilities can be radical, nothing less
and not probably that, but not less possibly that.

'More'   (Beckett, *Rockaby*, p. 9)

In the face of this, what do we make of Lenin's fear more of the
mechanistic materialists than the idealists, whereas now we must
fear the reverse, an anti-Stalinist liberal allowance of the
bourgeois interest, defining all questions in terms that disallow
any answer outside of the current capitalist patriarchal
hegemony's adumbrations of site, technique, apparati, and end.

By example: the question of the movement of (the) Mouth in *Not I*
as pleasure. Pleasuring the self and the not only need but *want* to
deinvest the psychical from this is one process of *Not I*. In *Not I* the
showing of teeth is the 'quoting' of mouth, mouth quoting itself in
'stop'-moment, frozen wait. This is done by Billie Whitelaw by the
opening of Mouth, showing teeth fully, frontally, though gritted, in
an unhidden admission of physical pleasures of that bodily
function, its sexuality. The monologue rattles on, ten words per
second. Then stop, quote, continue speaking, stop, show teeth,
etc., then block the stoppage, return to Mouth's movement,
speech. It is always the Mouth present as apparatus to transform
a process *in* process. The language, the gesture, the look, and the

speed of the Mouth are not in this case suppressing the function of its process. It is never merely mouth *used*, vehicle for something else, alterior, communicated, out of process, out of hearing, out of sight, out of time.

It is possible to eat, chew, pleasure oneself, vigorously, whilst a similar vigour can be applied to not eat, chew, pleasure oneself or to eat, chew, and *not* pleasure oneself! *Use*, again, becomes the critical concept.

The *gestik* of Mouth is in relation to its minute size on stage, negating spectacle by the difficulties of location and locution. *Gestik* does change the dramatic function. 'Be honest in a dishonest world' is analogous to 'Be logical in an illogical one'. The question of the logic of language comes up here, and of languaged logic in the gestural. In this monological/gestural bypass, no suture is operated; a place is produced for the operations of the *work's* processes.

(See Illus. 19–21.)

The moving-forward of a hand in Godot, in *Footfalls*, in Karl Valentin's and Liesl Karlstadt's pieces, is to both emphasise a word, a point, a meaning, and to question it through the undermining possibilities of gestural questioning, where the questioning is given as the pull-back of assertion, undermining as in certain *dialect* (dialectic streetspeech), *emphasising and simultaneously* (hilariously) *contradicting*.

> offer it up plank it down . . .
> . . . the whole misery diagnosed undiagnosed misdiagnosed
> . . . we'll make sense of it . . .
> we'll put it in the pot with the rest . . .
> (Samuel Beckett, 'Ooftish', in *Transition*, no. 27, 1938)

This is an opening of possibilities by demonstrating (via a *personalisation* which denies any legitimising 'objectivity' its illusion) the colloquial's determination against the ideology of

[text continues on p. 212]

Illus. 19   (*Left*) Max Wall* and (*right*) Trevor Peacock as Didi and Gogo
in *Waiting for Godot*, Royal Exchange Theatre, Manchester, 1980

*'I am fascinated by Sam Beckett's mind . . .' (Max Wall, 19 March 1977, letter
to author)

Illus. 20 (*Left*) Winston Ntshona (Estragon) and (*right*) John Kani (Vladimir) in *Waiting for Godot*, Baxter Theatre Company, University of Capetown (1981), directed by Donald Howarth

Illus. 21 (*Left*) Karl Valentin and (*right*) Liesl Karlstadt in *Der Sonderling* (1929)

academic speech. What Bunraku is in earnest, certain streetspeech is,in supposed disearnest, namely the intrusion of the subject, and the *subject's guilt*. It is affirmation *and* negation, demand *and* question; it is statement *as* question, which is both an absence of any 'true'[48] and an obsessively paranoiac hystericising of truth. All representation is thereby questioned in its articulation; the claim is being made for a stylistic analogue in a different discourse, the colloquial.

In *Not I* the *gesture's* suppression of function works together with voice's suppressions, the negating-of-ululation. This latter persists in the work of voice plus memory, together with the latter's *inabilities*, which counter any imaginarily conjured figure's possible 'presence'. It is a come to end, comic through the running down and out (death) of both voice and gesture. Beckett's pieces have no end; Valentin could not end his pieces; but it is not a matter of not being able to find endings. Rather, no matter how the writer felt it or thought it, or the critics, the process of such monological discourse as Beckett's *Not I* or *Footfalls* or *Rockaby* is an inculcating by the structure of articulation: the structuring precisely of voice and memory, gesture and memory, and its inability, the work of that, and its constant countering and not countering of the figure's attempts, its processes, with no finality beyond that.

> Practice equals turning into a determinate product a determinate raw material. (Louis Althusser, *For Marx*, trans. Ben Brewster (London: Penguin, 1969) p. 166)

The 'product' so far described is precisely not a product, consumer-durable, in the theatrics described; but neither is it simply unendurable. Rather, the 'product' is a process, reification written out, thereby redefining 'product' and practice.

> Yes, I saw K.V. in a shabby cafe-theatre outside Munich. Evil days for him. I was very moved. (Samuel Beckett, letter to author dated 12 September 1972; the time referred to is 1938)

XXXV

Quote: Valentin and Karlstadt's 'Yesterday's Papers'

Repression

'Why?!'

Karl Valentin's *Lehrstück*/Context in History

Human Body and Language

Functioning

Slowness

'Yesterday's Paper'

MAN: Hey, did the man who wanted yesterday's paper get
it yet?

WOMAN: Yeah, I've given it to him.

M: Yesterday's?

W: No, today's.

M: But he wanted yesterday's!

W: I didn't have yesterday's so then I gave him today's.

M: When?

W: Today. I promised him yesterday's for tomorrow.

M: Me too; so you don't have to get him yesterday's,
because I'm getting him the same one.

W: Neither of us can get him yesterday's, because the
editorial offices don't have any left. So the man will
have to take one from the day before yesterday!

M: But the day before yesterday's won't be of any use to
him!

W: Well, if he anyway wants an old paper, then the day
before yesterday's is even older than yesterday's!

M: Some idea you've got! There might've been
something in yesterday's paper which wasn't in the

213

> day-before-yesterday's, something that isn't even in today's!

W: Well, well! That's what the man had said too, and then he bought today's from me, and then he said, 'Oh god, it's not in here!'. Probably it was in yesterday's! But what it was that was supposedly in yesterday's, that he didn't tell me!

M: Well that'll most probably be in yesterday's.

W: What?

M: What the man was looking for in today's.

W: That I don't believe since such things often aren't in the papers at all!

M: What kind of things?

W: Well you know, such secret things.

M: How do you know he's looking for secrets?

W: Well, if it wasn't any secret then he'd've told me what he's looking for!

M: What he's looking for! Wati! Wati! It's not a secret it's a sickness!! You can read about medicines in the paper too! Maybe it's in tomorrow's!

W: But you can't get tomorrow's yet today!

M: But tomorrow you can get today's!

W: But the man wants yesterday's!!

M: Oh, you're driving me crazy! The man was here *yesterday*, not today! And yesterday he wanted yesterday's, in other words in this case he wanted the day-before-yesterday's!

W: No! – the man only *assumed* that; he thought, if it isn't in yesterday's, then it could possibly be in the day-before-yesterday's.

M: You don't understand me! Let's say the man had come tomorrow, and wanted yesterday's paper, then today's would've already been yesterday's and yesterday's the day-before-yesterday's! In reality though the day-before-yesterday's would've been yesterday's; did you get that?

W: (*very loud*): Yes, not in the slightest!

M: (*grouchy*): Well that isn't of any importance! The man needs the paper that's printed what he's looking for.

W: Then he has to look in the day-before-yesterday's!

M: Well is it in the day-before-yesterday's?

w: Well how should I know, the man doesn't even know himself!

M: But if he doesn't know what's in it, then how should *we* know!

w: Of course he knows *what's* in it, only where it is, in which paper, *that* he doesn't know. To me he said, in yesterday's ... Hello! Hello! You, Mr! – hey, there he is – Mr! I couldn't get yesterday's paper, the one that has what you're looking for ...

MR: Oh, that's not so important – I just wanted to know the ticket-price at the Zoological Gardens! (Karl Valentin and Liesl Karlstadt, 'Yesterday's Paper', in Karl Valentin, *Gesammelte Werke* (Munich: Piper, 1981) vol. 1, p. 168)

Papa didn't write at his desk – he usually wrote in bed. Mama and I were his first-night audience. Even after the actual premier the pieces would be rewritten three or four times. Even if the best parts were pretty much kept to, there was still ongoing improvisation. (Bertl Valentin, *Und Zwar Sofort* (Munich: Piper, 1971) p. 61)

Immer denkt's in mir! (In me it always thinks!) (Karl Valentin, quoted in Bertl Valentin, ibid., p. 108)

I have fear of fear! and it's coming at me like a black cloud! (Karl Valentin, ibid., p. 111)

In fact he was very courageous, when it was a matter of enduring pain whose cause he knew. He only got nervous when he couldn't explain the causes. Uncertainty disturbed him. (Bertl Valentin, ibid., p. 111)

'Effect X' remains troubling if 'Cause X' is the problem, displaced onto 'Cause Y'. Repressing it and concentrating on something else not only means the wrong item ('Effect Y') is focused on, but as thereby the cause remains undealt with, it is therefore still functioning as cause unresolvable. The wrong item ('Effect Y') onto which it was displaced thus continues to obsess too, as *it* can not be solved, as its cause, 'Cause Y', was not the cause (of the obsession, fear, whatever) of 'Effect X'. The same goes for the continual effect of another cause ('Cause X'), unless the correct cause is resolved.

The living-through (living-*out*) of the process of that *angst*, and manifestations to counter it in paranoid language, monologue, gesture, in the face of the cause's undeterredness, maintains the repressed's functioning, the obsessions' continuances. Thus, for example, Valentin's question '*warum*?! [why?!]' interjected loudly and hastily *whilst* Karlstadt is speaking, situates the 'persona' of Valentin as a negative presence, countermanding *any* intended meaning. A 'why?!' spoken that way therefore *also* counters Karlstadt's specific, intended meaning without setting forth an alternative meaning, and thereby the other fictions of description which he, she, and we encounter. The speed of the spoken response '*warum*?!', which in other pieces is '*nein, warum*?! [no why?!]' or '*ja warum*?! [yes why?!]' in all three cases overdetermines through *speed* any *specific* positivity or negativity. So, (a) Valentin's presence is interjected, this technique thereby subjectifying discourse, taking it out of the hold of the imaginary world of *re*presented truth, and (b) his presence is interjected with a speed, a dynamic, which undermines any direct correspondence, or synchronicity, of his subjectivity with *what* is said. His *speaking* is in conflict with language's attempts to represent.

The dynamics cited belie the possibility for interpretation, at the primary level of the spectator's involvement and response, because within this dynamics it is impossible to exhume instantaneously what the represented meaning was that was so hurriedly, in such paranoiac resistance (*Abwehr*), taken issue with. On the structural level Valentin's '*warum*?!' is negation as negation. Valentin hereby poses the *Lehrstuck* ('Teaching-play') as a psychoanalytic politics wherein language is not given its hold; identifications split; the authority of language's dominant meanings is disallowed a synchronising authority and function. Such interrogations as those in Beckett and Wittgenstein, Gertrude Stein and H.D., remove language from an essentialist position of phallocentric truth's authority. The socialisation of the viewer–listener through a materialist usage of language is socially produced as such a rarity that such language-labour and its socialisation is a problem.

This materialist function of language is never outside of history; yet it is not directly engaged with its momentary context, as that would be to yet again assume that meanings are *not* made in history and its social context*s*, but are determined primarily by a happenstance context's specificity. Such a notion of 'specific context' believes nothing exists but the meaning momentarily projected onto any production, whereby anything can mean anything at anytime in any space. In that case meanings, paradoxically, are seen to pre-exist separate from *any* process, they simply get *projected*, any object of pleasure finally suitable; this reactionary system is suitable for much of academia. Opposition to this is a process *in* history: *process as history*.

> My name? ... Wedlpf ... What?! ... Wrdlpf!   (Karl Valentin, *Die Filme des Karl Valentin*, ed. Michael Schulte and Peter Syr (Munich: Piper, 1978) p. 103)

As to (b) the psychoanalytic functioning of negation, due to the *structure* of resistance via the human body's larynxial wedge: Valentin's *speed* of speech-intervention is aligned to a *slow* body. It is a body–mind separation which produces, in Beckett's work too, the *weight* of discourse, the gravity of the attempt of trying to resurrect what's left of the nothingness, the all, and discovering by that resurrection-attempt the impossibility of sublimating one discourse for another. There is no coherence of the two, the word and the act, or the intention and 'its' manifest, or the word and the thing. Language is a barrier, thus, but not *to* some 'true' or final perfection or essence (religious ignorance).

> On the buses in Ireland they'll cross themselves soon at the sight of a crucified pig.[49]

There is no *unmediated* access, communion, presence, or transsubstanciation, in or outside of language. Rather, language as problematics unsuppressable, the exigencies of *social* discourse.

Nothing is to be done away with in the interests of 'functioning'. Artifice, construction, process, meaninglessness, are produced always in relation to, and against, the ideological-political oppression of the given meanings of 'pure function'.[50]

That the dominant ideologies' readings and understandings of works of negative dialectics are often over-determined (by a will borne out of need) is understandable. Valentin's and Karlstadt's concretions are abstract philosophical materialism in the real, condensing the practices of modernism/post-modernism and social realism.

More on (b). That *slowness* is also a slowing-down of meaning; for example, someone asking for something and having it mis-understood by Valentin and Karlstadt over and over again, constantly getting it wrong, the *it* thereby becoming lost in the rage of wanting to get it right, which either never happens or when it happens finally, has lost its purpose. It is too late. It is, finally, non-sensical, an arbitrary construction which via that durated extension loses the cohesiveness of 'necessity', its micro-rational world-view (as when the newspaper, or the record, are 'not *wanted* anyway', or when the baker's laboriously worked-at frosted letter 'B' is painfully perfected according to Valentin's endless demands, and then with one lunge taken and eaten). Other than that, Valentin finds no way out, no way to end his pieces. They have no end.

XXXVI

Quote: Valentin and Karlstadt's 'In the Record Shop'

Quote: Valentin's 'The Aquarium'

The 'End'

Quote: Valentin's 'I Am a Poor Thin Person'

Quote: Valentin's 'The Loveletter'

Association

Quote: Valentin and Karlstadt's 'Theatre Tickets'

Hopelessness and Time

The Impossible

Gestik against Speech

Questions of Class in Valentin and Karlstadt

Material Practice, Turning Raw Material into 'Product'

'In the Record Shop'
  After Karl Valentin listens to various records, the saleswoman
  says, trying to sell him a record of Valentin and Karlstadt,
  'You'll like this one, a nice homey scene'. (*Heard from the record:
  voices, as follows*):
  KV: Clara, I can't find my glasses. Do you know where my
       glasses are?
  LK: I saw them lying in the kitchen yesterday.
  KV: What do you mean yesterday? An hour ago I was still
       using them to read.
  LK: That may be, but yesterday they were lying in the
       kitchen.
  KV: Don't talk such rubbish, what good is that to me if the
       glasses were in the kitchen yesterday?!

LK: I'm only telling you because you've already left them lying in the kitchen a few times.

KV: A few times! I've left them more often than that! I want to know where they're lying now!

LK: Well, where they are *now* I have no idea, I'm sure they'll be somewhere!

KV: Somewhere! Of course they're somewhere, but where?! Where is somewhere?!

LK: Somewhere?! That I don't know. I guess they're somewhere else!

KV: Somewhere else! Somewhere else is still somewhere!

LK: Oh don't babble such stupidity, somewhere else can't be at the same time 'somewhere else' and 'somewhere'! Every day this search for the bloody glasses! Next time just remember where you've put them, then you'll know where they are!

KV: But woman! Only someone who has no idea about glasses can talk like that. Even I, I think I know where I've put them, yet that doesn't help at all, as I can't *see* where they are! Because I can't see without my glasses!

LK: Simple! Just get another pair, so that you can search for the one with the other!

KV: Hm. That would be an expensive joke! A thousand times a year I misplace my glasses, if each time I needed a pair of glasses – the cheapest costs 3 Marks – that would be three thousand Marks worth of glasses each year!

LK: You sheep! For that you don't need a thousand pairs of glasses!

KV: But at least two. One shortsighted and one longsighted. No, no, I'd rather not even start with all that. Imagine, I've mislaid the longsighted ones and am wearing the shortsighted ones, but the longsighted ones are far off, so that with the shortsighted ones I can't see the ones lying at a longsighted distance!

LK: Then just keep the shortsighted ones on, and go so close to the spot where the longsighted ones are that you can see them with the shortsighted ones!

KV: But I don't know the spot where the longsighted ones are lying!

LK: The spot is obviously there where you've put the glasses!

KV: That's what I mean! I don't know the spot any more! I

just don't understand it! Perhaps they're in the case! That's it! That's where they'll be! Give me my case!

LK: Where's the glasses-case?

KV: Where the glasses are, they're in it!

LK: But the glasses aren't *always* in the case!

KV: Yes they are. They're always in the case. Well, not to be found!

LK: The case?!

KV: No the glasses!!

LK: Welllll. What do I see there. Just look at your forehead for a second!

KV: I can't see up there!

LK: Then touch up there! You've pushed the glasses up your forehead!

KV: Right, there they are! But unfortunately!

LK: (*very quickly*) What unfortunately?!!

KV: Without the case!!

LK: (*as saleswoman*) Did you like that disc?

KV: An optical disc has nothing to do with humour. I myself am a passionate glasses-wearer, I know what a catastrophe it is when one wants to read something and can't find one's glasses. I envy those people thousands of years ago before there were glasses, they didn't have to bother with them!

LK: (*as saleswoman*) But a thousand years ago there weren't any newspapers, so people didn't need glasses.

KV: True, newspapers didn't exist ...

LK: (*as saleswoman*) But the bible did.

KV: True, the bible did ... simple ... if someone couldn't read the bible without glasses, then someone who could see well read it to them!

LK: (*as saleswoman*) Wait, here I have something sweet about a dog.

(The piece continues with another KV/LK record). Much later:

KV: What does a record cost?

LK: Three Marks

KV: Now look, for three Marks I can buy a hat! And how much is a gramophone needle?

LK: (*showing him various types of gramophone needles*). A box like this is 60 pfennig.

KV: I'd only really need *one*. Don't you sell them by the piece?
LK: No, that is most certainly, most certainly not a possibility, that'd be some business!!!
KV: So, a box like that costs 60 pfenning. And that (*he points to the large gramophone with amplifier*), that costs 500 Marks?
LK: Yes.
KV: (*sees catalogues lying on the table, takes one, and asks*) You, what does a catalogue like this cost?
LK: That costs nothing! You get that for free, just like that!
KV: Just like that? So? Then I'll take a catalogue! (*He goes off, leaves the shop*).
LK: (*Standing at the shopdoor, watching him walk off*) Well, that does it!!![51]

The Aquarium

As we're speaking about the Aquarium, as I lived earlier – not in Spring, *earlier!* – in the Sendlingerstrasse, not *in* the Sendlingerstrasse, that would be laughable, one couldn't live *in* the Sendlingerstrasse, because the streetcars *constantly* drive through it, I lived in the *houses* in the Sendlingerstrasse. Not in all the houses, in one of them, in the one that is sort of stuck between the others, I don't know if you know the house I mean. And that's where I live, but not in the whole house, but only in the first floor, on the first floor, that's under the second storey, and above the paterre, like that, in between, and there's a stairway going up to the second floor, well it goes down too, the stairs don't go up, we go up the stairs, well one just says it that way.

And there I have, in the living room, where I sleep, I have an extra living room, where I sleep, and in the bedroom I live and in the bedroom I have for my private amusement an Aquarium, standing sort of in the corner, it fits wonderfully into the corner.

I could've also had one of those round Aquariums, then the corner wouldn't've been filled out. The whole Aquarium isn't bigger than this (*gesturing*), let's say these are the two glass walls, these are my hands, I'm just explaining it, so that you understand it better – and these too are two walls, and underneath is the floor, which holds the water, so that the water doesn't flow out the bottom when one pours it in the top. If the floor weren't there, on top you could pour ten, twenty, thirty litres, all of it'd come flowing through and out the bottom. It's a completely different matter with a birdcage. With a birdcage the walls are similar to an Aquarium, only with a birdcage they're not made of glass, they're wire. That'd be a huge stupidity if it'd be the same with an Aquarium, because then the Aquarium couldn't hold the water, the water would run out between the wires constantly. That's why everything is so wonderfully organized by nature! Yes! And in that Aquarium I have goldfish, and in the birdcage I have a bird; the other day I was plagued by some stupidity and I put the goldfish in the birdcage and the bird in the Aquarium!

Of course the goldfish kept slipping off the swing in the birdcage and the canary would have soon drowned in the Aquarium, but then I put the whole thing as it was and put the bird back in the birdcage and the goldfish back in the Aquarium where they belong!

Now the fishes swam happily around in the Aquarium, first up this way, then down that way, they swim differently nearly every day. The day before yesterday a Malheur happened to me, I saw that the fishes needed more water, and added a full pail of water, in the meantime that turned out to be too much, now the water was this high (*gesturing*) above the Aquarium, but I only noticed it the other day, and a goldfish swam off over the edge and fell on the floor, because in the room where the Aquarium stands, we have a floor underneath, and that's where it then lay, but only after it stopped falling.

Now, the fish didn't have any water on the floor, because we don't really have *any* more water in the room, apart from in the Aquarium. Then my housecleaner said, 'You'll see, the fish'll get broken on the floor down there, it'd be best if you kill the fish.' So that it wouldn't have to suffer so long, I thought to myself – do it with a hammer? In the end you'll hit yourself on the finger – so shoot it. But then I thought: In the end you'll miss, and it'll really start suffering, it'd be smarter, I said, if I just take the fish and carry it to the river and drown it.   (Karl Valentin, *Das Aquarium*, 1908)

The *end* is always a dead end in Valentin; it is neither beginning nor end, it is the interminable non-analysis of the verbaged. It is the impasse of the impossible end, the continued beginning, another routine, another difficulty constructed; impasse is the only ending not neatly fictionalised.

Filed, thus, are a series of incidents, produced as accidents; they are enacted, associated to language, but never concretely adequately measured or given over to the viewer–listener by language. This relies finally on the inescapable conclusion that the act is as much artifice as the word that tries to capture it.

The ceaselessness of materialist non-convergence of language and act motors the contradiction: *language* (as act) and *act* (as language unsufficed).

During these Valentin/Karlstadt pieces, the attention span is held to circumstances in conflict with, though not beyond, control, in a system the very opposite of suspension-of-disbelief. What is railed at in these anti-metaphysics is the lack of nature's or culture's cohering force, or goodness. Valentin's exasperated anger is the vehement refusal to relinquish the ideology of the first-person (as) subject. That non-relinquishing (surrounded by words and acts which refuse Valentin's desires!)[52] is a constant contract with the impossible, resulting in the release of laughter for the viewer–listener *and* resulting in the latter's equal lack of power and authority over cause-and-effect. The separation of cause from effect, as mythologised in these theatrics *and* as evidenced in concrete everyday petit-bourgeois existence represented as the basis from which Valentin and Karlstadt take their cue, functions as elaborate disharmony. It is the dualism of thought and act, word and meaning, desire and need, no sooner one thing said than another undone.

The *undoing* paralleled by the saying (speech) means the theatrics of Valentin/Karlstadt are not a series of snares for the viewer–listener, but the manufacture of the lack-of-synchronicity of day-to-day existence. All speech then becomes the demand to have what is not (here), elucidating the absence of the speaker's power, and speech's power: indisposed by speech. And the enactment of this problematic is outside any psychoanalytics, outside any *individualism*.

The (im)posture of death equals the End; but it is the endlessness of the discourse of endlessness here. Brecht liked the 'round' *Ein Hund ging in die Küche* ('A Dog came in the Kitchen'); he brought out its emphasis when recorrecting *Baal* (1922) in the early 1950s, after reading *Waiting for Godot*:

VLADIMIR: A dog came in –
    (*Having begun too high he stops, clears his throat,*
    resumes):
    A dog came in the kitchen
    and stole a crust of bread.
    Then cook up with a ladle
    And beat him till he was dead.

    Then all the dogs came running
    and dug the dog a tomb –
    (*He stops, broods, resumes*):
    Then all the dogs came running
    And dug the dog a tomb
    And wrote upon the tombstone
    For the eyes of dogs to come

    A dog came in the kitchen
    And stole a crust of bread
    Then cook up with a ladle
    And beat him till he was dead.

    Then all the dogs came running
    And dug the dog a tomb –
    (Beckett, *Godot*, p. 37)

> *I am a poor, thin, person.*
> Oh it's terrible it's true
> When a person's truly thin;
> I am thin, what pain,
> Thin as a soupbone.

What law must I've broken, that nature put me together so awfully. I just don't understand it, it can't come from my family, as my father weighs over three hundredweight, my mother over two hundredweight, and my sister married a freight manager! And of all people I have to be so thin! Well, now it's manageable, but you should have seen me earlier, right after being born, I looked like a salami. That's why I didn't need scales as a small child. . . . In spite of that, my father's proud of me, he doesn't like fat children, and just because of that, because I am so thin, he thinks so well of me. He says, fatter I can always get, once my sister's married. . . . In spite of which the thinness saved my life, when I was once in Africa, with the cannibals, these people-eaters caught me and wanted to roast me. They made a fire and undressed me – when they saw me undressed they all ran away, because they got the horrors, and my life was spared.   (Karl Valentin, 'A Poor Thin Person' in *Alles von Karl Valentin*, p. 14)

'The Loveletter'   January, the 33rd Munich 1925 1/2
Dear Darling!
With crying hands I take the pen to hand and write to you. Why haven't you written for so long, as you recently wrote that you'd write me, if I don't write you.
    My father wrote me yesterday. He wrote, that he wrote you. But you didn't write me a word about that, that he wrote you. If you'd written me a word about my father's having wrote you, I'd have written my father that you'd wanted to write him, but didn't have time to write, otherwise you'd already have written him. As to our writing it's gotten very sad, because you haven't written me as to any of the writings which I wrote you. If you couldn't write, that'd be something different, then I wouldn't write you, but you can write and don't write, when I write you. I'm ending my writing and hope that you'll finally write me, otherwise this is the last writing which I've written you. But if again you're not going to write, then at least write me that you don't want to write me, then at least I know why you never wrote me. Excuse the bad writing, I always get writer's cramp from writing, you of course never get writer's cramp, because you never write.
Love and kisses,
Your N.N.
(Karl Valentin 'The Loveletter', in *Alles von Karl Valentin*, p. 28)

In the works of Valentin/Karlstadt, association is used to deny association and negate it, to deliberate against the colonisations of language. Narrative possibilities and expansions are disallowed by the obsessive-compulsive insistences upon isolated detail, the meaning and usage of a single word-concept or thing-concept (the word *yesterday*; the misplaced glasses). The severe logical interrogations brought to bear force the reductiveness of the anti-narrative further; rather than narrative expansion we are faced with endless contraction. This systematic functioning in the works of Valentin/Karlstadt works against any concept of 'truth', as the endless interrogations do not allow any 'true answer' to maintain power and acceptability. There is always another denial, difficulty, interrogation, reduction. Language is used as a monological/dialogical *gestus* against the true; as such it is outside the moral tradition of the Judao/Christian icon and its patriarchal representations. In the Valentin/Karlstadt structure, sexual hierarchicalisation is abolished. It is thus a materialist practice at once encumbered constantly by the associative/narrativistic values of the history within which it (mal)functions *and* is dialectically posing their impossibility at every concert. The end of each word, each breath, each pause denies a harmonious finality, as the immediacy of misunderstanding is inscribed as soon as spoken, gesture-by-gesture, word-by-word. Thus this is an oxymoronic splitting of language both from its own uses as 'free exchange and communication outside of power' (the myth of ideological naturalism) *and* from its hinge-function in a mechanistic-humanistic teleology of some reified 'real' represented world.

FRAU   (Liesl Karlstadt): Hey, old one, just think, *just* as I was coming up the stairs I ran into our landlady and she gave me a present again – guess what it was.

MANN   (Karl Valentin): Don't be silly, just tell me.

FRAU: Well, two theatre tickets for *Faust*! – what d'you have to say about that?!

MANN: Thanks a lot! Why doesn't she go herself, that old bother?!

FRAU: Oh well, she probably just doesn't have the time.

MANN: Oh, I see, she doesn't have time, but *we* have to have time!

FRAU: Don't be so ungrateful.

MANN: Now it's really clear, the woman has something against us, otherwise she wouldn't have given the tickets to us, of all people.

FRAU: But she just wanted to do something nice for us.

MANN: She us?! Have we ever done anything nice for her?! Never!

FRAU: Well do you want to go? Yes or no?!

MANN: When does it start?

FRAU: I don't know. I'll go downstairs and ask her again.

MANN: Well, it probably starts at 7.30.

FRAU: But it's already 6.45, we'd never make it. But the theatres usually start later ... at eight o'clock.

MANN: Well, between seven thirty and eight they start.

FRAU: Well, not before eight o'clock, the theatres always start later; do you remember four weeks ago we were at the Frühschoppen and that started at ten.

MANN: What'll we do there?

FRAU: Don't think about it for such a long time, just come!

MANN: And we haven't eaten yet ...

FRAU: Dinner's ready.

MANN: I'll manage, combing'll only take me a second.

FRAU: You can do that later, now we'll just eat quickly (*she goes off*). (*The man takes a mirror and places it on the table, the mirror keeps falling down. The woman comes with plates and knives and forks.*)

FRAU: Well, let's get a move on. I don't believe you're doing that! Just set it up. (*The mirror stands, but only when facing the wrong way*).

MANN: I can't look into it that way!

FRAU: Turn it around then!

MANN: (*The man turns the mirror around, but again it doesn't stand up, it repeatedly falls down. The woman sets it up correctly for him. The man combs his hair*).

FRAU: Now I'd just like to know, what's there to be combed?! You can't make a part on a bald head! [*'Mordstrumm Plattn'*]

MANN: I'm still used to it from before!

FRAU: Just how can a person be so vain – for whom are you making yourself so pretty? I'm satisfied and no one else has to be.

MANN: Perhaps in the theatre a goodlooking woman will be sitting next to me.

FRAU: And of all things she'll be watching *you*? She'll be there to watch *Faust*.

MANN: But I mean during the break.

FRAU: (*goes and gets the dinner, a bowl with Kraut and Würstchen*).

MANN: That again!

FRAU: We've never had anything else!

(*Each plate receives one Wurst, Valentin grabs them both, takes a measuring tape out of his pocket, measures both, gives the smaller one to Karlstadt and keeps the longer one for himself; then both hastily dig into the Sauerkraut dish with their forks, which get intertwined, each pulls back hard to disentangle the forks, without result. Finally Valentin pries the forks apart with his knife. During this confusion he is looking at the barometer on the wall.*)

FRAU: Now my fork's bent, at least I know now who wrecks our forks! But eat quickly now, hurry!

MANN: It's unhealthy to eat quickly.

FRAU: You've got gall! (*She gets up and serves lots of Sauerkraut, onto his plate*).

MANN: (*Pushes it back angrily with his hand*). I'll take my own stuff!! (*He takes some Sauerkraut from the bowl. He then looks in the mirror*).

FRAU: Don't make such a fuss, while you're eating you don't *have* to look in the mirror.

MANN: Just then is when I've *got* to! Then one gets two portions! But what do we do with our boy when he comes home from work?

FRAU: I've thought of that already. We'll warm him some dinner, and before we go, we'll write him a note – just keep eating, I'll write it. (*She goes to get paper from the commode, and ink*). I'll write that we're not home.

MANN: That you don't have to write him! He can see it for himself! But you've got to write him that we've gone out.

FRAU: That's what I mean! I'll write him that we're not here because we're gone.

MANN: Write. Munich, the . . .

FRAU: No, I'll write: Dear . . .

BOTH: Um, what's his name?

FRAU: You as father ought to know the boy's name!

MANN: You as mother ought to know it all the more!

FRAU: Well, it's because we call him boy; well, what's his name?

MANN: Wait ... I'll ask the neighbour.

FRAU: No ... we'll figure it out for ourselves ... Jesus Christ! . . . oh ... Josef is his name. So: My dear Josef.

MANN: You can't write that, he belongs to me too you know.

FRAU: Then I'll write, our dear Josef, to keep you quiet. Our dear Josef ...

MANN: My dear Sir, our dear Josef ...

FRAU: Your food is in the kitchen at the oven, warm it up for yourself as it's already cold ...

MANN: It's December already.

FRAU: I mean the food – it's cold; and because we have to go to the theatre ...

MANN: Well we don't have to go if we don't want. . .

FRAU: Then I'll write may ... could, would ... should ...

MANN: Will ...

FRAU: But we'll be gone already by the time he reads the note.

MANN: Then write: have gone

FRAU: Should the theatre be finished, then we'll perhaps certainly come home. With best regards ...

MANN: Yours Most Sincerely. . .

FRAU: Your having-gone-out-parents as well as mother. . .

MANN: The mother's included when you say parents!

FRAU: Then I'll put a fullstop, otherwise the idiot will keep reading.

MANN: Now just add: should you prefer the food cold, then you don't have to warm it up.

FRAU: Otherwise it'll be too hot. There, we'll put that on the table. Or maybe he won't see it there right away – he usually enters through the door, so we'll put it on the floor there.

MANN: Then he'll stand on it with his dirty boots and won't be able to read it! (*He puts the letter on a side table, leaning against a vase*)

FRAU: That's no good, with that flowerbouquet, he'll think it's his birthday!

MANN: But it isn't!

FRAU: But that'll irritate him, so it's no good.

MANN: (*leans the letter against the mirror*): That's fantastic, now look, when he comes, he'll stand there, look into the mirror, and he'll think: what kind of a note is that? Then he'll see it.

FRAU: We look into it because we know that there's a note there, but he'll have no idea now about it if he doesn't look in!

MANN: That's the main thing, that he looks in.

FRAU: Yes but what if he doesn't look in, then we've put the note there for nothing.

MANN: Yes, well, hold on, I've got it. Now, write another note: When you get home, look into the mirror immediately!

FRAU: OK: When you come home, look into the mirror ... immediately ... then you'll see something. I've written it. So, now we've wasted so much time with all this writing, it's almost 7 o'clock, it's just as well the theatre starts at 8.

MANN: At 7.30 it starts.

(Karl Valentin and Liesl Karlstadt, 'Theatrevisit', in *Alles von Karl Valentin*, pp. 472–5)

The repetitive difference of reattempted feasance is given here via the perturbing absence of any possible security in the empirical. Thus *any* decision has *as* little hold over the consequences and manageability and *success* of its enactment as any other, thereby rending as hopeless the sureness of a universe which such a decision could give its subject and object: hopeless but not useless. At some point one's subjectivity takes a position without though having to see it as *true*; it is a stop to indecision. The political is a dialectical engagement against overwhelming odds against defeatism and decadence, and, when countering oppression (separate from any 'rights' or morality), against consuming (and being consumed by) the given as is.

Many uses are manufactured from the space in which the narrative-attempt is taking place, but none *hopefully*, none in any probability of the possible. The being-on-time/being-in-time, is no more probable (though possible) than that the boy sees the note. The constructions of fear produce such effects of paranoid articulation of order and ordering, to no avail. All this is an availing itself of the multifarious permutations of its process, other

than which an earlier dead-end would result. That only happens
when the piece is deemed over, and the artificiality of that decision
is foregrounded. The piece ends when it is realised that it is, in any
case, the wrong *day* for *Faust*, though not the wrong *time*. That
which is *right* has, finally, no place in the Valentin/Karlstadt
universe; the impossible is the motor of the apparatus of the
Valentin/Karlstadt process of figuration and disfiguration of plot.
It is not as if the possible and probable were in conjunction
denied, but rather, that producing that conjunction is a
narrativised fiction, *simultaneous* valorisation and impossibility, the
attempt towards which both motors and empties each scene.[53]

The *gestik* of each sequence, each 'take', with its ostensible
contents, plays a part in the meanings which complexly produce
laughter. But it is *not* a matter, simply, of the gesture, for example,
being of a 'throwaway'-expression *against* a particular line of
speech. Thus the gesture is not made subservient to the thread of
speech-continuity. Nor is the thread of speech continuity made
subservient, diminished in relation to the laughter-producing
gesture. *Gestik* is not simply gesture. But *gestik* in Valentin/
Karlstadt dialogues functions to naturalise, not to *de*naturalise. It
functions to distanciate, but here, unlike in the works of Brecht
and Beckett, through the naturalisation of the scene, its
'realistic-ness', the lapidary casuistry of the Bavarian petit-
bourgeoisie. The latter is the group naturalised to the Valentin/
Karlstadt theatrics, the group laid off, dispossessed of the
property acquired by class and culture. The home as produced in
the *mise-en-scène* of Valentin/Karlstadt is only nearly a kitsch,
petit-bourgeois home; it is not one with plastic flowers but with
pride of place and pride of property alienated from power and
authority. The images' semiotics foreground themselves forcefully
and constantly in the absence of a theatrically stable unity of sex,
class, position-in-the-world, position-in-language; Valentin and
Karlstadt's *gestik* is to function against the petit-bourgeois
surround nevertheless without a given coherence of stolid
subjectness and ego; the attempt (dialectical and dialecticising) is
always frustrated. The loss of the fictive unity, being-in-the-
world, in power and authority, *and* the inability of new fictions and
strategies by Valentin/Karlstadt to over-determine their loss of
the petit-bourgeois (fictions of) power, permeates their modes of
behaviour, the breakdown of which (in the absence of a binding,

cohering, ideological imaginary) produces in the audience a communal laughter at powerlessness and the impossible, at Valentin/Karlstadt and at oneself and one's social space.

> Und sie sitzen ernst und lachen sich selbst aus [And they sit earnestly, and laugh at themselves]. (Brecht, commenting on Valentin/Karlstadt's audience, *Das Grosse Karl Valentin Buch*, ed. Michael Schulte (Munich: Piper, 1974) p. 91)

The fragile hold by a class onto its precarious power-relational fictions (in language) produces an anxiety-effect in the audience, contradictorily constituted as it may be. The audience exists as ab/*surds* in relation to power over space, time, language, narrative, social relations and anything conclusive of anything but the redundant non-capitulation to the capitulable. The audience as the you, I, is not constitutive of (in the sense of primary to) the materiality of the text or the specific social relations presented; the social that theatre is and the social that monologue is, are the primary materiality of the specific theatric social relations. The only non-idealist, historical way in which to conceptualise and theorise the relation of the process *theatre* is one in which context is not fetishised. The move of the viewer to the text is both constituted and constitut*ing*. The uses of language, its meanings, have meanings within the culture and history of their time, and have other meanings in different places and times not because the time and the place outside of the theatric-material is over-determining, but because it is not. Those material meanings, in other words, in another time and place, in another culture, are a *different material history* to begin with, prior to any specific 'contexts' of difference.

How is this a practice, i.e. turning a determinate raw material into a determinate product? Is the product the material in the crude sense, or the material of laughter, or the material of efficiency's impossibility? Certainly what is expostulated is that exchange is, here, impossible; use is all that can be given or asked for. Nothing increases in value, here; no amount of work (labour) produces an artifact, commodity, which can be exchanged and to which value, and surplus value, have 'accumulated'. There is in that sense no allowance for the (petit)-bourgeois' *hope*, nor for hope sublimated onto movement 'up' the ladder of class. It remains an impossible enterprise. What we are left with is the production for use, for *its* effects, as a laboriousness which itself is a materialist dialectic of the non-metaphysic *of* labour and its power, and the relations *in* labour of language.

The '*Plumpes Denken*' ('clumsy thinking') of Brecht, Beckett, Valentin and Karlstadt makes weighty the invisible – it produces laborious relations for probable (though by no means therefore necessarily possible!) *use*.

Ladders are taken away as soon as used. Each moment-to-moment move produces determinate effects, laughter, anxiety, waiting, insecurity, etc. Is such a material practice social, other than mere laughter-production? Is it all mere presence, or is there use to this? It must be carefully noted that mere happenstance presence opposes interventative presence; productive *use* opposes us*age* in which process is lost. Thus the concept of *presence vs usage* is important here, calling for lack of knowledge, lack of illusionist inculcation into the fictional, lack of anything but the theatrically laboured material, for literary thinking, theatric thinking, dialectic thinking, philosophical thinking, political thinking, etc.[54]

XXXVII

Quote: Karl Valentin's 'Letter to a Theatre Director'

'Clumsy' Thinking and Petit-bourgeois Ideology

The Social Real/Against Seamlessness/the Audience

'Letter to a Theatre Director' (written 1934)
Munich, September 1934
Dear Herr Direktor!
If I allow myself to criticize yesterday's performance, then surely you can permit me to express my impressions. You have actually yourself to thank that yesterday a performance took place in the almost new *Volkstheater*-theatre, even more so as in the afternoon one wasn't yet sure whether in the evening definite premiering could take place, yet you managed it, with steadfast energy and a will of steel, to transform a down and out theatre into a jewel, even the Herr Mayor was to be seen amongst the guests. Above him, in the fourth row, an old schoolfriend of my humbleness amused himself similarly at this wonderful play, he who was happier about the two complimentary tickets than about the play itself, which isn't hard to understand, as he also has already just like the 'Hauptmann' in the play, embezzled not only in dollars but in pounds of pain. I myself don't want to practice criticism of the play, as I'm not justified in doing that, as an ex carpenter and vegetable merchant – but it was good – gooder it shouldn't have been, otherwise it'd have been too good, and with that one coddles the audience that is present in the auditorium, then when the next following play is not as good, I mean not good at all, ungood, then one can't make good anymore so easily. The only thing I do have to add was at the end the sudden end. Even though the whole audience assumed (me too, of course) that now the Hauptmann was going off to kill himself, it still was a

235

terrible shock. One old lady behind me lost her dentures from the hollow of her mouth out of pure shock, and it fell unfortunately into the hands of the young woman sitting next to her, and she thought they were her own and shoved them into her mouth; naturally she immediately noticed that there wasn't any more room as she had hers in. It would only be a suggestion of mine, if just before the end from behind a curtain a man would step forward to the ramp and in a short speech explain that the honourable audience should get ready for the pistol-shot to come – or couldn't one just leave the end off, and the Hauptmann could poison himself with Veronal? Then the man could save himself the explanation, as the audience then couldn't get shocked, and such unlovable events such as the one with the dentures would be once and for all time banished from the world of theatre. That you have only bottled beer in the refreshment room is a disgusting thought for a *Münchener*, but probably not to be avoided, as the breaking of the kegs during the performance would make too much noise.

Terrible directorial mistakes were noticeable in the play. At the point where the young banker Raaz is sitting in a highly modern room with steel furniture and a telephone, the young man's wearing a bowtie made of Plastron, the way my great grandfather wore it when he went for his first day of school as a child. You, honourable Herr Direktor, have put so much in the New Theatre – go buy Raaz a modern tie, the September 1934 model instead of one from January 1866.

It's not to be missed that in this play there's lots of phoning (even if only faked), but in any case yesterday the audience was insulted that the telephones on stage were finished and the new telephone booth in the anteroom of the theatre is without a phone! When will there finally be help in this matter? Other than that everything was wonderful, especially the new theatre-furniture, like the expensive carpets in the auditorium. It's too bad if this wonderful floorcovering gets used up by the audience. If I were you I wouldn't let anyone in.
Love and Kisses
Your
Karl Valentin.
(Valentin, *Gesammelte Werke*, p. 409)

The 'clumsiness' with which he allows himself to say what isn't to be said, to break the rules of social behaviour, has to do with a slow, gruff, Bavarian 'characteristic' which insists on knowing, in apparent transcendence of class and sex, of matters which are not one's own socially sanctioned areas of knowledge. The varying and unapprehendable status of art in relation to the demeaned social status of the petit-bourgeoisie's non-aesthetic realm, forces in Valentin's work a critique *of* the Bavarian petit-bourgeois' critical position, with nothing but its own laughableness as a substance and rationale. The audience must thus perforce laugh at itself in that Bavarian context, in both its assumption of cultural power and knowledge in the face of its representative's (i.e. Valentin's and Karlstadt's) obvious and highly stylised and recognisable ignorance, *and* in its refusal to be condescended upon (by certain cultural class-pretensions).

The audience for the work of Valentin/Karlstadt was contradictory; it could never merely consume contradiction, though, because of the way the Valentin/Karlstadt process worked. The social fabric of different classes, at moments 'united' via Bavarian ethnicity and the denial of class and sex difference, made Valentin/Karlstadt popular, yet this was not at the expense of Valentin/Karlstadt's materially defined subject and class position as outside, powerless, *impossible*. And it was for a unification as *that* that the audience's ethnicity was utilised. Thus it could also never become a matter of some 'resolution', neither through an assumed 'education' of one segment of an audience, nor through a de-elevation and exclusion of another segment of the audience. Such resolutions, assimilations to power, were denied. What was worked through in the Valentin/Karlstadt pieces was each time an aesthetic production insisting on a process of conflict-enactment *in situ*, in such and such a time, in such and such a place.

Seamless consumption is thus made difficult, then impossible; this is due to the real exigencies of the social-real of the audience and the hilarity of its conflict with the identities given to it in the Valentin/Karlstadt enactments, identities which never succeed. In 'The Letter to a Theatre Director' the production of absurdity is the result of comparing the effect of an event in the play with the shock-effect in the audience of a suicide on stage: thus play and

audience are at odds, and Valentin's language here does not let
that become the repressed of culture. This is a very real theatrics, a
socialising theatre, which is of no small use in realising the
necessity of not over-valuing the cultural artifact in its
hierarchicalised position within culture (the play referred to in the
'Letter'), whilst at the same time disallowing ignorance any
legitimacy as criticism. Thence the laughter produced by the
circumlocutions and assumptions of Valentin as letter-writer
from one class-position, to the theatre director of another assumed
class, the represented theatrics referred to again of another: the
codes of all three are used, then presented as always in conflict
with one another. The hierarchicalisation of such socialised codes
is refused; the 'subject' (Valentin or Karlstadt) as socially difficult
is materially positioned against 'the' social. The imaginary unity
of subject and object is smashed.

Valentin was hated by Leon Feuchtwanger, in whose book *Success*
he is lambasted, as much as Brecht, in the persona of Pröckl, is
heroized. Feuchtwanger was Brecht's first, and main, champion,
and a leading intellectual left writer and critic in Munich. His
contemporaneousness with Valentin/Karlstadt allows one form
of negative reaction to them.

XXXVIII

Quote: Leon Feuchtwanger, *Success* (Fictionalised Valentin/Karlstadt)

Slowing Dowing and Speed, in Valentin/Karlstadt, *Footfalls*, *Not I*, etc.

'Content'

Structure and Repetition

Science?

Burlesques' Asynchronicity

Lack of Narrative

The Return of the Same, Stein, H.D., Beckett, Valentin/Karlstadt

The simplest things became complicated problems. One couldn't manage it with words. Besides, one had two instruments to play, and one couldn't manage it with hands only, nor with feet, nor with one's tongue. It was a difficult world to live in. The only thing to do was to sit there sad and busy, a little obstinate too, and impenitent, for one had one's own thoughts. But the others either didn't or wouldn't understand them. For example, one thought of a bicyclist, and whoop! there was a bicyclist rushing past. Now, that was remarkable. But the others wouldn't admit that it was remarkable. Yes, they said, oh yes, my dear chap, if you had thought of an aeroplane, for instance, and it had been an aeroplane that flew past, that would have been remarkable, if you like. But it *wasn't* an aeroplane, Himmell Kreuzakra! it was a bicyclist. And then there were the instruments, the drum that always had to be played when one was busy with the violin, and there was that man on the stage hammering and hammering,

239

and one couldn't let him go on without a word of advice, and there was the conductor's tie that one couldn't let come undone, and there were the thoughts that it was hopeless to explain, but which one had to persist in explaining. The problem about the bicyclist that one couldn't forget. It just wasn't an aeroplane, it was a bicyclist. . . . The strange thing was how the simple pathos of this comedian reduced all the spectators to the same level. Their individual joys and sorrows disappeared. No more did Johanna think of Krüger, nor Herr Hessreiter of his fatuous, long-bearded gnomes and gigantic toad-stools, nor Minister Klenk of certain imminent and important changes in personnel, nor Privy Councillor Kahlenegger of the last annoying attacks on his theory about the stuffed elephant. As their heads followed in unison the comedian's movements, so their hearts were moved in unison by malignant delight at the struggles and failures of the cantankerous creature on the stage. All the other diverse interests of the thousand intelligences crowded in the hall were submerged by a single burst of joy over the misfortunes of the painted, gloomily labouring clown.   (Leon Feuchtwanger, 'Hierl, the Comedian, and his Public', in *Success* (Munich and London: Martin Secker, 1930) pp. 209 and 213)

Pathetically he stood there, with his bored hollow-cheeked face, gaunt and sullen in his long slip-shod drawers, drinking his beer and blinking at his partner, grumbling steadily the while. At last he suffered himself to be led to the tramway; for although he made good money he was very stingy, and shrank from the luxury of a taxicab. On the platform, he wedged himself close to his companion, for contact with strangers worried and upset him.   (ibid., p. 216)

Hierl is Valentin. Hierl's act is related as one which unifies the audience, but with such biting satirical politics on the part of Feuchtwanger that the implication (and simplification) is that this individualist performer Hierl is the cause of the illusion of classlessness amongst the audience and, in direct causality, that Hierl collaborates with Nazism and the audience's potential or crypto-Nazism. In fact, Valentin was always an anti-Nazi. One of his routines, seemingly 'spontaneous' but not, was performed when SS officers entered the cabaret during his acts. He would stare at them, salute in the Nazi fashion, arm outstretched, shout

Illus. 22   Karl Valentin and Liesl Karlstadt

'Heill!!!' then 'Heil! Heil! ehh, uhh, Heil, uh ... what's his name again?!', the audience roaring with laughter. Also, he did not work during the war years, a kind of semi-self-imposed exile of silence, whilst remaining in his beloved Munich. The story goes that he kept a photograph of Leon Feuchtwanger above his toilet, for scatalogical reasons.

> Ich bi'ka antisemit, aber'n Feuchtwanger, der ka mi mal! [I'm no anti-semite, but Feuchtwanger can kiss my ass!]

(See Illus. 22 and 23.)

The speed with which the foot falls in *Footfalls*, the speed of the moving of Mouth, the one hour slowness reading four pages in *A Piece of Monologue*, the Valentinesque '*why*?!' interposed with a suddenness unexpected, and the Bavarian drawl which slows down expectation or represses it (in a complex movement of neither denying expectancy nor utilising it in the narrativisational teleology of expected conclusions) forms the work of play. The time to take its time and play its part in the function of meaning in the text, and the function of interpellations of an audience, is a foisting which remakes the audience; a different convention had at first been expected.

Slowness or its inverse high speed allows for a convention with which a spectator can both attempt to synchronise as to its general and knowable *form* and be constantly asynchronous to in terms of any assumption of a meaningfully conventional continuum ('in such and such a style, with such and such a speed of delivery', etc).

Content is not a stated concept here, as it would read as that which fills up the form, whereas what is meant is that which makes and breaks meaning, not within but against. This posits neither transcendental nor transcendant possibilities, but the positioning of each moment in the history of its process, whilst *not* separating structure in such a manner as to mean that it could have its own set of significations *in vacuo*. A structure having 'its own set' of significations is patently inoperable as to its meanings/ meaninglessnesses, without recourse to *a* relation (synchronous, asynchronous, desynchronous) to its signified concepts. *Concepts*: meanings given, meant, in the momentary transparency of the

Illus. 23   Karl Valentin and Liesl Karlstadt

word's placement in the convention of narrative fictional/factual discourse, as in: a house is burning *means* such and such. Categorical knowledge of a *minimum-intent* is expostulated via such transparent language usage (communication). The structure invariably, *finally* (when speaking as if such a phrase, *x*, means such and such) is neither neutral nor can be seen as 'addable' (thus somehow amenable to 'changing meaning'), but suppressed (consciously) and repressed (unconsciously) *in the ideological interests of being able to speak* (as above) *a phrase as if it were outside of (its) structure* (or as if it were natural) in relation *to* its structure. What this is is a naturalisation of the 'absence' always already unattributed, though not unattributable, of structure.

Endless repetition/reiteration in the works of Valentin/Karlstadt, and Beckett, thus can lead to the asychronous relation of the 'content' to the structure, but only when the two are seen absolutely as *co*present, empirically and theoretically. This is not just a strategy or tactic (it is that too) in the 'philosophy/politics/ideology of language-discourse' but rather the result of culturally specific language-use.

Structure and content as elucidated above are really a euphemism for *form* (giving validity under *these* conditions to another term, *content*, and opposing it to form leads to the defunct necessities to continue the debate religiously, against a process of materialism). *Form* as defined here solves a particular unending problem, as, for example, entropy solves certain problems for a closed system (Gödel, Godin, *Godot*). Matter is lost, the world will end in four billion years (or sooner!). That is a scientific fact. In fifty years, other scientific facts may exist realigning the concept universe, its entropicity, or other entropies.

> I venture to call Kafka's stories latent grotesques. The flywheel of an obsession has taken hold of thinking and continues to rotate until its end, in the void. We have reached a turning-point in the conceptual history of the term grotesque. Its reduction to the fantastically comic [which] was ultimately to lead to its identification with . . . the burlesque (Burlesk-Komisches). (W. Kayser, *The Grotesque*, trans. V. Weisstein (New York: Columbia University Press, 1981) pp. 150 and 103)

In terms of the relation to time and asynchrony, Beckett's and Valentin/Karlstadt's burlesques coincide at times. The theoretical model of asynchronicity in a dialectical/materialist process allows for language discourse and gestural discourse to procede along definitions not aligned to nor maligned by some narcissistic need. The rough, clumsy, *time* Beckett's *Rough for Radio* (1975) signals collapses in an irreversible humoristic. *Who* is being spoken *to* is always in question; the same goes for its uses of plastic conventions. The forward movement narrative demands is obliterated, and therewith its *reversibility*. Except for Valentin/Karlstadt's, Beckett's and Stein's dead-ends, narrative is predicated upon reversibility.

What is equally important is that a lack of narrative is not somehow *per se* an absolute function against suspension of disbelief The temptation to the true, which both 'fiction' and 'documentary' encode (truth, beauty, desire, caesura-lessness, etc.), is not so much determined only by narrative/ narrativisation, but rather cannot be *necessarily* opposed by its lack. Thus lack of narrative is no guarantor or authority for a position outside of the imaginary's hold over you by an it, language, image, structure.

A paragraph by Gertrude Stein may be a force against the narrative hold (a bourgeois patriarchal economy) subjecting and subjugating an implicit reader in its formation. But the abstract, and abstraction, are not necessarily productions of literalisation/ the literal. The prose and the poetics of Stein, H.D., Beckett, some of Joyce, some of Kafka (*Betrachtungen*) are not by their *general* conventions of necessity literalised materials of the process of their techniques, functions, apparati. Rather, their *specificity* functions in determinate instances as such. Auteurism for this reason is a fiction too: one work by one artist can and must be oppositioned (or not) to another by same which in its general aesthetic outlines may be 'the same'. The specific work has a structure which militates for, against, etc., determinate functions, responses, aesthetic/political/psychoanalytic effects, affects, etc. The return of the same in the quick, sharp, clipped, stopped, phrase projects suddenly another subjectivity as a wedge where there was a semblance of continua (in Stein's *Tender Buttons* (1914), H.D.'s *Hedylus* (1928), Beckett's *How It Is* (1964) or Valentin's *Nein* and *Der Regen* (1920s).

XXXIX

Quote: Re-quote, *A Piece of Monologue*

Quote: David Warrilow on Acting/Speaking the Latter

The Slip

Duration, and Farce

Viewer (Male/Female)

The Anti-narrative

Moving Time/Regress/Anonymity

Anonymity

> Loved one ... on his way ... her way ... 30 seconds ... fade ... gone ... stands there staring beyond into dark ... whole again ... note ... no such thing ... as whole ...   (Beckett, *A Piece of Monologue*, p. 78)

The gaps in *A Piece of Monologue* as spoken: 2 seconds each; 6 pages equals one hour's speaking. In *Not I*, 6 pages equals 11 minutes' speaking).

> ... a stumbling block often in dealing with Beckett's work is to involve oneself with psychology whereas the language itself is such powerfully compressed psychology that the only way to treat it is like either music or pure sculpture; if you treat the words as being sculptural and you deal with the sounds of each one, what I find when I do that is that it starts to have emotional repercussions on me *without* my necessarily *getting involved* in known personal references.   (David Warrilow (actor/speaker of *A Piece of Monologue*), in conversation with the author, December 1980, in New York)

(See Illus. 24.)

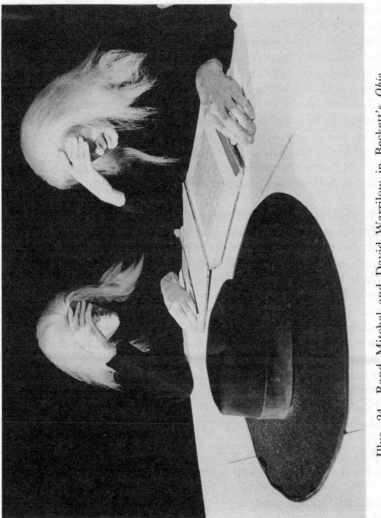

Illus. 24 Rand Mitchel and David Warrilow in Beckett's *Ohio Impromptu* (1983), directed by Alan Schneider

Max Wall slips on a banana-skin (in *Krapp's Last Tape*), the Bunraku-like figure helpless in its fall whilst willing; this music-hall comic is in this play '*acting-for*'/enacting for, the audience. He is not a psychologisable 'human' but an apparatus whose function will be to slip. The slipping/looking-at-the-audience is simultaneous: fixing of the look and its impossibility, the point-of-view towards you, and from you. Your need to follow the usual star (Max Wall) producing the usual (laughter). The latter is caused by Max Wall's/Krapp's loss of the figment, and the concretion, of being whole, in control. The control of the substance 'body' is lost, as is any self's adequate reassurance thereof. At the same time, the characterisation by known-quantity Max Wall and his music-hall history disallows any to-be-identified-with 'loss of self' (complications for suspension-of-disbelief notwithstanding!). It is less a sadism, more a collusion. That is the contract between actor and audience here.

The tension (investment) is in the duration played prior to the slip; the release in laughter is at the expense of the performer, as the voyeur is always again in the position of power no matter how much he/she is manipulated *by* the object of the gaze, i.e. Max Wall. The collusion with the audience, and the audience's with the actor, does not mean there is an essential psychoanalytical equality when an enactment releases laughter and guffaw. Yet in *such* a performance* nothing of any personal sentimentality of the 'story' of Krapp maintains itself, it is all *vis à vis* the possibility of objective and subjective fissure and breakdown, and of the impossible contract constantly renegotiated to continue the characterisation and its non-slippage. The 'material' is thus transformed to this, from what was 'The Story of Krapp's Last Tape'.

More likely than not in patriarchy a male viewer will respond to the unavoidable demands of language through the female Mouth in *Not I* with the kind of fear and despair which in 'life' is produced by and produces systems of power and authority aimed at relegating that woman's language to irrelevance, or to 'personalize' it, or to make it a hysteria, or to concoct a structure for it as a wall against the force of its discohering power. The

---

*Max Wall's is the complexly, precise, perfect one.

desire will be to more likely than not enforce reactive/reactionary codes for the reproduction of those (dominant) power-relations most consumable and reproducible, i.e. least harmful to the structure as is. Yet the strategies to reconstruct and reproduce systems of power and authority if not reproduced *revolt*. Sex can never absolutely determine the product, any more than an intention can cover its effects, but likelihoods exist, as they construct positions, and come from such constructions in culture, history, ideology, polemics, theory, politics.

Each sex's problematics is established; the solution which certain of Beckett's works pose operates in a way that does not reproduce the hegemony of dominant power-relations. The fragmentation spoken by Billie Whitelaw in *Not I* is spoken through a voice that is separate from any humanisation of, and by, a full figure. That disembodied cathexis is not a necrophiliac passion but rather a 'dehumanisation' liberating the female voice from the ideology of the essential, wholeness, *body*, the 'feminine'. *And thereby is constituted the voice of a female as not the biologistic female voice*; it is not 'woman'. A mode of address is produced (always via the *specific* actress) which no longer pretends that an ostensible figure must be metaphorised, as symbol for the caricature: hysterical, lonely, passive, outside language, humiliated, anti-intellectual, resigned, etc. The possibilities for an audience given by the theatrics of *Not I* are two-fold: either *leave*, or work with this no matter how fracturing (for good or bad) of the expectations that you operated within (whether you expected satisfaction(s) is another matter). Male and female viewer will thus, more likely than not, enter this production process differently.

The staged fragment is never *in* a scene, but making a scene. The scene's reduction: short sentence, speech as much as silence, uneffaced movement as laborious, head-on at the you, unhumanised unnaturalised slowness and /or speed. If, finally, the anti-natural is what the viewer–listener, as male, is contracted to, the contract is for loss of power and authority, a disenfranchisement of identities for the duration of this theatrics. For the audience as female, it is a fracturing of expectations, but not a loss of power and authority; rather it is 'the power of a woman's speech and gesture as materially dialectic' (though it is the loss of the illusion of certain male-defined forms of power and powerlessness which naturalistic representations had functioned to maintain).

Narrative is evicted, again and again, whilst being simultaneously the last pretence for that theatrics through which the operations outlined above can materialise. Narrative is the last pretence, whilst anti-narrative attempts persist here. If one function of the artist, producer of writings, paintings, textile pieces, films,[55] sculpture, music, performance, poetry, theatre, etc., is simply to *work* via experiment and theory, then one mode of the work of such description can be a practice of non-regression. Whence a kind of infinite regress, by a relativistic trace of entropy and anonymity, making difficult time's seamless 'forward'-movement. Yet the anonymity of a materialist work must be *produced*; simply absenting the traces of the artist for *a priori* 'anonymous' texts is to deny the production process in the interests of a crude mechanistic materialism that does not anonymise authorial 'truth' but simply represses it. The instruments of production, the apparatus-in-use, have specific objective and subjective histories and specific contradictions and effects in the material of the aesthetic/political (*material* ideologies, and *ideological* material).

What we are left with after all is said and done is not any more the question, because the inextricable dialectical object is now no longer in stasis, *and* no longer an energy somehow outside of subjectivity and its real objective histories. That this may be the end of reproduction is another matter. The limitless recourse of the viewer–listener's ideological intercourse produces nothing so much as so little seen as much. It is, though, not the little to regret, just the seeming muchness. The consequent procedures of the constant erasure of succour might lead not to wishes' consumptions but to theatre not prepossessed. The work inculcated thereby may produce effects of negativity, denial, silence, loss, lack, regress, even, but the material (notwithstanding attempts at its annihilation) retains its tissue.[56]

Notes

1. *Oxymoron*: in this concept, each portion is persistently weighted against an other. Thus the 'unity of opposites' must be understood without any concept of balance or harmony. Additionally it is to be understood without the possibilities of an interpretation leading to the choice of one or another (of the) contradictory positions to 'end up' with. Thus it is a matter of oppositionality *per se*, rather than a given and another against that as 'different'. The contradiction then inculcates a position to be made and taken rather than simply a 'choice'. The clash of opposites forces a result, and inherent in the concept of oxymoron is that of the *closeness of opposites*. Still a position *is* taken, is a product, is the specific effect and affect but always, even then, contradictorily and in *closeness* precisely to its opposite; it is never an autonomous finality, which the individualistic concept 'choice' would denote.

    Equally, it is not equivocal which of the 'two' opposites is positioned in and through one (the subject: *you*). What in the Karl Valentin/Liesl Karlstadt pieces is termed '*dummer Gegensatz*' is precisely in order to force thought about a specific referent's *function* and productive force. Valentin's 'and what if it doesn't get dark?!' when in dialogue about fireworks at the Oktoberfest, forces thought about the function of the Feuerwerk, about 'lighting up the sky', about the judgement of time in relation to 'when it is time to start the fireworks', about the definition of night (by time, by colour) etc.

    > Ask of all-healing, all-consoling thought
    > Salve and solace for the woe it wrought.

    Chamfort's eighteenth-century anti-theses (six were translated by Beckett for the Italian journal *The Blue Guitar*, Messina, 1975) are examples of the use of oxymoron.

    Ingenious reflexion belongs to the favourite expressions of Marx. And it is the structural principle of Heartfield's photomontages! It's no miracle that the montage 'Stützen der Gesellschafft' ('Pillars of Society') finds the basis for its worldview and its rhetorical analog in the Marxian acknowledgement, that only banditry could save civil society: 'Only theft property, perjury religion, bastardy the family, disorder order' [Marx, *MEW*, Bk 8, Berlin, 1969, p. 204]. (Hilmar Frank, 'Heartfield's Bildsprache: Visuelle Rhetorik, Zur Theorie der Fotomontage', in Eckhard Siepman, *Montage: John Heartfield, Vom Club Dada zur Arbeiter Illustrierten Zeitung* (Berlin: Elefantenpresse, 1977).

The minuscule change of text, which changes the meaning, parallels the visual oxymoron   (ibid., p. 232).

2.   It was published without the repeat of the first word *birth*. On-stage and in the radio version it was 'Birth. Birth was the death of him.' I spoke it so that the experience would be like the experience of listening to a tape, the voice not loud but (it) reaches everyone. So the stage experience was: distance but intimate, no facial features, no personality. I stood in a 40 foot deep black box, barely discernable light on stage   (David Warrilow, to whom *A Piece of Monologue* is dedicated, and who acted/spoke it in December 1979 in New York, in conversation with the author.

Character is sacrificed to temperature. . . . At first we are not sure if Mr Warrilow's mouth is actually moving. Is he speaking, or is he being spoken for? Is his voice live or recorded. The light is dim and we must adjust our eyes – and our ears.   (*New York Times*, 19 December 1979)

3. *Producing* meaninglessness is not the same as 'the empty signifier'. This crucial difference is often elided in recent theoretical/critical work. For further discussion of this problematic, see, for example, 'Modernism, Phantasy and the Avant Garde Film', by Michael O'Pray, in *Undercut 3/4* (London, 1982) pp. 31–3.

4.   I was never afraid of animals or the dark but I always began to tremble when I heard that trade was bad.   (Bryher, *The Heart to Artemis* (New York: Harcourt Brace & World, 1962) p. 15)

Exchange-value and use-value

The wealth of societies in which capitalist production prevails consists of commodities. A commodity is a thing that has *use-value*; the latter exists in all forms of society, but in capitalist society use-value is, in addition, the material depository of *exchange-value*.   (Friedrich Engles, *On Marx's Capital* (1868) (Moscow: Progress Publishers, 1972) p. 51)

Just as a commodity is something twofold (use-value and exchange-value) so the labour contained in it is twofold determined: on the one hand, as *definite productive activity*, weaving labour, tailoring labour, etc. – '*useful labour*'; on the other, as the simple expenditure of human labour-power, precipitated abstract (general) labour. The former produces use-value, the latter exchange-value; *only the latter is quantitatively comparable* (the differences between skilled and unskilled, composite and simple labour, *confirm* this). . . . Only in the equation of two concrete products of labour does the property of the concrete labour contained in both come to light as abstract human labour . . . materialisation(s) of abstract labour. . . . Exchange-value is impressed upon the use-value of a commodity by definite historical relations. Hence the commodity cannot express its exchange-value in its own use-value, but only in the use-value of another commodity.   (ibid., pp. 51–3)

A commodity proves that it is a commodity in exchange. . . . A commodity is a use-value for its non-owner, a non-use-value for its owner. Hence the need for exchange. . . . Every commodity owner considers *his own* commodity as the universal equivalent . . . no commodities possess a general relative form of value. . . . Therefore, they do not confront each other at all as commodities, but only as products. . . . The immanent contradiction in a commodity as the direct unity of use-value and exchange-value, (thus) as the product of useful private labour and as the direct social materialisation of abstract human labour – this contradiction finds no rest until it results in duplicating the commodity into commodity and money. . . . The process of exchange gives the commodity which it converts into money, not its *value*, but its *value-form*.   (ibid., p. 53)

[But] the capitalist does not want the use-value produced for its own sake, but only as the depository of exchange-value and especially of surplus value. . . . [But] in no case can an instrument *of* labour (a machine, a brain/ed) transfer (from itself/ed) *more* exchange-value than it possessed itself – in the labour process it acts only as a use-value, and hence can give only the exchange-value that it possessed previously. . . . Only the labour-*process* adds new value.   (ibid., pp. 69, 71)

Marx argues that the epistemological principles he outlines in *Capital* are applicable to all sciences, and have been applied to most. 'All science would be superfluous if the outward appearance and the essence of things directly coincided' [*Capital*, vol. iii, p. 797]. . . . It should be said straightaway that this relation between essence and phenomena is not that prescribed by the empiricist problematic of a 'real real' and an 'unreal unreal', attacked by Althusser in *Reading Capital* . . . his [Marx's] aim here is not to suggest that the invisibility of the commodity form is purely subjective or specifically ideological, but that the commodity form has *no intrinsic link* with the use-value of the useful good-as-commodity . . . Marx's scientific theory of the economy is not established by a change of perspective enabling him to see behind the illusory reality to the real movement, but by the establishment of a new conceptual space redefining the supposedly visible but illusory *concepts* of the reality.   (Ben Brewster, 'Fetishism in Capital and Reading Capital', *Economy and Society*, August 1976, pp. 347–8)

Brewster's complex analysis formulates the theoretico-ideological problems of Marx's epistemology and criticises the latter in relation both to the Copernican Revolution and his concept of illusion and reality, 'the existence of things'. Brewster then asks 'what are the consequences in *Capital* of this displacement of the property of concealment/manifestation from the *process of knowledge* to the (concepts of the) "real" object itself?' This matters precisely in relation to the question of use-value and exchange-value (and the use and exchange of the Beckettian speech, the appropriation of such speech to use and/or exchange, in duration, and how). The process by the viewer/with the viewer/through the viewer 'of' the appropriation and transformation of, and positioning via, meaning-attempt, is a social, aesthetic-political process as much as any.

5. Isn't one a bit bewildered, that to that which is brought forth there is also a bringer-forth, a creator to the work, an artist of the oeuvre – one has this feeling a bit only with very autonomous works. But it is always again comfortable to know that this was made by people. (Adam Seide, 'Visiting Beckett', *Theatre (Yearbook)*, *1964*, p. 37)

The critic, here, seems to need to find an author perversely present via the unpresent, unintentionalised text.

> AS: 'No, no. One must be going.
> SB: He had felt sorry that he'd had so little to say.
> AS: No, why?' (ibid., p. 37)

6. (The publisher) thought Beckett's time shouldn't be taken doing the translations. And I was chosen for this task. And I did an initial translation which took me months. It was so hard. But I thought that I had done a reasonably good job. And so I finished it off – I think it was THE EXPELLED, and sent a note to Beckett saying that I have a draft of the translation ready and can I send it to him? And he wrote back saying well I think it might be better if we got together so that we can discuss any minor changes that I might care to make. And we met at The Dome at Montparnasse. And spent probably 4 or 5 hours of an afternoon going through it and by the time 6 o'clock came we had progressed through about a page and a half. And he would always begin 'Now that's a marvellous rendition of this sentence – Oh I like that very much. Do you think, however, we might change the word such and such into such and such – do you think that might work better?' And I would say 'Well sure that sounds good to me.' But he would never change anything – he would suggest that we might change it. But of course all the changes in it – by day 3 or day 4 it became totally ludicrous that I had even undertaken this task. And I said when it was finished I just don't think I can put my name to this it just wouldn't be fair. 'Oh', he said, 'Yes, if it makes you feel better you can say in collaboration with the author.' (Richard Seaver, 'Samuel Beckett', BBC Radio 3, 17 August 1980)

7. In this hour too he was an Adamur. . . .
The spirit of the community. . . .
They were pulled towards him like irondust to a magnet, as with magic strength he carried them with him, far, far, through the lane, through the city, over valleys and hills, over seas and deserts. . . .
And his eyes lit like the Adamur's eyes, and his hands worked therewith like the Adamur's anointed feet.
I am sitting as in a dream, suddenly someone touches my shoulder.

I look around – the Adamur!
'You see, this is how I danced; but a melody naturally did not come along, it remained outside the door: he is a student of the Wilnaur Gaon...ä!'
The *ä* drove into my heart like a knife.
Suddenly he said:
'Go, Chaim, and give the uncircumcized ones at the machineworks some mead!'
But what this meant I had not the faintest idea any more.   (Leib Perez, 'Chassidic Mischna', *Chassidic Stories* (Berlin: Schocken, 1936) p. 37)

The Wilnaur Gaon is a sharp opponent of the Chassidim. Mischna means repetition, oral passage. It designates the oldest part of the Talmud (these stories though were written in the late nineteenth century).

Adamur is a shortened version of 'Adonenu Morenu Rabbenu, Our Teacher, Our Master'.

The yiddish language tends in any case to considerable change of tense, and the use of the present in stories. In Perez this tendency is raised to the limit; always again the moment is made present so that it stands out from the unravelling of the recollected past; it confronts the listener like the present, so that those sections told in the past tense often function as short pauses between various presents pressuring against one another. Perez always has the listener in mind, like a man of the people, who tells with lively mimetic movement; he addresses the listener and brings the events close to view (*dicht* = densely). Gesture and countenance of the storyteller the listener seems to see, whether it be a character of the writer's imagination or the writer himself. (Afterword by the Yiddish-to-German translator, Ludwig Strauss, ibid., p. 8)

8. '*Subject*' here is the speaker/enunciator, not the 'subject' as in 'the subject of the play is . . .', not the 'object' as in 'the object of the exercise'.

    For to watch them is to face what all if they could, would willingly forget.   (Bryher, 'G. W. Pabst, A Survey', *Close Up*, December 1927)

    What will it do with us? (Dorothy Richardson, 'Continuous Performance', ibid., December 1927)

9. In a letter to DB, October 24, 1974, Beckett stressed that he did not study philosophy at Trinity College Dublin, 'let alone Wittgenstein'. He felt compelled to add this information 'because of the many comparisons between his writings and the philosophy of Ludwig Wittgenstein, which he abhors' (Deirdre Bair, *Samuel Beckett: A Biography* (London: Jonathan Cape, 1978) ch. 4, 1929/30, n. 5, p. 655)

10. 'Against sexual identity would be, then, neither *difference* ('woman-as-other' against a male norm, outside language and power) nor *homogeneity* ('woman-as-same', assimilating the male role in patriarchy, identifying

with it, such a role denying both women's subjective and objective histories, ideologies, powers.' (Peter Gidal, 'Against Sexual Representation in Film', *Screen*, November–December 1984, vol. 25, no. 6, pp. 29–30)

Are not the *Sefirot* also, and all of Kabbalah, an incarnation of the desire for difference, and for an end to Exile. *To be different, to be elsewhere*, is a superb definition of the motive for metaphor . . . defending against death. Kabbalah is a theory of *writing*, but this is a theory that denies the absolute distinction between writing and inspired speech, *even as it denies human distinctions between presence and absence* [italics mine]. . . . Derrida, in the brilliance of his *Grammatology*, argues that writing is at once external and internal to speech, because writing is not an image of speech [but writing is an image of writing, not a pure 'source': author] while speech itself is already writing, since the trace it follows 'must be conceived as coming before being'. (Harold Bloom, *Kabbalah and Criticism* (New York: Seabury Press, 1975) p. 52)

At the same time it must be seen that such a religious ideology is not autonomous from other coterminal ideologies: 'Kabbalah is nothing if not sexist' (ibid., p. 29).

11.   If we can't keep our genres more or less distinct, or extricate them from the confusion that has them where they are, we might as well go home and lie down.   (Samuel Beckett, in a letter to his American publisher, 27 August 1957, quoted in Clas Zilliacus, *Beckett and Broadcasting: A Study of the Works of Samuel Beckett for and in Radio and Television* (Abo, Finland: Abo Akademi, 1976) p. 3)

Beckett's specificity as to genres is clarified in the letter as a whole, referring to *All That Fall* and *Act Without Words* but really to be seen as general principle. In full:

All That Fall is a specifically radio play, or rather radio text, for voices, not bodies. I have already refused to have it 'staged' and I cannot think of it in such terms. A perfectly straight reading before an audience seems to be just barely legitimate, though even on this score I have my doubts. But I am absolutely opposed to any form of adaptation with a view to its conversion into 'theatre'. It is no more theatre than *Endgame* is radio and to 'act' it is to kill it. Even the reduced visual dimension it will receive from the simplest and most static of readings . . . will be destructive of whatever quality it may have and which depends on the whole thing's *coming out of the dark*. I think really we had better call it off, if it is not too late. I would have said all this before if I had known you had such a performance in mind and I am distressed at having to burst in on you with my wail at this late hour. But frankly the thought of *All That Fall* on a stage, however discreetly, is intolerable to me. If another radio performance could be given in the States, it goes without saying that I'd be very pleased.

Now for my sins I have to go on and say that I can't agree with the idea of
Act Without Words as a film. It is not a film, not conceived in terms of
cinema. If we can't keep our genres more or less distinct, or extricate them
from the confusion that has them where they are, we might as well go
home and lie down. *Act Without Words* is primitive theatre, or meant to be,
and moreover, in some obscure way, a codicil to *Endgame*, and as such
requires that this last extremity of human meat – or bones – be there,
thinking and stumbling and sweating, under our noses, like Clov about
Hamm, but gone from refuge.   (ibid., p. 3)

12. Thus it is not another which is *not* him/her magically at one with him/her.

13. Let me try a quick outline of the polarity of these two great masters (Diego
and Orozco). I offer an original response by finding the same polarity at
the core of myself and of my cinema – of my moving frescoes (for we also
work on walls!). *Potemkin* bursts through the screen into the auditorium.
The General Line pulls onto the plane of contemplative space both the
vertical
and
the horizontal –
such is the definition given me by Fernand Leger (see *Le Monde*).
That is what gives me the possibility of seeing their work *in this way*.
This is what forces me to see them *in this way*.
Perhaps it's a vision, a prevision.
Is a synthesis possible on a wall's space?
Can it contain the furious tension that pulls across its surface like a bow
about to let fly its arrow, like a balloon about to burst – can all this be put
on a wall? – and (it) still be a wall?   (Sergei Eisenstein, 'The Prometheus
of Mexican Painting', in *Film Essays and a Lecture*, ed. Jay Leyda
(Princeton, N.J.: Princeton University Press, 1982) p. 229)

14. *Footfalls* in German entitled *Tritte*, meaning 'kicks' or 'steps'. Both 'kicks',
the (German) colloquial, and 'steps', within High-German speech, have
coequal strength within the language, an equal immediacy of association.
One concept is thus not a less than contradictory subtext of the other, and
vice versa; this necessitates, even on the level of the title, moment-to-
moment disentanglement as much as it is impossible.

15. WAP (Women Against Pornography) and WAVAW (Women Against
Violence Against Women) are politically opposed to *reproducing* sexual
violence against women, which so-called 'pro-sex' libertarians and
pro-S&M lesbians are not. This 'debate' has very real effects.

Libertarianism whether espoused by men or 'Socialist feminists' has
reactionary effects which its individualist proponents either deny or are
quite happy about. Their ideology and practice is supportive of and in
harmony with right-wing politics (whether they 'like' it or not); 'freedom' is
seen as outside of power relations. One of the effects of this right-wing
position is sexual violence against women.

16. This is regardless of what momentary stylistic is chosen for its consumation, and regardless of the *order* such stylistics would find opportune.

17. A current philosophical fashion which ex-leftists seem particularly attracted to is one that says, first, that representation is impossible and, secondly, predicated upon that (as if logically!) that since nothing can be represented, no political entities can exist to constitute demands. In such a schema, there is no last instance of the economic, or the political/ideological, etc., in the Althusserian sense. The impossibility of absolute representation (of anything – therefore also of political demands) is used to 'depoliticise', and voluntarise towards notions of individual freedom. This Western concept of individualism is embraced for reasons of sex and class interests, and academic acceptability ('status') within the bourgeoisie. It is opposed by one that states that no practice remains autonomous, representation included, and each practice is semi-autonomous in its functioning and sociality. The semi-autonomy of each practice and each's economic–political–sexual last instance means that any attempt to place it in an idealist void is an unspoken, and reactionary, politics in certain interests: to maintain the *status quo*. Patriarchal power can only constantly reinstate itself through such strategies. Philosophical purity states, then, that, 'nothing can be *re*presented so let's keep everything the way it is'. The other fashion which ex or current leftists seem unfortunately attracted to, when they are encumbered by bourgeois ideology, is one that does not even begin to deal with and see the materialist dialectic politics of questions of representation in the first place, opting instead to accept the forms of representation of the dominant sex and class as eternal. That both currents are vociferously taking or attempting to take power in a backlash against any radical feminist and Marxist aesthetic/political (or simply political!) practice is not a coincidence.

A male can not *be* a feminist or a radical feminist, but can attempt to not reproduce the power-relations of his sex (or sex class), his economic class and his race (objectively he is still part of that sex, class and race).

18. As to *any* implication that Beckett is not polemicising:

Not for me these Grotowskis and Methods. The best possible play is one in which there are no actors, only the text. I'm trying to find a way to write one.   (Samuel Beckett to Deirdre Bair, letter dated 19 June 1973, quoted in Bair's *Samuel Beckett: A Biography*, p. 722)

19. No more. The slipping signifier.

20. This does not imply less repression, but less of that kind of repression. As the unconscious is a constant process, repression is operative.

See *Sigmund Freud and Lou Andreas-Salome: Letters*, ed. Ernst Pfeiffer (London: Hogarth Press, 1972).

21. The situation of women is a cause of revolt. This is a platitude, but this platitude entails a corollary which is much less frequently admitted. People do not revolt against what is natural, therefore inevitable or inevitable, therefore natural. Since there is revolt, there is concurrently and necessarily a notion of a resistible process. That which is resistible is not inevitable; that which is not inevitable could be otherwise; it is arbitrary, therefore social. The logical and necessary implication of the women's revolt, like all revolts, is that the situation can be changed. If not, why revolt? Belief in the possibility of change implies belief in the social origin of the situation. (Christine Delphy, *For a Materialist Feminism* (Paris: l'Arc, 1975), reprinted in *Feminist Issues*, no. II (1981, Berkeley, USA) pp. 68–76; and in *Close to Home* (London: Hutchinson, 1984))

I do not say that women who have children are 'mothers' and therefore liable to be exploited. I say rather that because their work is appropriated women must raise children for nothing. I do not say that 'motherhood' explains the appropriation of women's labour, but on the contrary that the appropriation of their labour, effected among other things through unpaid childcare, constitutes women as mothers. Thus motherhood, far from being a natural fact giving birth to exploitation, is a social construct created by exploitation. (Christine Delphy, 'A Materialist Feminism is Possible', *Feminist Review*, no. 4 (1980, London) p. 95; and reprinted in *Close to Home*)

In relation to 'the viewer' and 'the woman's body', see also the excellent ' "Phallomorphic Power" and the Psychology of "Woman": A Patriarchal Chain', by Monique Plaza, in *Ideology and Consciousness*, no. 4 (Autumn 1978, London), reprinted in *Feminist Issues*, no. I (1981, Berkeley, USA); originally published in *Questions Feministes*, no. 1 (Paris, 1978).

We don't need or want a mother's look against the father's look, 'difference', but the not mother, not father, looking or not. In a previous formulation, 'I consider the possibilities of the not-mother, not-father, (looking or not)' (the author quoted in Stephen Heath, *'Difference'*, *Screen*, vol. 19, no. 3 (Autumn 1978) p. 97).

Yesterday it occurred to me that I did not always love my mother as she desired and as I could, only because the German language prevented it. The Jewish mother is no 'Mutter', to call her 'Mutter' makes her a little comic . . . for the Jew, 'Mutter' is specifically German, it unconsciously connotes together with Christian splendour Christian coldness. Also, the Jewish woman who is called 'Mutter' therefore becomes not only comic but strange . . . I believe that it is solely the memories of the Ghetto which preserve the Jewish family, for the word 'Vater' does not approximate to the Jewish father either. (Franz Kafka, *Diaries 1910–23*, ed. Max Brod (London: Penguin, 1982) p. 187, entry for 24 October 1911)

Julia Kristeva writes 'Der platonische aufnehmende Raum ist Mutter und Amme [The platonically receiving space is Mother and Nurse]' (*La Revolution du Langage Poetique* (Frankfurt: Suhrkamp, 1978) n. 18) and, in her search for the constantly final (maternal or not) signi*fied*: 'She [Mouth in *Not I*] experiences jouissance in nonsense through repression' ('The Father, Love and Banishment', in *Desire & Language* (New York: Columbia University Press, 1980) p. 154). Simultaneously, somehow 'In *Not I*, Mouth, leaving behind an obsessional labyrinth, becomes a mirage of this possible serenity, shielded from death, that is, incarnate in the mother. Here I see the averted, disillusioned eyes of radiant Madonnas' (ibid., p. 157). That women must be mothers, not to mention the bourgeois-ideology-infested notion of what it means to be a mother, can cause *nothing but* acceptance of Kristeva's theses by dominant patriarchy. Which leads, together with her glorification of her husband's pro-Church statements, to:

And here is finally a certain feminism called to the rescue [of antisemitism]. I was already struck at the moment when feminist theoreticians pronounced themselves on the role of women as exchange value, or on language as if made up of abstract and phallocentric antiwoman signs, by the resemblance of these themes with the cliches of nazi propaganda against 'money' and 'abstraction' of an essence at that time not patriarchal but rather jewish. . . . the modern antisemite is a Marxist who doesn't know it.   (Julia Kristeva, 'Anti-Semitism Today', *Art Press* (1979, Paris) pp. 33–6; see also Peter Gidal, 'On Julia Kristeva', *Undercut* 10/11 (London, 1983)

In other words she sees feminism as Nazism, and Marxism as anti-semitism.

Against this, an anti-phallocratic position, a feminist position is possible:

When Juliet Mitchell translates this arbitrary nature of the sign from the sphere of linguistics to that of psychology, the differences between men and women completely float away from biology and become purely social constructs. This happens because society 'needs' it [a trace of Juliet Mitchell's functionalism here]: . . . '*for human society to exist at all men and women must be marked as different from each other*' . . . Yet the logic of this locks us as securely within the structures of phallic power as does 'biologism'. Instead of simply accepting certain biological distinctions between the sexes, of which the psychological and cultural consequences are not necessarily very great (we do not really know how important they are) we appear condemned perpetually and for all time to recreate – or to *create* – the distinction *culturally* because otherwise we could not survive *biologically*, or could not survive at least as distinctively human. Thus the touchstone of human culture itself becomes the difference between 'masculine' and 'feminine'. Strangely, this is both wholly arbitrary and absolutely inevitable. It seems odd to demolish the tyranny of biology only to put in its place an imperative equally tyrannical and unalterable. And I question whether the whole of human culture should necessarily be seen as resting primarily and predominantly on the creation of heterosexuality in this way. . . . Mitchell writes: 'The woman's task is to *reproduce* society, the man's to go out and *produce* new developments. There is an obvious link between the security of Oedipal father-love (the girl's destiny) and the happy hearth and home of later years'. . . . To say this is to argue that the sexual division of labour as we know it in an industrial capitalist society has some *permanent* correspondence with the creation of 'masculinity' and 'feminity'. . . . It is implied that psychoanalysis enables us to understand how we internalize . . . ideology. This in turn assumes (and Juliet Mitchell certainly *does* seem to assume) that women are in general *successfully* constructed as 'feminine' in our society. Women, according to her, *do* end up narcissistic, masochistic and the rest. This is rather curious since Freud himself laid great stress on the difficulty of this process and its incomplete success in many women . . . psychoanalytic theory is odd in its mingling of the highly particular (the details of an individual's biography to elucidate an individual's current psychological state) with the universal and general (the general 'law' of the Phallus, and the necessity for the individual – and for all individuals – of entering culture via the Oedipus complex enacted in the nuclear family). At both these levels it misses the historically specific; that is, it can be 'true' of one individual and of all human history; it has little to say about one particular historical period. This makes it especially difficult to integrate with Marxism, since Marxism precisely deals with what is socially particular at a given historical period. . . . More generally feminist interest in psychoanalysis has not in practice led to a sharpening of feminist political struggle. On the contrary it has validated reactionary positions amongst feminists. . . . If anything, psychoanalysis seems to have been used implicitly to justify heterosexual relationships at a period in the women's movement when women who wanted to relate to men sexually felt under pressure from feminists who were lesbians. . . . The last thing feminists need is a theory that teaches them only to marvel anew at the constant recreation of the subjective reality of subordination and which reasserts male domination more securely than ever within theoretical discourse. (Elizabeth Wilson, 'Psychoanalysis: Psychic Law and Order?', *Feminist Review*, no. 8 (Summer 1981, London) pp. 63–78)

Such concepts are inseparable from, precisely, *forms* of identification, and the material-ideological positioning inculcated.

22. In relation to the question of teleology, and historicism, the following note by Rene Gimpel, originally written with reference to such concepts in film theory, is I think apposite:

I don't think that to historicise is to give a teleology – I think that there already exists a teleology inscribed within capitalism which is masked under different ideological headings, e.g. the search for truth, for more 'efficient' goods/services/lifestyles whatever, happier computer programmes and so on. Each little 'separate' area, nicely disconnected from the other, intent on finding its own virtuous path to a more fulfilling self. Virtually none of the developments (*virtually* because economics is sometimes the exception) in any branch of science or knowledge in capitalism is recognised by the bourgeoisie as tending to improve exchangeability (which is a definite teleological goal). While acknowledging (sometimes) that improvements lead to increased exchangeability, the bourgeoisie present improvements as improvements *qua* improvements. To paraphrase Tony Fry – it follows from this that the (Arriflex) as an exchange commodity, is bought and sold as product, representation, and labour process. When Peter Gidal heroically misuses an Arriflex to good purpose, he is in danger of showing Arriflex SA, Berne and Liechtenstein, that there might be a new market, however modest, as yet untapped amongst structural materialists.   (Rene Gimpel, letter to author, dated December 1982, referring to p. 161 of Gidal's article 'Technology and Ideology in/through/and Avant-Garde Film: an Instance' which appeared in *The Cinematic Apparatus*, ed. Teresa de Lauretis and Stephen Heath (London: Macmillan, 1980) pp. 151–65)

23. As to, for example, a staging of the prose piece of 1970, *Lessness*:

So we disagreed – though having discussed the play and having agreed on how it should sound he sat back and said 'well first do it your way' (as in less than a week we were opening) 'and then do it my way' and then he just laughed pleasantly. He would then have just one voice – whose rhythms never change, and the lighting – everything, is repetitive, and *without* change . . . he would have the image of the little body upright in the midst of ruins and the same voice coming from different angles of the stage, according to the themes (Ruins, Earth, Man, Mindlessness, etc.). The central little body he would possibly represent by just a mask with two lights for the eyes. The whole thing would be mechanized and inhuman. In discussing it he then thought one could make it more effective if one differentiated the themes by different lighting as well as the different areas. . . . He said I was mad to think of staging the play, but when pushed he revealed that he had of course a definite visual picture of it – and one that was simply related to the text . . . the piece re-written in terms of the 6 separate themes. The 6 themes are obviously one voice, but for theatrical purposes I chose to differentiate them – even sexually – 3 men, 3 women, which Beckett disagreed with.   (Lucy Bailey, letter to author, dated 26 February 1982)

24. This is the break between thought and feeling, or rather, the non-dialectical proceduring of the imaginary non-break, *a* plus *b*, glue, cement as language, a mechanistic materialism crudely aligned to idealism in practice.

25. 'He and Suzanne were now totally dependent on her dressmaking' (Bair, *Samuel Beckett: A Biography*, p. 373; the time referred to is 1946–8).

26. The same language that is the language thus worked against is also the language and power used in the transitional stage to obtain immediate communicate action. In this transitional stage no idealist jump is possible, and at the same time neither is the illusion that transparent language could be radical whilst encoding transparency. This was brought out in conversation between the author and Jonathan Rosenbaum in 1980 in New York.

27. But during *Rockaby*, I wasn't thinking, I was playing someone rocking backwards and forwards. The way I use Sam's words – the way a musician uses music – in relation to *Not I* – I felt it has got to be so fast, like talking backwards into hell making strange animal noises, though every time, on the night, it was like starting blind. The fact that the lady was 70 and didn't remember who she was was neither here nor there, just a hook to hang emotion on. Recently a sister's niece had committed suicide, impaled herself on barbed wire, kept thinking of that in the sense that in each life there's one humdinger – either you survive or you don't – and it's so awful you're paralysed, 'looking out through' as Beckett would say 'unseeing eyes'. In *Rockaby* the 'more' is a 'not yet, not yet'. And the white face – it's something I do, a process I go through – flesh and bone – to get to when it's the crunch. What Beckett calls 'prematurely aged'. And – in *Not I* – not concerned whether she was a man or a woman. That didn't matter to me. What mattered, particularly with *Not I*, was dropping everything off, skin, flesh, bone ... I seem to understand what Sam Beckett means, and knew from the start it had to be fast, very fast. In Germany Brecht's daughter did a forty-five-minute version, a 'gentle walk through the fields' – *Not I*, awful, Beckett fled the country! I kept having an idea in my gut about where I have to get to with it, then step back, and the thing grows. Just have to keep working, shedding all the *stuff* that gets in the way. For the reading of *Enough*, which preceded *Rockaby* in the programme of two pieces, I didn't want to dress up. That was my idea. And throughout the rehearsals for *Rockaby*, talked to Sam nightly on the phone. Actually I still owe him a letter, I've had two since then, must tell him how it went. He still doesn't know. I want to do it again.   (Billie Whitelaw in conversation with the author, 1981)

Also as to *Not I*:

It goes at this tremendous pace. I've been practising saying words at a tenth of a second, I could see myself spelling them out like an Olympics clock. No one can possibly follow the text at that speed but Beckett insists that I speak it precisely. It's like music, a piece of Schoenberg in his head. Every muscle is put to the test. And at the end of the five-week run, I'm going to lay carpets. Tidy the house. Then nothing.   (Billie Whitelaw, *The Times*, January 1973)

[Rehearsing *Not I*] I began to suffer what I think is called sensory deprivation. I got through about three pages, and then I just broke down. I was sobbing, I felt I was tumbling through space, and I could hear my own voice getting faster and faster. It's true I broke down, it's true Sam said afterwards 'Billie, Billie, what have I done to you'. . . . But then I said 'that's another hurdle over, now lets go on.' I told Sam he would have to let me have slits in the hood for my eyes, so I could see.   (Billie Whitelaw, *Guardian*, 30 May 1979)

Beckett muss ja uralt sein. Schreibt der überhaupt noch? [Beckett must be age old. Is he still writing?]   (Friedrich Dürrenmatt, *Der Spiegel*, 12 January 1981)

It [*Not I*] is a most extraordinary piece of writing. I didn't understand it at all when I first read it. Going to see him in Paris and talking about it made it much clearer. Not the metaphysics of it, but just the tone, which is a terribly compulsive, feverish one. He was generous and concerned enough to read it to me as he thought it should be, and it sounded like the right voice. I felt I knew what it should be like. But he's changed his mind in rehearsal about the tone of voice. It's a terribly difficult thing to do. It's a stream of disconnected thoughts – in a sense – except that they aren't disconnected when you begin to work at it. . . . Billie's play [*Not I*] is really for a voice. He said the psychological thing was completely invalid in approaching it, it's an athletic feat. The intensity it demands is enormous – the actual intensity the actress has to generate – but the range of voice and the range of volume is very disciplined. He gets terribly frightened of an excess of emotion flooding the style of it which is quite severe. It's like a painter who chooses to use a very narrow palette.   (Anthony Page (the credited director of *Not I*), 'Working with Samuel Beckett', *The Times*, interview with Ronald Hayman, January 1973)

28. This point was brought out by Mary Pat Leece in a discussion with the author in 1981.

29. The question of various kinds of realism takes on import as does the relation to, for example, Socialist Realism, realism in certain transformational revolutionary interests, leading to communism, as a realism not necessarily unproblematically to be appropriated.

> the two contradictory ways one can conceive Eisenstein's theory, the one that's fairly conformable to a notion of Socialist Realism, and the one which in some respects is radically different. That what happens in a work of art is that reality, or reality simply reproduced, that is photographs of reality, which in the end the film strip in one sense can be regarded as, is reorganised through the vision of the artist so what in fact you produce is a reality which relates to a theme, and it is reorganised from within a perspective defined by the world view of the artist, which is also for the work to be good, the historically progressive one at any particular point, which is that which points forward towards the further transformation of the relations of production and social relations in general towards communism. That is quite easily read as a Socialist Realist Theory of Art. The two contradictory views build in the already then quite common distinction between a purely naturalistic or documentary type of realism where simply whatever is real outside is simply recorded (and the word 'photographic' here is used, in its pejorative sense, in these descriptions, 'the mere photographic reproduction of reality' . . .) – *that* is contrasted to reality which has been in some way reorganised through a world view, a vision, a socialist world view, and in some way the essence of reality is obtained, which is that reality is moving toward communism, that essence is obtained in a way that is not obtainable by mere external (photographic) reproduction. . . . (and I'm not saying photography, whether still or moving, does reproduce the surface of reality, just that

that's how the argument was put in the 30s).   (Ben Brewster, lecture on Eisenstein for Peter Gidal's seminar, Film Department, Royal College of Art (1978), London (tape transcript)

The further problem of the (seen or not) author(ial presence) specifically can lead to the possibility of the subjective intervention *not* necessarily fracturing and problematising but rather forming (finally) via omniscience *a continuum* of subjectness (however 'fragmented, interruptive, contradictory'). This (possible) effect in theatre/performance art/cinema can be the retrogressive harking formed by unhistorical and non-materialist subjectiveness, that *meta*discourse as opposed to radical (even realist) subjectivity.

30. Several nude women seen at the 'Sphinx', while I was seated at the end of the room. The distance which separated us, the polished floor, seemed insurmountable in spite of my desire to cross it, and impressed me as much as the women.   (Giacometti, letter to Pierre Matisse, *Catalogue of the Tate Gallery's 'Collection of Modern Art Other than by British Artists'*, ed. Ronald Alley (London: Sotheby/Parke Bernet Publications, 1980) p. 280)

See Illus. 17 on p. 175.

Here, in a reversal, bits of material are added, the process of additiveness and the not-knowing, the process giving no evidence of any knowing, of how to add to 'it' (and the body never separate as an 'it') eyes, chest, etc. Here it is not the usual matter of matter pared-down, away and subtracted 'from'.

Das gilt auch für Beckett's Regiearbeit, bei der 'Zurücknahme', Reduktion des Ausdrucks, der Bewegung, Mimik und Gestik, eines der Leitprinzipien ist [This is true also for Beckett's theatre-directing, for which 'taking back', reducing of expression, movement, mime, gesture, is one of the main principles].   (Michael Haerdter, 'Szeniker Beckett', *Das Werk von Samuel Beckett, Berliner Colloquium*, ed. by Hans Mayer and Uwe Johnson (Frankfurt: Suhrkamp, 1975) p. 239, n. 10)

Als ich eines Tages mit Sartre esse, wiederhole ich ihm meine Formulierung über die Statuen, 'Die Bronze hat gewonnen'. 'Das würde ihm die grösste Freude machen' sagt Sartre zu mir. 'Sein Traum wäre, vollkommen hinter seinem Werk zu verschwinden' [One day whilst eating with Sartre, I repeat my formulation about his (Giacometti's) statues, 'The bronze has won'. 'That would give him the greatest pleasure', Sartre says to me. 'His dream would be to disappear completely behind the work]. (Jean Genet, *Alberto Giacometti* (Zurich: Ernst Scheidegger, 1962) p. 34)

31. Fortunately, the Gotha Programme has fared better than it deserves. The workers as well as the bourgeoisie and petty bourgeoisie read into it what should rightly be in it but is not, and it has not occurred to anyone from any side to investigate publicly a single one of these wonderful propositions for its real content. This has enabled us to keep silent about

this programme. It comes to this, that nobody can translate these propositions into any foreign language without being *compelled* either to write down palpably crazy stuff or else, whether friend or foe, to inject a communist meaning into them. I myself have had to do so in a translation for our Spanish friends. (Friedrich Engels to Wilhelm Bracke, 11 October 1875, in Karl Marx, *Critique of the Gotha Programme* (New York: International Publishers, 1938) p. 48)

32. Roland Barthes, *Writing Degree Zero* (London: Jonathan Cape, 1967).

33. Beckett can be termed 'the last expressionist' in the sense that his work realises that the extreme though pared down to voice and body subject-matter rather than the mundane is the only way into the question of language *vs* image, whereas a cool existentialist modernity of what is in fact incredible melodrama leaves one with current British and American consummable middle-class decadences, accepting the deathlikeness of life in its most bourgeois, least historical forms, and never 'simply' a body, a voice, two voices, never a politics of the difficulty of that. Rather, what is given as theatre is continuing melodrama annihilating any process or mechanism in the constant mesh of narrative and the illusions of the 'dramatic world', television onstage, standard evenings (some termed political, some not).

34. See my earlier formulation of 'presentation not usage', London Filmmakers Co-operative Catalogue (London, 1969).

35. As to the concept, and the physicality, of the *fragment*, it is to be noted that the most radically constructed, unseamless productions of post-Beckettian theatre, theatre which produces processes of constant dialectical anti-teleologies (and no little laughter), is that of Cunning Stunts, an all-women theatre collective in Britain, in whose productions (for example, of Gogol's *The Overcoat*) the characterisations are not only in a constant process of post-Beckettian 'absurdness', but there is materially produced an impossibility to hold to 'type' or to 'sex' or to 'character' any person or act or scene. The seamless flow is non-existent; rather, a series of endless reconstructions, reprocesses, interactions based never on the psychologistic, but rather on the production in the act of roles, poses, movements, gestures, speech-segments, fantasies, which, though bound to a 'primary text' and though rehearsed (as perfectly as any Beckett or Valentin/Karlstadt piece must always be, must always have been, to function), nevertheless formulates an impossible signified. The meanings of any moment of such theatre, and the reference in the 'real' world referred to, is never unmitigated, unquestioned, communicated. The production qua production is always that process, but only rarely do such lessons of materialist theatre become evident in the supposedly unconventional, 'off-Broadway, off–off Broadway, Public Theatre' stagings in the United States, or, similarly, the 'alternative' or 'lunchtime' or 'fringe' theatre acts in Britain or on the Continent. Cunning Stunts' radical materiality of theatre process, never losing sight of their feminist polemic and theory, *material* in every sense of their (*hilarious*) productions, is the most advanced example of the possibilities of both undermining the transparency of the theatric

signifier *and* functioning ideologically/theoretically, that is, within a political space and position.

From the concept and materiality of the fragment, too, can be ascertained positions in literature. An example.

Emily Dickinson, although she did not publish, wrote nearly eighteen hundred poems, and organized the largest portion of them with her own form of bookmaking: selected poems copied onto sheets of letter paper that she bound with string. In her isolation and poetic silence, these manuscript books, known as fascicles, may have served privately as publication, a personal enactment of the public act. Formal features, like her unusual punctuation and capitalization, line and stanza divisions, and display of alternate readings, are a source of continuing critical concern. Because she saw no poem through to press and left her manuscripts unprepared for print, judgments must be informed by the manuscript conventions themselves. Perhaps no less important, interest has developed in the fascicles as artistic gatherings – a gathering intrarelated by theme, imagery, emotional movement. In general, we need to understand why she assembled the fascicles – by what principles and for what purposes – and to have them available in the way she viewed them. The variorum edition, *The Poems of Emily Dickinson*, edited by Thomas H. Johnson, translated the mechanics of the poems into conventional type and, in presenting them chronologically, obscured the fascicle structure.

One motive Emily Dickinson had in constructing these books was to reduce disorder in her manuscripts. [But it should be noted that that does *not* mean she conventionalised type or chronology: the author.] As she copies poem after poem onto uniform sheets of stationary, she destroyed earlier versions. . . . A sense of the disorder thus forestalled may be gained by examining the manuscripts left from the last years of her life, after she had stopped copying onto fascicle sheets. Mabel Loomis Todd, the first Dickinson scholar, called them 'scraps' – a profusion of shapes, sizes and materials, from brown paper sacks and used envelopes to notebook pages and the backs of recipes. . . . Because she did not number or otherwise label the fascicles, did not index them or apparently maintain them in a particular order, one may wonder how she found her way among them. . . . To assemble a fascicle she stacked several copied sheets on top of one another. She started out in 1858–59. . . . The sheets, copied separately, were not inserted inside each other, but were stacked and then sub-bound; she punched two holes through their sides, from front to back, and threaded them with string, tied on the front. That completed the construction of a fascicle, as there was no title page or pagination, and no contents list or other apparatus to lead to specific poems. (R. W. Franklin (ed.), *The Manuscript Books of Emily Dickinson* (Cambridge, Mass.: Belknap Press of Harvard University Press, 1981) vol. 1, pp. ix–xx)

See Illus. 15 on p. 157.

36.   I often could have written out a fine cheque for myself and write his name
       on it for a couple of pounds a few times he forgot to lock it up besides he
       won't spend it Ill let him do it off on me behind provided he doesn't smear
       all my good drawers O I suppose that cant be helped Ill do the indifferent
       1 or 2 questions Ill know by the answers when hes like that he cant keep a
       thing back I know every turn in him Ill tighten my bottom well and let out
       a few smutty words smellrump or lick my shit or the first mad thing comes
       into my head ... I suppose thats what a woman is supposed to be there for
       or He wouldnt have made us the way He did so attractive to men then if he
       wants to kiss my bottom Ill drag open my drawers and bulge it right out in
       his face as large as life he can stick his tongue 7 miles up my hole   (James
       Joyce, *Ulysses*, 1922 (London: John Lane, The Bodley Head, 1937) p. 740)

       Yes. Carry me along, taddy, like you done through the roy fair! If I see him
       bearing down on me now under whitespread wings like he'd come from
       Arkangels, I sink I'd die down over his feet, humbly dumbly, only to
       washup. Yes, tid. There's where. First. We pass through grass behush the
       bush to. Whish! A gull. Gulls. Far calls. Coming, far! End here. Us then.
       Finn, again! Take. Bussoftlhee, mememormee! Till thousendsthee. Lps.
       The keys to. Given! A way a lone a last a loved a long the   (James Joyce,
       Finnegans Wake, 1922–39 (London: Faber & Faber, 1964) p. 628)

       Den Verfremdungseffekt benutzt Joyce in Ulysses. [Joyce uses the
       distanciation-effect in Ulysses.]   (Brecht, *Gesammelte Werke*, vol. 19
       (Frankfurt: Suhrkamp, 1967) p. 293, first publicised by Brecht in 1952)

       I shall speak of Joyce, who has preoccupied me much this year, only to say
       that he is the simplest consequence of a refusal – such a mental refusal! – of
       a psycho-analysis, which, as a result, his work illustrates.   (Jacques
       Lacan, *The Four Fundamental Concepts of Psychoanalysis* (London: The
       Hogarth Press, 1977) p. ix (Preface), 17 May 1976)

       any shelter in which may be established a viable, temperate relation of one
       sex to the other necessitates the intervention – this is what psychoanalysis
       teaches us – of that medium known as the paternal metaphor.   (ibid.,
       p. 276, 24 June 1964)

       The phallocentric signified is reproduced and solidified as much by such a
       conservative (and hysterical) psychoanalysis as by a polyvalent language
       production (Joyce) which, in the end, as throughout, relies on the hold of the
       signifier by the (profusion of) signi*fieds*. This is in direct opposition to the
       productive process of the signifier in Beckett and Stein, for example.

       Beckett's writing also tries to disintegrate a phrase with a word.   (Pierre
       Chabert, 'Beckett as Director (from personal experience)', *Gambit 28*
       (London: Calder, 1976) p. 61, n. 13)

Is there any reason why that terribly arbitrary materiality of the word's surface should not be dissolved (Samuel Beckett (1937), quoted in Lawrence Harvey, *Samuel Beckett: Poet and Critic* (Princeton, N.J.: Princeton University Press, 1970) p. 434)

Joyce's reliance is on the signified, and its infinite capacities for the colonisation of all meaning, complex, expansive, possessive, rather than reliance on the signifier, its capacities for inculcating a production-process of/in/against meaning, and meaninglessness, complex, contractive, dispossessive, exposing the ideology of expansiveness and possessiveness in and via language. *Ulysses* and *Finnegans Wake* (1922 and 1939) are opposed by *Tender Buttons* (1914) and *Not I* (1971).

37. Thus we get an extreme anti-expressionism, the superficies of which remind the illustrators and their journalistic counterparts of Bacon and godknowswhat.

38. What both above issues share is the question of literalisation in specific relation to women's discourses of work, languaged as such or not. Similar misrecognition of Marxism allows under the rubric orthodox the launching of a critique of Christine Delphy's materialist analysis of women's oppression. That critique having finally proved issueless, a new tack is tried, namely one of post-Marxist 'ideology'. That too is proven issueless by her clear enunciation of patriarchy as material in every sense, no less ideological for her domestic labour-relation emphasis, in this specific conjuncture an emphasis against the academic 'left's' fetishisation of 'pure' ideology as saviour not from vulgar materialism but from politics both personal and public.

39. Freudians and Lacanians could say: 'profoundly disturbing lack of the Imaginary, however imbibed the initial rocking and rockaby-ing may be'. But they *would* say: 'profoundly disturbing lack of the symbolic'. Either way, the lack of metaphor scares them silly.

40. Beckett's laconic tone fascinated Brecht so that he wanted to produce and direct a version of the play [*Godot*], Werner Mittenzwei has explained how: 'Brecht intended in his version to take Beckett's position and extend it *ad absurdum*. The play was to be cut up into many small parts between which he could then introduce film segments and pantomime sequences, which would tell of the great social revolutions, whilst Beckett's heroes continue waiting. Brecht wanted to replace [*preisgeben*] the dogmatic acuteness of the thinker Beckett with the joyous laughter of his audience. The tragic Beckett pose of the 'eternally alienated person' was to be shown up as untruth, even more as exemplary lie, in the face of those people who had broken the chains of alienation through revolution. (See John Fuegi, 'Brecht and Beckett', anthologised in *Berliner Colloquium* (Frankfurt: Suhrkamp, 1975) pp. 185–205, for more information on the interrelation, and on biographical material as to Brecht's position on staging *Godot* and filming it.)

The stage, which looks smaller than usual, reduced the country road and the tree to palpable artefacts; and the moon, when it appears, is cranked to its correct position behind a gauze by the heavenly stage manager. This is not a representation of nature; it is another of Beckett's dungeons. . . . Each [Vladimir and Estragon] has his own walk: Estragon's a nautical roll, Vladimir a splay-footed shuffle. But once the time-killing game gets under way, their routines flash across with mirror-image precision. I doubt whether the piece has ever received such physical counterpoint before. . . . Accelerating rows subside into blank dejected intervals in a living rhythm of engagement and detachment.   (Irving Wardle, 'The Hand of Beckett, *Waiting for Godot*', *The Times*, 1976 (re: the German-language Beckett-directed production))

The movements are delicate and ceremonious: precise melancholy clowning which counterpoints the dialogue with solemn hilarity and musical exactitude. Observe the actors' hands: they signal spare but eloquent desolation. Behind them the moon rises, small, blue, and toylike, as in a landscape by Klee.   (John Peters, *Sunday Times*, 1976)

One will have to discover a mode by which the poor [*armselige*] end-result becomes enriched, without thereby disturbing or erasing the discoverably simple starting point [*Anlage*] (p. 16). . . . I am switching to the realm of music. Fundamental structure is the measure. The measure is pretty much latent for the ear, nevertheless becomes experienced [*durchempfunden*] as structural net, on which musical ideas are quantitatively and qualitatively played out (p. 33). . . . Material is thereby assumed [*Voraussetzung*] for the area of action; it must be everywhere (p. 48). . . . From now on, let us present the organism as moving machine [*Bewegungsmachine*] (p. 48). . . . [The muscle] obeys when the order reaches it, *does not want to act, must act.* (p. 49). . . . The brain dominates the muscles with its will, via the nerves; through the muscles' tendons the orders reach the bones, till finally the whole material does move after all, in spite of being earthbound (p. 50). . . . The function of a pictorial work is the manner in which it betrays to the eye its structure-in-time (time-based structure), and how characteristics of movements in each case inherent to the pictorial work are foisted onto the eyes and the receptive capacities underlying them [*dahinter liegenden*]. In this way the old story as to effect is broached, but not the general effect or the effect as such; rather, the in each case specific type of effect due to the emphasis of the characteristics of movement in each case inherent to the pictorial work. To order and differentiate *these* types of effects means as much as organizing a pictorial work as to type. As we saw last time every work even the quickest [*allerknappeste*], both arising (productive) and taken-in (receptive), moves in time. The construction of our eyes is based on a touching-in-time [*Abtasten*] of every image-perception (p. 59) . . . (Quotes from *Paul Klee: Contribution to the Pedagogy of Visual Form* (1921/22) Appendix to the facsimile of the original manuscript of Paul Klee's first cycle of lectures at the State Bauhaus, Weimar (Basel: Schwabe, 1979).

41. Beckett's friendship with the brilliant communist Nancy Cunard started
    when she published *Whoroscope*, in 1930, for her Hours Press, having
    awarded it first prize in a competition she organised with Richard
    Aldington. Cunard's friendship with Beckett lasted until she died in 1965.
    Her immense labour on the radically important *Negro Anthology*, in which 19
    articles were translated into English by Beckett, and her tireless political
    organising, writing, publishing, 'as well as' working on her own poetry and
    essays, has been largely elided. She has been erased from history, even in the
    biography of her life, which is so thoroughly nasty (by a writer for *Time*
    magazine) as to damn and damn again with faint praise (at best) and to
    attempt to reduce her to some kind of dilettantish nymphomaniac (at
    'worst'). She was, and remained, one of Beckett's closest friends throughout
    his life, and they remained in touch through thick and thin, meeting often for
    all-night talks, then corresponding through letters and via friends mutually
    held. In 1956 he wrote to her:

    > I am so glad you saw the play [*Waiting for Godot*] and that it wound its way
    > to you, but the French production was more like what I wanted, nastier.

    > I still have *Negro* snug on my shelves, unlike most of what I once had, and
    > even a few Whoroscopes. . . . I shall not fail to be in Paris round about the
    > 20th and hope you will keep an evening free for me. The dog is duller than
    > ever but its friends know it doesn't mind if they get up and go away. If you
    > are organizing subscriptions for your African Ivories, put me down.

    > He also wrote, that year, 'Godot reopening Broadway November with an
    > ALL NEGRO CAST! That's my best news' (Anne Chisholm, *Nancy Cunard*
    > (London: Sidgwick & Jackson, 1979) p. 305).

    > [he] . . . particularly liked parts of [her poetry volume] *Parallax*; he also
    > found her an excellent talker, and they would meet for a drink at the Café
    > d'Harcourt on the long summer evenings, or drive with Crowder to
    > Montmartre in an open car to listen to music or have dinner *á
    > trois*. (ibid., p. 152)

42. As in film, where the profilmic as *a* cinematic signifier results in a trace on
    film (and results from a trace on film) after the filming has taken place: *a
    photochemical trace*. This point has been repeatedly made by Malcolm LeGrice
    in the interests of problematising experimental film radically.

43. 'Character is labile in Beckett *and* Brecht' (John Fuegi, *Berliner Colloquium*
    (Frankfurt: Suhrkamp, 1975) p. 191).

44. What tantalizes Madge about Echo's response, just as it informed her
    curiosity about . . . is the recalcitrance of the word, its refusal to yield up
    meaning, its emptiness of signification, as well as its ambiguous status as
    silent sound . . . 'like an echo of an echo in a shell – very far away yet very
    near – the very shell substance of my outer ear and the curled involuted or
    convoluted shell skull, and inside the skull, the curled, intricate,

hermit-like mollusk, the brain-matter itself' [H.D., *Tribute to Freud*, p. 90]. . . . H.D. hides her private meaning behind public words, so her story is always 'different yet the same as before' and therefore 'only' a repetition. Herein lies both the courage and the anxiety of her art, as well as the reason why the echo is yet another infinitely decipherable (and therefore indecipherable) palimpsest. (Susan Gubar, 'The Echoing Spell of H.D.'s Trilogy', in *Shakespeare's Sisters: Feminist Essays on Women Poets*, ed. Sandra M. Gilbert and Susan Gubar (Bloomington, Ind.: Indiana University Press, 1979) pp. 215–16)

Her eyes go black suddenly like the black wings of a swallow . . . her eyes go shut, are shut. Will they ever open? Her seemed to be dragging beat on beat out of that heart by her very static will-power. I will not have her hurt. I will not have Her hurt. She is Her. I am Her. Her is Fayne. Fayne is Her. I will not let them hurt HER. (H.D., *Hermoine*, in *Montmora*, no. 8 (1981, New York) p. 54)

Hermione's nickname 'Her' – always grammatically awkward as a subject – signifies her object status within conventional heterosexuality. (Susan Friedman and Rachel Blau du Plessis, 'I Had Two Loves Separate: the Sexualities of H.D.'s *Her*', in *Montmora*, no. 8 (1981, New York) p. 7)

H.D.'s usage of repetition and the interjection of the subjectivity of the speaking subject precludes the phantasmed linear illusionism that narrative demands for its closures of both content and form, roughly said. And the humanisation, the defictionalisation of the language anthropomorphs of conventional story-telling is materially fractured; the remnant, the skeleton 'of' language enforces the ideological historicity of the reader in process, without the collapsing of reader (subject) with read (object) in some imaginary, willed or not, 'act'.

45. See the *Redstockings Manifesto* of 7 July 1969:
    After centuries of individual and preliminary political struggle, women are uniting to achieve their final liberation from male supremacy. . . . Because we have lived so intimately with our oppressors, in isolation from each other, we have been kept from seeing our personal suffering as a political condition. This creates the illusion that a woman's relationship with her man is a matter of interplay between two unique personalities and can be worked out individually. In reality, every such relationship is a *class* relationship, and the conflicts between individual men and women are *political* conflicts that can only be solved collectively. . . . Men have controlled all political, economic and cultural institutions and backed up this control with physical force. They have used their power to keep women in an inferior position. *All men* receive economic, sexual and psychological benefits from male supremacy. *All men* have oppressed women. (Redstockings, 'Feminist Revolution' (New York, 1975))

Such an analysis is basic to a study of the relationship between patriarchy and capitalism. It means that we must know what patriarchy is in order to understand to what extent it is theoretically independent of capitalism. Only such an understanding can enable us to account for the historical independence of these two systems. Only then is it possible to establish the material basis for the connection between the struggle against patriarchy and the struggle against capitalism. . . . This analysis should be followed by a class analysis which integrates individuals into both systems of exploitation (patriarchal and capitalist) according to their objective interests. This is necessary in the short term to enable us to mobilise for the immediate struggle, and in the long term to enable us to see how the dynamic of the struggle against patriarchy and the struggle against capitalism can be oriented to combine them in revolutionary struggle. . . . For now we can say that women will not be liberated unless the patriarchal system of production and reproduction is totally destroyed. . . . Our strategy should be centred on patriarchal oppression and should therefore include all individuals who are oppressed by patriarchy and hence interested in its destruction, that is all women. The work of mobilisation must emphasise the solidarity of all people oppressed by the same system. To do this we must:

- attack the problems of false consciousness, that is class consciousness determined according to membership in capitalist classes rather than in patriarchal classes, and the identification of women under this pretext with the enemy patriarchal class;
- show how this false consciousness serves the interests of patriarchy and detracts from our struggle. (Christine Delphy, 'L'Enemi Principal', *Partisans*, no. 54/55, October 1970 (Paris))

This article appeared in English as *The Main Enemy: A Materialist Analysis of Women's Oppression* (London: Women's Research and Resources Centre, 1977; mimeo-translation, 1974, WLM Conference, Edinburgh).

the widespread theoretical schizophrenia of the left on the subject of women's oppression. The contradictory analyses they produce are due to a desperate desire to continue to exempt men from responsibility for the oppression of women . . . men (as) the class which oppresses and exploits women. . . . For a long time the socialist feminist current has represented within the Women's Liberation Movement an expression of a tendency to protect our enemies. (Delphy, 'A Materialist Feminism is Possible', *Feminist Review*, no. 4 (1980, London) p. 102; rept. in C. Delphy, *Close to Home* (London: Hutchinson, 1984)

The brilliant work of Delphy, in both constructing a materialist analysis and theorising/polemicising it, *in detail*, in the two above-mentioned publications, is taken further in 'Patriarchy, Feminism and their Intellectuals' in *Nouvelle Questions Feministe*, no. 2 (1981, Paris), reprinted in *Close to Home*.

Socialist feminism and cultural feminism, despite surface differences,

manage to coexist very well. That is because they have very similar
political views on feminism. Like cultural feminism, socialist feminism
deradicalises feminism by opposing its political element. They censor
political feminism out of their publications [and] also attack the ideas of
radical feminism – such as an independent women's movement, men as
the oppressors of women – . . . they use the obvious errors of cultural
feminism to attack radical feminism. Socialist feminists do not use the
radical portions of either, and they end up with a liberal, opportunistic
doctrine. ('Brooke' in 'The Retreat to Cultural Feminism',
Redstockings, 'Feminist Revolution', p. 65)

The line put forward as 'Marxist Feminist' is neither Marxist nor
Feminist; and if it handicaps the antipatriarchal struggle, it does not serve
the anti-capitalist fight for all that. [This] socialist feminist tendency . . .
presents a replacement enemy: capitalism. The refusal to consider women
as a class and to consider men as the antagonistic class relates back finally
to its 'unthinkability'. If we dig a bit at these unthinkables we will notice
that they themselves relate back to the set of confused representations
which turn around the *belief* that there must necessarily be close and
permanent relations between most females and most males at all times.
This makes a structural conflict 'dysfunctional', hence unthinkable. But it
might be said that this is a question of reality, not of a 'belief'. But this
'reality', or this 'belief' – the belief that such is reality – is not only
ideological, but is the very heart of the ideology (i.e. of the representation
of the world which supports the patriarchal system). There obviously
also, there *above all*, the ideology does not appear as ideology but as *the*
reasonable presentation of reality, as reality itself. (Delphy, *A Materialist
Feminism is Possible*, p. 103)

46. Peking used to fight against the USA to the last Vietnamese, then fought
Vietnam to the last Cambodian, and now seems to want to fight
Cambodia to the last Thai. The aim is raw material in the area. (Alexei
Leontev, Radio Moscow, 12.15 a.m., 28 January 1981)

47. For further elucidation of this concept, and the problematic aesthetic/
political questions of formalism, see especially *20th-Century Studies 7/8*,
Russian Formalism, December 1972 (Faculty of Humanities, University of
Kent, Canterbury) and *Russian Formalist Criticism: Four Essays*, ed.
Lemon/Reis (essays by Shklovsky, Tomashevsky and Eichenbaum)
(Lincoln, Neb.: University of Nebraska Press, 1965), as well as *Screen Reader I*
(London: Society for Education in Film and Television, 1977), which in
some chapters takes up these issues and translates several key texts
(unfortunately, those who were responsible for these translations never
developed any of the notions further nor found a way to utilise them
productively in relation to contemporary film, theatre, performance,
textiles, dance, music or writing).

48. As to the 'true' in *Ghost Trio*:

The script states 'faint'. It grows louder. In any case, the camera this time has *not* moved in, but the music nevertheless comes on, and F and we hear it. V: 'Stop'. Music stops. V: 'Repeat'. Sound comes on; image cuts to near shot; and *moving camera equals louder sound*. F raises his head sharply, as if hearing something: at that instant the sound stops. Head back into opening pose, sound returning with it. Thus the Figure controls the sound now – an effect without cause, *but given to be seen by us as without cause*. Thus we are not given an effect, some image magically produced and, therefore, an idealism, without cause. We are given the causelessness itself. Just prior to this sequence *Voice* controlled the sound with its (her) 'Stop'.

In viewing this durational section, and in allowing for the contradictions of the controlling element to reinforce our *lack* of knowledge *in direct conjunction with the precision of our perception* we are placed in a position of no longer searching for a kernel of truth. No longer is a layer of meaning being unveiled to show underneath some fabrication given as unfabricated, some whole and cohesive analogue to the real or metaphor for such. Instead – as if we had a choice, given the material at hand – we are placed, contradictorily, in the face of such confusion, or rather, of such lapses in the internal coherences of the narrative. We are disabled in the figuration of the plot. We are disabled in the figuring-out, the figuring-in: both are denied. Thus a fragment is given that is for once *not* a fragment of a whole that can be 'spontaneously', 'immediately' reconstituted in imagination. A fragment is given that does *not* control the meaning and stand for the meaning of the reconstituted whole.   (Peter Gidal, 'Samuel Beckett's *Ghost Trio* TV Play', *Artforum*, May 1979 (New York) p. 54; reprinted in *Transmission: Radical Video*, ed. P. d'Agostino (New York: Tanam Press, 1985))

Similarly, or rather, analogically, for the radio play *All That Fall*, Beckett preferred natural sounds to the idea of human impersonators for the animal sounds: 'their brevity and incongruousness would be enough *to keep conventional realism at a distance*'   (Clas Zillicus, *Beckett and Broadcasting*, p. 70; italics mine)

Thus a naturalistically reconstituted whole *militated against* was Beckett's intention, though the apparatus which would allow this to him was, paradoxically, in the specificity of radio-ideology, to use natural sounds which would oppose the codes and conventions of radio's 'natural'.

49. I cannot find the original of this quote, so it is left unattributed.

50. There is no such thing as pure functionalism.

51. Seine Antwort auf die Frage, warum er die leere Brillenfassung ohne Gläser immer auf der Nase trage: 'Besser als gar nix is es!' [His answer to the question why he always wears the empty frames, without lenses, on his

nose: 'It's better than nothing!'].   (Quoted by Theo Riegler, Friday, 4 June 1982, 'KV's 100th Birthday', *Münchener Stadtanzeiger*, p. 5)

To which Beckett's response would have to be 'Impossible!'

52.   The consistently philological might already in and of itself streak the border of the comic. . . . Once I received a letter from Valentin at the end of which the formula for the final greeting created philological headaches for him. What it said literally was 'Many Regards' ['*Mehrere Grüsse*'] – the previous formula 'Some Regards' having been crossed out, presumably as too miserable. . . . One of the main modes of acting for Valentin, the dialectical, was caused by his nervousness. The dialectical in Valentin developed into a controlling artform altogether, one that not rarely attained a socratic radicality, a socratic depth. One could speak in relation to Valentin, all in all, of a nervously sprinkled [*gesprenkelten*] dialectical pedantry, underlying the Munich [*Münchnerische*] folkiness as well as bluntness. . . . The heights of Valentin's dialectic were reached in the three dialogues about the 'Duck's Dream', the 'Coincidence', and the relationship between fireworks and darkness. In the first of these dialogues which one wants to call eternal as examples of this genre, it was the goings-on of an absurd interlocking of dream and waking reality. Valentin dreams he is a duck, discovers at the edge of the river a yellow worm three inches long and is just about to grab this worm as he is awakened. The awakening Valentin regrets the disturbance – he didn't begrudge the dreamer the worm!; but finally Valentin has to be thankful that one has woken him, because, if he had eaten the worm in the dream, he 'would now be feeling quite sick'. One sees in which direction the dialectic aims: onto the question as to the identity between the dreamer who is awake and the one dreaming of himself as a duck, the identity between '*der Ant'n*' and Karl Valentin. 'Well, was it *that* duck which dreamt it?!' – 'No, I dreamt it, me!' 'Whether – whether a duck dreams, no one knows – that'd be [then switching from Bavarian to high German] pre*cis*ely a zoo*log*ical as*sump*tion, so to speak. Of course with a parrot it's different, it can say in the morning: I've just dreamt! But a duck can't talk – and now leave me alone . . . !' Enough. It is impossible to adequately represent the metaphysical subtlety of the dialectical back-and-forth. One has to read the dialogue, it is printed; one can hear it as well as it exists as a phonograph record. . . . The dialogue about the 'coincidence' also exists in printed form and on record. Here the question is whether it is a coincidence in the banal sense or rather more likely a mysterious causal event (coincidence as anti-coincidence) when a bicyclist passes by really *just* as Valentin and a friend were crossing the Kaufingerstrasse and were speaking of a bicyclist. A listener, onstage, interposes: 'But on the Kaufingerstrasse there are bike riders every day, thousands pass by!' Excited response from Valentin: 'Thousands! – *One* came by!!' Valentin had this manic way of isolating things. Thereby this dialogue reached the last depths of dialectical philosophising.   (Wilhelm Hausenstein, *Karl Valentin* (Munich: Karl Alber, 1948, pp. 22–4)

53. The signified is finally over-determined by the signifier, to put it another way.

54. Iser 'suggests that modern texts may often be assimilated by viewing as a consistent pattern their very resistance to the formation of illusion' (Vicki Mistacco, 'Reading Nouveau Romans', in *The Reader in the Text*, ed. Susan Suleiman and Inge Crossman (Princeton, N.J.: Princeton University Press, 1980) n. 46). The point to be made, though, is that those that don't, those modern texts that can*not* be assimilated by viewing as a consistent pattern their very resistance to the formation of illusion, may or may not allow for a unified consciousness of *reading*. One must add the related opposite of this, that those that *do*, those modern texts that are assimilable 'by viewing as consistent pattern', aren't *necessarily* assimilable *due* to 'consistent patterns'.

55. He read books by and about Pudovkin, Arnheim and Eisenstein, and as many issues of the journal *Close-Up* as he could find. Suddenly he was filled with a new excitement and sense of mission: he would go to Moscow to study with Eisenstein. He had never been cut out to be a writer anyway, he rationalised in a long letter to McGreevy. Perhaps work as a cameraman was what he had been intended for all along – certainly no harm could come of a year in Moscow learning the fine points of cinematic photography. He went to see a local expert, 'father of Jelly Fitzgerald', who used a sixteen-millimetre camera and projector, but Beckett was disappointed to find that although the elder Fitzgerald was familiar with the methods of creating photographic montage and illusion, he had no interest in them and refused to teach them to Beckett. This convinced him that he needed to apprentice himself to a major studio to learn the latest techniques; but the time had come to leave Cooldrinagh and return to London, and, like so many of his other ideas, this one was superseded by the activity or demand of the moment.

Yet he continued to talk about going to Moscow for more than a year, usually when he was casting around desperately for some direction to give his life. In the summer of 1936, when he was particularly depressed, he actually wrote to Eisenstein and suggested that he come to Moscow at his own expense and live there for a year as the master's unpaid apprentice, doing whatever Eisenstein wanted him to do.* Eisenstein did not reply, and Becket turned his attentions to Pudovkin. From him he hoped to learn how to edit film and perfect the zoom technique [*sic*.: this outrageously silly biography adds to its sins by getting the 'zoom' twenty-five years early: the author]. He wrote a long letter, saying he wanted to revive the . . . two-dimensional silent film, which he felt had died unjustly before its time. Even though dramatic advances in colour and sound had been made in motion pictures by this time, Beckett had little interest in them and preferred to concentrate on techniques of the rudimentary silent film, unquestionably a major influence on his own dramatic technique as well as on his one film script. (Deirdre Bair, *Samuel Beckett: A Biography*, pp. 204–5)

*In fact he wrote, contrary to the above, of the wish to study at the Moscow State School of Cinematography with emphasis on the scenario and editing. The letter's existence and authenticity have been comfirmed to the author by Jay Leyda, the leading Eisenstein scholar, and by Beckett. This information came initially from Anne Friedberg, whose doctoral dissertation (1983) on *Close-Up* was under Leyda's supervision, at New York University. And as to 'why it didn't happen':

Beckett's letter would certainly have attracted Eisenstein's attention (that closeness to Joyce was recommendation enough) – and action – if it had not arrived in the last half of 1936. That was a year that turned bad for Eisenstein. Most of *Bezhin Meadow* had been shot when he and the production were stopped by smallpox. The forced interval grew more fatal as it grew longer. Even before the smallpox there had been official murmurings – 'Isn't the imagery getting too biblical?' 'Why does the Father look and behave like Pan?' While still in his quarantine hut Eisenstein began modifications in structure and 'story', and by the time he left the hut he invited Babel to collaborate with him on a drastically revised script that would answer his own doubts as well as those from above. Beckett's application was lost in the shuffle.   (letter of 22 February 1984 from Jay Leyda to the author)

56. A final footnote. I guess I should say that I have loved Beckett's work since first reading *Endgame* and *Krapp's Last Tape* in 1963, have been involved with it mentally consistently since then. So this isn't some academic 'choice' for a book; there was no choice for me.